JOURNEY FROM OBSCURITY

JOURNEY FROM OBSCURITY

HAROLD OWEN

ABRIDGED AND EDITED BY

H. M. GORNALL

INTRODUCED BY

JOHN WAIN

Oxford   New York

OXFORD UNIVERSITY PRESS

1988

Oxford University Press, Walton Street, Oxford OX2 6DP

Oxford New York Toronto
Delhi Bombay Calcutta Madras Karachi
Petaling Jaya Singapore Hong Kong Tokyo
Nairobi Dar es Salaam Cape Town
Melbourne Auckland

and associated companies in
Berlin Ibadan

Oxford is a trade mark of Oxford University Press

Unabridged edition originally published in 3 vols:
Childhood, 1963; Youth, 1964; War, 1965.
This abridged edition first published 1968
Reprinted 1975
Reissued, with John Wain's Introduction,
as an Oxford University Press paperback 1988

British Library Cataloguing in Publication Data
Owen, Harold, 1897–
Journey from obscurity—Abridged ed.
1. Great Britain. Owen, Harold, 1897–
I. Title   II. Gornall, H. M. (Hilary M.)
941.082′092′4
ISBN 0–19–282258–6

Library of Congress Cataloging in Publication Data
Owen, Harold, 1897–
Journey from obscurity.
1. Owen, Wilfred, 1893–1918—Biography—Family.
2. Owen, Wilfred, 1893–1918—Biography—Youth. 3. Owen
family. 4. Poets, English—20th century—Biography.
5. Birkenhead (Cheshire)—Social life and customs.
6. Shrewsbury (Shropshire)—Social life and customs.
7. Owen, Harold, 1897–
I. Gornall, H. M. (Hilary M.)   II. Title.
PR6029.W4Z8   1988   821′.912 [B]   88-18015
ISBN 0–19–282258–6 (pbk.)

Printed in Great Britain by
The Guernsey Press Co. Ltd.
Guernsey, Channel Islands

Preface

This abridgement of Harold Owen's *Journey from Obscurity* has been made so that some part of the autobiographical trilogy is available in one volume. Alterations to the text occur only to provide continuity, and there are few, since the various incidents are frequently complete in themselves.

Harold Owen covers the years 1890–1920. He writes of his parents' early struggles to bring up their family, Wilfred, Mary, Harold and Colin, in straitened circumstances, first in Birkenhead and later in Shrewsbury, and of how the lack of financial security was offset by the atmosphere of the home. He relives the past with intensity, whether describing his own excitements and disappointments and those of his family, or the scene around him—the mean and wretched streets of Birkenhead, the poverty-dulled schools, the docks and their shipping, the country round Shrewsbury. There is the same vigour of response in his accounts of the places and experiences of his travels at sea, in India, along the South American coast and elsewhere when, at the age of fifteen, he joined the Merchant Service.

The family and the relationship between its different members is present throughout and, in selecting incidents from the three books, I have tried to retain the sense of this family background. Here Wilfred is seen, not as a poet in embryo, but as the eldest son in a closely knit family through the eyes of a critical, often rebellious, but warmly affectionate younger brother. However, while letting the pattern of events and of relationships follow its natural development, Harold Owen satisfies the particular interest that Wilfred and his emerging personality will naturally arouse.

The account ends when Wilfred's poetry is just being published; Harold, his career at sea brought to an end by tropical diseases, is setting out to study art in London, and Colin is starting to farm. Though the future was full of uncertainties, Harold and Colin were in fact beginning the work in which they were to find success and satisfaction, and Wilfred's stature as a poet was to grow steadily.

I should like to thank Mr. Owen for the enthusiastic support and generous help which he has given to the making of this abridgement.

H. M. S.

Contents

WILFRED OWEN 1893–1918   vi

INTRODUCTION   ix

1. EARLY DAYS   1
2. HOLIDAY IN IRELAND   4
3. SHIPS, SEA AND THE DOCKS   13
4. WILFRED   17
5. SCHOOLS   20
6. UFFINGTON   35
7. ART SCHOOL   41
8. HOLIDAY INTERLUDES   44
9. PROBLEMS OF WILFRED'S FUTURE   50
10. DISAPPOINTMENT AND UNCERTAINTY   56
11. SEA-GOING DECISION   59
12. LEAVING HOME   71
13. JOINING SHIP   77
14. AT SEA   85
15. CALCUTTA   94
16. HOSPITAL   119
17. RETURN TO SHREWSBURY   134
18. MY FATHER'S OFFICES   152
19. AT SEA AGAIN   161
20. THE HULK   180
21. THE DREAM   193
22. PANAMA ZONE   204
23. THE MADAM   214
24. WAR   220
25. ARMISTICE DAY   227
26. CAMEROON COUNTRY   234
27. BUTTERFLIES   238
28. ELEPHANTS   243
29. RETURN TO ENGLAND   254

Wilfred Owen, 1893-1918

Wilfred Owen was killed on 4 November 1918 while trying to get his company over the Sambre Canal. At this time his poetry was known to very few and only four of his poems had been published. In 1917 he had been invalided home and during this period had met Siegfried Sassoon who recognized the quality of his work and gave him encouragement and also introduced him to others interested in modern poetry. Wilfred returned, as he had hoped, to France for, as he said, 'It's the only place I can make my protest from' for 'my subject is War and the pity of War', and it was between August 1917 and September 1918 that his greatest poetry was written. In 1919 Edith Sitwell, later Dame Edith, published seven of his poems in the poetry publication *Wheels*; these were *The Show*, *Strange Meeting*, *A Terre*, *The Sentry*, *Disabled*, *Dead-Beat*, and *The Chances*. In 1920 an edition of twenty-three poems was published, edited by Siegfried Sassoon; in 1931 a new edition, with notices of his life and work by Edmund Blunden, was published; and in 1963 the collected poems were published, edited by C. Day Lewis and containing Edmund Blunden's Memoir. These three editions were published by Chatto and Windus. In Benjamin Britten's *War Requiem*, which was commissioned for the consecration of Coventry Cathedral in 1962, settings of nine of the poems are combined with the words of the Mass for the Dead, including *Anthem for Doomed Youth*, *Futility*, and *Strange Meeting*.

The Owen Children

Wilfred Edward Salter	b.	18 March 1893
	d.	4 November 1918
Mary Millard	b.	30 May 1895
	d.	27 November 1956
William Harold	b.	5 September 1897
Colin Shaw	b.	24 July 1900

Introduction

Literature faces so many competitors these days that any book has to scramble for attention. In that scramble, Harold Owen's *Journey from Obscurity* starts with several distinct advantages. To begin with, it is an enormously 'good read', continuously interesting from beginning to end. The present edition is slightly shortened, but comparison with the original three-volume narrative will soon show that the shortening was motivated simply by the wish to make one manageable book out of three large ones, not by any tendency to loquacity or overwriting on the author's part. His prose needs no wringing out. It makes the same impression as the man himself made. He was a spare, sailor-like figure with something of the tautness and decisiveness of the quarter-deck in his manner. I remember his kindly hospitality and his penetrating but modest style of talk.

Another advantage for the book is that it is an invaluable historical document. It takes us into the society of the early years of this century, when Harold Owen was growing up in an intensely respectable but cramped and pinched household. All the family were intelligent and gifted, and these early chapters are a salutary reminder of the hard, often overwhelming struggle that faced gifted young people from such families. The Owen boys longed for a good education. Harold yearned for art school, Wilfred for Oxford. But they lived fifty years too soon for the grant system, and forty years too soon even for the Butler Education Act, which conceded the right of the whole population to at least secondary schooling. I am far from suggesting that the life of a present-day student living on a government grant is all jam, but it would do no one any harm to read carefully this account of the painful toil of the Owen brothers to get their minds trained to full effectiveness. In the end that training had to be largely self-administered.

Harold Owen's decision to follow the sea was not, then, his first choice. It was *faute de mieux*. And even his entry to the world of ships had to be at the cut-price end. Not for him the scrupulous professional training given to young men who could afford to sign articles with the proud passenger lines, steaming to timetable over the main routes of the oceans. The best that could be found for him was to be an apprentice on a cargo ship destined to spend most of her time tramping with miscellaneous cargo in the far places of the world. It was a rough, dirty, hard novitiate. But, sensitive though he was, his 'native hue of resolution' often 'sicklied o'er with the pale cast of thought', he found the strength and stubbornness to survive it, and that he did so is our gain, for very few of the men who sailed on those ships, carried those cargoes, and explored those water-fronts had the ability to recapture their experiences in words. Harold Owen's seafaring days coincided with the tail-end of the period in which Joseph Conrad wrote his immortal novels of the sea. And heaven knows, to have a Conrad is close enough to a miracle. But Conrad, scion of the minor Polish aristocracy, and with a French literary education behind him, went into the seafaring life at a higher level than Harold Owen, and from 1884 onwards held a Master's ticket, which, as far as I know, Owen never aspired to.

Conrad shares with Rudyard Kipling the honour of being the chief literary chronicler of imperialism. Kipling wrote about India under British rule, and it was surprising enough that British India, with its narrow provinciality of mind and its restricted social horizons ('India,' as he calls it, quite possibly with perfect seriousness, 'where everybody knows everybody'), should have contained within its ranks a writer of first-rate abilities. But if we had only the work of Kipling our imaginative grasp of the imperialism of the later nine-teenth century would be limited to one half, the official, military, flag-waving, speech-making side. There was another half, the nakedly economic. While Kipling's soldiers were square-bashing and polishing their brass and fighting punitive engagements with tribesmen and all the rest of it, Conrad's schooners were nosing among the islands, his tramp-steamers battling across typhoon-torn seas, in search of nothing more high-minded than simple profit. As Kipling shows us the reality behind the platitudes of Empire, Con-rad shows us the reality behind the network of international trade. It is, as I say, an extraordinary piece of luck that a captain engaged in that casual and multifarious trade, plying those seas and putting in at those strange, far-off anchorages where the writ of 'civilization' did not run, should have written novels, and great novels at that. But before that trade finally died in the convulsions of 1914–18, it drew to itself one more observer with a gift for words.

Harold Owen is not, of course, a Conrad. He is not in competition with Conrad. But his work is an invaluable sidelight on the pro-found fables of the master. He shows us the same world, seen from a humbler vantage-point. We hear a voice that might so easily never have been heard, a voice from that habitually inaudible fringe of background figures, the young Third and Fourth Officers in Conrad's streaked and wallowing tramp-steamers. At this period of his life he resembles a character from one of Conrad's early sea stories: *Youth*, say, or *Typhoon*.

But of course, behind the book that rises so readily from the page to greet us, there is the diagram of another book, the biography of one of the best English poets of this century. Being the younger brother of Wilfred Owen inevitably coloured Harold Owen's life from first to last. In his later years, as Wilfred's fame grew and grew, he knew that people sought his acquaintance because he was Wilfred's brother rather than, at any rate to begin with, because he was Harold Owen. And in the earliest years his situation must have been even more trying. For a family perennially struggling to make ends meet and to plaster over the cracks in shabby-genteel poverty, having a genius in the family is an expensive luxury. Geniuses are not well adapted to earning money, and they have expensive tastes. Harold, who so longed to paint, would have liked to occupy that position. But Wilfred, who needed to write poetry, had arrived first and already staked it out. Harold was given firmly to understand that the family could not afford a second genius. He must earn a living, either at some indescribably dreary job or (in fulfilment of his father's frustrated secret dream) at sea.

On its first appearance, Harold Owen's autobiography had many readers who went to it primarily to read about Wilfred Owen. It would be insincere to pretend that this will not be the case always, even though the book has proved itself in its own right. Wilfred Owen's standing as a poet, everywhere in the English-speaking world, is deservedly very high. Primarily, of course, he is honoured as one of that group of poets who managed to convey, to people back home who could scarcely imagine it, what the insane hell of the 1914–18 war was like for the men who actually took part in it: civilian-soldiers, hurled straight from a society that enjoyed a peace and stability never seen before in world history, to be the first to experience modern war. Owen's purpose was, in that sense, documentary. He wrote to convey an experience in all its rawness, not to be 'concerned with poetry'. But at the same time his work demonstrates that an artist can devote himself single-mindedly to communication, can strip away any kind of play-element and any ornamentation, and still find that he works better by not deserting the path of art. He finds, that is, that the procedures of art, as distinct from the procedures of journalism or advertising, are not merely ornamental, but practical.

There has been, all through the twentieth century, but with particular insistence since the early 1960s, a body of opinion to the effect that art oughtn't to seem like art—oughtn't, that is, to seem studied, deliberate, shaped, planned, worked at. Human emotions (this school of thought maintains) are best conveyed by utterances that give first and foremost the impression of spontaneity, of having been forced out of the utterer by the sheer pressure of the immediate situation. I have a certain amount of sympathy with this view. It has respectable antecedents. It is, after all, only the Romantic doctrine of individuality and openness of soul in a crude and watered-down form—Romanticism, one might say, in deliquescence. Among its ancestors we may discern Wordsworth's famous statement that poetry at its best is 'a selection of the real language of men in a state of vivid sensation', or Blake's 'Damn braces: bless relaxes'; or, with a slightly altered emphasis, Keats's notion of 'negative capability'.

It is when we meet this doctrine in its extreme, mid-twentieth-century form, which maintains that painting ought to resemble the impulsive daubing on a wall that might result from the release of pent-up feelings at a political meeting, music the whoop or yell of immediate simple emotion, poetry the stuttering or maundering that precedes any kind of composed speech, while narrative, shaped narrative purposefully leading from one episode to the next, has no right to exist at all ('the novel is a cop-out')—it is when we meet it in this form that we begin to notice that the doctrine does not square with our observable experience. In actual life, when we feel a need to convey something that comes from deep inside us and involves our most cherished values, we weigh our words carefully, choosing the ones that will most forcefully carry our meaning to the centre of the target. Who ever made a declaration of love, or a serious statement of intention, or perhaps launched an attack intended to devastate an adversary, without taking pains over the choice of expression? Without pondering, not only the words, but the placing of the words to form cadences, rhythms, high and low points, all aimed at total effectiveness? This has to work, we say to ourselves. If it fails there will be no second chance.

'Above all,' wrote Wilfred Owen in the Preface to his solitary collection of poems, the only one he lived to write, 'I am not concerned with poetry.' No, of course not. A surgeon operating on a desperately ill patient is not concerned with surgery; he is concerned with restoring a sick person to health. And a poet writing about an important human event, be it of glory or of tragedy, is not concerned with poetry. He is concerned with doing justice to the subject, containing it, letting none of its essence run out through leaks and cracks. But the surgeon has spent many years in the careful study of surgery. And the poet was traditionally seen as spending many years in the careful study of poetry. 'The lyf so short, the craft so long to lerne.' Only in our time has it become usual to think that the way to produce poetry is to open one's mouth and let it all run over.

Wilfred Owen held the traditional view. He knew that, if he were to become a poet, it would be necessary for him to train himself as carefully as a surgeon is trained, or a musician, or a physicist. And in Harold Owen's book we catch glimpses of him doing this, putting himself through the long, arduous training. He was young; he was friendless; he had no allies in the struggle he was waging with the drab money-earning society around him, and whose values he impatiently brushed aside as a tissue of irrelevances. Only one thing mattered to him—the shining dream of being one day a great poet. In the pursuit of that dream he could be single-minded to the point of selfishness. He could be intolerant to the point of arrogance. On the gentle and sensitive younger brother this selfishness and arrogance fell like the lashes of a whip, for it was he to whom they were oftenest shown, and most nakedly.

And of course, like everything else that happened to the young man, these things have found a place in his honest and open narrative. When the work first appeared, I remember some people speculating as to whether the younger brother, in some devious way, were not purposely trying to blacken the character of the elder. Stuff and nonsense. It was not in his nature to play tricks, to pretend to admire Wilfred while actually showing him in a bad light. He knew only one method of telling his story—to say, in an unvarnished and truthful way, what happened.

These touches of detail about the irascibility and aloofness of the youthful poet are, in any case, highly effective in the architecture of the book, though I would find it very hard to say whether this effect was planned or simply the result of happy accident, a reward for Harold Owen's straightforward honesty. But surely the closing section of the book, in which the central episodes are the Armistice and, simultaneously, the news of Wilfred's death, would not be so deeply moving if we had not journeyed with Harold through the troughs and shallows of a relationship with Wilfred, as well as its fine, dashing waves. Just because he has not tried to sentimentalize his brother, just because he has drawn him warts and all, the grief at their sundering is the more deeply etched. The First World War, even when seen across the war-torn landscape of the twentieth century, still seems one of the worst disasters that ever befell the human race, and its sadness has found many echoes in literature, but surely none sadder than the young Harold's vision of Wilfred, khaki-clad, sitting in the chair in his cabin, in that ship anchored off the port of Victoria in the Cameroons. The very setting of this vision has its own deep, tragic irony: the Cameroons were once, briefly, the pride of Bismarck's African Empire; the town of Victoria had been built in the ornate German colonial style; and now the German defeat had emptied the place of its white governing class, and left it a ghost town full of echoes of a vanished German past. That was one irony. Another was that, with the slowness of communications and the lingering disorganization of wartime, the news of Wilfred's death had still not reached Harold, though the telegraph had spread the news of the Armistice and the end of the fighting weeks earlier. If he had been in home waters, Harold would have known about Wilfred's death long before this, when the rest of the family knew about it. And now that the ordinary means of communication had failed, the two brothers, because of their deeply entwined closeness, found a way to be together, a way they both believed in and understood, the way of imaginative vision. And so the book glides, like a ship coming to her right moorings, to its ending: the home-coming, both touching and comical like all Harold Owen's descriptions of his family circle, and finally the almost unbearably moving moment when Harold, left alone in Wilfred's empty and silent room, dips into his books as a last link between them.

There seems to be only one more duty that a humble introducer of this memorable book can perform. The book itself, while totally convincing in its presentation of Wilfred Owen as a young man whose being is dedicated to the service of poetry, quotes not a line of his verse. It assumes, and rightly of course, that anyone interested to know what Wilfred actually achieved out of all those years of self-forgetful sacrifice (and surely if they are not interested at the beginning they will be by the end), can easily get hold of Wilfred's poems, which are very widely published, anthologized, quoted, mentioned, discussed. Quite right. And yet it also seems right that this reprint, as it starts its journey into the world, should take on board just one of Wilfred's poems. He should be present in what he made as well as what he was; in his authority as a poet as well as in his longing and aspiration as a penniless apprentice. Read this poem. No matter how

many times you have read it before, read it again. Let the majesty of
its rhythm, the slow sonority of its music, the perfectly achieved poetic art with which it can afford 'not to be concerned with poetry', do
what this essay, or any essay, could never do.

Anthem for Doomed Youth

What passing-bells for these who die as cattle?
   Only the monstrous anger of the guns.
   Only the stuttering rifles' rapid rattle
Can patter out their hasty orisons.
No mockeries for them from prayers or bells,
   Nor any voice of mourning save the choirs,—
The shrill, demented choirs of wailing shells;
   And bugles calling for them from sad shires.

What candles may be held to speed them all?
   Not in the hands of boys, but in their eyes
Shall shine the holy glimmers of good-byes.
   The pallor of girls' brows shall be their pall;
Their flowers the tenderness of silent minds,
And each slow dusk a drawing-down of blinds.

1. *Early Days*

My father's life had always been one of struggle in which personal ambition and inclination had to be sacrificed to family needs and financial necessity. Although he came of a family of some standing, circumstances were such that at an early age it was indicated to him that he would have to fend for himself. So when he was fifteen he applied for and obtained a post as a junior clerk with the railways. As time went on, my father realized his lack of prospects, and made up his mind to get out of England in the hope of finding better advancement; and, as this also fitted in with his ambition to travel, especially in the East, he set himself to find some post abroad. While still a minor, he was offered a post with the Indian Peninsular Railway in Bombay. The post stipulated payment of his own passage out. My father, of course, had not got this considerable sum, and knew nobody at all from whom he might borrow it. Nevertheless, he accepted the job, went to Liverpool, and hunted the docks until he could find a ship's captain who would sign him on as a deck hand for the single voyage. One September morning in the eighteen-eighties he signed on as an Ordinary Seaman in the ship *Benalder*, 1,330 tons, Captain Buchanan. After an adventurous voyage of considerable hardship he reached India, took his discharge certificate from the ship, and before Christmas took up his new appointment in Bombay. He did well during his four years there and established himself so securely that his prospects for a career that might have been spectacular, and anyway would have been of real importance, were very bright indeed.

Before he left England he had met and fallen in love with Susan Shaw, the sister of his somewhat profligate friend, Edward Shaw. My father was accepted and so much liked in my mother's home that his suit was permitted, although I think there were designs for her elsewhere. My father loved his life in India, but set out for home on hearing from Susan of the difficulties she was having to face. Her mother was dying and her brother, Edward, was, through his wildness and uncontrollable drinking bouts, causing her terrible anxiety. As well as this she told him of her real worry about her father's financial affairs and things generally at Plas Wilmot, the Shaws' family home near Oswestry. Soon after this Edward disappeared— or rather ran away—leaving a message for his parents to tell them that he was alive and well and that he was making for America.

It was established that in 1893 he was in Denver, Colorado, but from that time nothing has ever been heard of him. This tragedy of Edward's running away, and all the other difficulties, my father found waiting for him upon his return to Plas Wilmot from India. In the circumstances he decided that a return to India was quite impossible and that the only thing to do was to reconcile himself to employment in England and give what help he could to my grandfather. To secure this end, he hid his disappointment and, abandoning all hope of an adventurous career in the East, obtained for himself a post with an English railway; and in 1891, with a salary of only seventy-five pounds a year, married my mother. After a short honeymoon my father and his bride returned to Plas Wilmot, hoping to bring about a more sensible economy which would place the family finances in a sounder condition, but it was too late to improve them, though the pattern of life seemed outwardly the same.

In 1897 my grandfather died. Plas Wilmot was sold immediately. As had long been suspected, my grandfather's estate, when realized, left no more than some few hundred pounds between his daughters. So my parents and their two children, Wilfred and Mary, had to leave Plas Wilmot, having to say good-bye to its gardens, fields, and coach houses and the gracious way of living that had given them a sense of security. Never again were they to live in such surroundings or perhaps find such peaceful happiness, and never again to the end of their lives were they or their children to have any feeling of security. It was here at Plas Wilmot that Wilfred for his first years could be, and was, so carefully nurtured. Here it was that my father and mother had peace so that love and gentleness flowed over Wilfred and, later, his young sister Mary. Upon all this, with their two small children, Tom and Susan Owen had to turn their backs and find a house or rooms and set about the difficult and uncertain task of rearing a family, and Plas Wilmot became—as such things will in families—a legend, much talked of amongst ourselves, and most likely, as legends do, gaining enhancement with the years. The transition must—although carrying more responsibility and anxiety —have been easier for my father than it was for my mother. While he had not yet faced real poverty, a lack of the finer niceties of life was not new to him: for my mother it was new—something which, until that time, she had never experienced. They moved first to Shrewsbury and in this town I was born in a tiny back bedroom of a small, rather shabby little house in a long street of other mean little houses—all exactly the same except that, in the tiny impoverished patch of ground in front of ours, a laburnum tree had somehow rooted itself. I was more fortunate than Colin, my younger brother. It was his fate to be born in another, even smaller, back bedroom; this time in the smelly July heat of a slum area of the sea-port of Birkenhead, some three years after my own birth.

It was at this period that acute lack of money began to exert its insidious influence upon our home, and, as a consequence, the corrosion of disillusion began to blunt my parents' ambitions. It became a time for us when existence—food, housing, and keeping free from debt—was the immediate problem, and so dominant was this preoccupation that the future for us children had to be something which must look after itself. All the usual additions to children's diets were unknown to us, as, of course, they were to hundreds of other children living around us who somehow survived in the dirty little houses and smelly streets, and, like them, we all of us developed a pinched, rickety look. My mother became unwell and Colin developed some bone weakness and it became necessary to encase the rickety legs in heavy iron splints to try to straighten the leg bones and prevent further deterioration. Expensive medical fees were therefore added to my father's anxieties. None the less, these hardships brought out the quality of my parents; in spite of their difficulties and the most uncongenial surroundings in which we lived, they were able to exercise a discipline which maintained a quiet dignity. In my father this showed in his love for a well-ordered family life, in his determination to pursue his cultural relaxations in his spare time, and in his engrossment with good reading and his passion for music. It showed too in his absolute insistence upon good manners in us in all circumstances. A grace before meals was always said; on weekdays my mother would proclaim this, but on Sunday my father was invariably invited to perform this small rite.

Upon looking back over all our childhoods, I am convinced that while perhaps seemingly trivial, this discipline, this observance of rites and small ceremonies, the ritual of splitting up the days into ordered routine was the most important thing in our young lives. It was through this that poverty, sickness, and pressing anxiety were all somehow, if not surmounted, at least kept at bay. Without this reinforcement of discipline and good manners, outside difficulties would have overwhelmed our structure, and, as a family, I think we would have crumbled away.

2. *Holiday in Ireland*

Soon a slight general improvement in our financial position came about. My father must have been promoted about this time, and before long he became a fairly senior official and head of his department. The house he was now able to rent was situated in a much better neighbourhood and, although it was very small and dark, we were once and for all out of the slum and tenement area.

During this time that we lived in Birkenhead, which lasted until Wilfred was fourteen and I between nine and ten, we were as a family able to take some holidays, such as the one in Ireland, in spite of shortage of money. I think my father must have budgeted for these very carefully and it was made easier by the actual cost of travelling never having to enter into the calculations. My father, in his capacity as a railway official, was entitled to free passes for the whole family once or twice a year. This gave us unlimited choice of district and it was possible in those days to get rooms for very small weekly sums.

For one of these holidays, when I was seven, my father took us all over to Ireland, to Tramore, a small village near Waterford. He had secured rooms in a fisherman's whitewashed cottage. It was perhaps the best of all our times. The fisherman and his wife were quite perfect hosts, and the accommodation, though tiny, was pleasant. The morning would be spent in bathing: my father and Wilfred, who was now good in the water, swimming, and we younger ones submerging ourselves in the surf and having occasional swimming lessons.

Almost every afternoon my father and I went out fishing, rowing or sailing miles out to sea to the dog-fish grounds. On one of these days our boatman, knowing the weather was set fair, suggested that on the following day we should make a dawn start, for if we did this they could take us to another fishing ground much farther out to sea. I was tremendously excited about this, so that when my father came to call me the next morning he found me already struggling into my shorts and jersey. He himself was not much less excited, and so anxious was I not to be late that I could hardly wait to drink our scalding tea, and, with our slabs of thick bread and butter still in our hands, we set off for the harbour.

For the first few hours we caught only the usual-sized fish, until suddenly my line tore through my hands, burning my fingers badly

—I was into a really big fish. My father and one of the men sprang to help me. I refused to let go, but the man forced my hands open and placed them over his own, and later they bound my hands with canvas so that I could hold on. It seemed to me hours while the fish was running until it turned and we hauled in the slack. . . . I remember shouting at the men not to let my fish go. . . . After a long struggle it broke surface, threshing the water into a boil ten yards from the boat. I was almost delirious with joy and excitement. The boatman proclaimed it to be a shark. It gave us many more furious runs before it could be brought nearer to the boat, but it was still fighting dangerously. Our fishermen now suggested we should cut the line. They thought it too dangerous to try to bring it over the side, and my father, for once, agreed, for these fish, unless handled with extreme skill, will tear a poisonous bite with their jaws and can inflict severe injuries with a flailing tail.

My cries of rage and disappointment at losing this marvellous prize—caught on my own line too—were so emphatic and so despairing that they all relented, and it was decided to get it aboard somehow. After many more runs the men took a turn around the stem with my line and made the fish take the weight of the boat until it began to tire, and the line was gradually shortened until they were able to bring it alongside. Telling my father to look after me, the fishermen with great skill somehow got it inboard, immediately partly smothering it with a heavy sail. The tail was then secured and the head hammered until it lay still. I could barely contain myself, and could not bear the idea of continuing with any more fishing that afternoon. All I wanted was to get ashore as quickly as possible and show my prize to the others, so we put about and headed for the harbour. When we had tied up at the jetty, of course the problem of disposal came up, but I quickly settled this by my determination not to be parted from the great fish, and demanded that we should take it up to our rooms. There was some demur about this.

The early return of the boat and rumours of a big fish had got about so that we were soon surrounded by everybody near the slipways. My intense excitement and refusal to be separated from the fish infected the crowd and they were touched as well, I think, by my enthusiasm for their own calling. They commenced shouting to one another, excitement began to run high, and very soon in their emotional Irish way they had created a sort of carnival atmosphere about the whole happening and were prepared to go to any lengths to see that I had my own way. A rope was secured to the head, a lighter piece of line was bent on to the tail, which I was given to hold to mark my ownership; the men laid on the heavier rope and the parade set off dragging the capture along behind us. Excitement spread and we were soon joined by most of the village men, women, and dogs, who, forming up behind us, cheered us on in triumphant procession until we reached our cottage.

My mother and the others were not quite as enthusiastic as I had expected them to be, and the woman from the cottage naturally even less so. She flatly refused to have the dead creature in the wide passageway inside the cottage where I wanted to keep it. However, there was an outhouse adjoining, into which it was finally hauled and the door shut. This was an even better arrangement for me and every half-hour or so I would run out to inspect it. At first one or two of the others would come with me, but when they tired of this I would go alone, which I liked doing very much, for then I could contemplate it with silent admiration and relive the excitement of the line running through my canvas-covered fingers. Wilfred showed a surprising interest, making much of my exploit, which gave me a nice warm feeling. I continued these visits of adoration until late in the evening. It was on my last visitation before I was to be put to bed that it happened.

It was almost dark now, I opened the shed door, my fish was gone—or so I thought until I heard a wet slithering noise on the stone floor, and peering into a dark corner I saw a greyish white upright shape. It was the fish standing on its tail. Even as I drew in my breath and cried out a bit, the wraith-like thing slipped to the floor with a wet slapping noise, but instantly it was up on its tail again so that it appeared to be walking around the shed. When with its next convulsion it lunged towards me it was altogether too much—the transition from death to life was somehow horrible . . . with a sob that was barely half strangled I leapt out of the shed, slamming the door behind me. I rushed into the cottage, calling out that the fish was walking about the shed. . . . Perhaps it was my unfortunate phrasing, anyhow I was met with utter disbelief; I was scolded, too, for making up such a ridiculous story and Wilfred was told to take me up to bed, but I was insistent. In the end—to pacify me—Wilfred came along to the shed, and when we got near he too heard the wet slam of the slapping fish as it fell about. Wilfred didn't like it any more than I did—holding hands very tightly we crept to the door, opened it a crack, saw the ghostly gleam as the thing reared and flopped; this time it was Wilfred who slammed the door, and we ran to the house calling out for them all to come quickly. My father, excited now, came running out, the fisherman following with a lantern.

Inside the shed the fish seemed weaker; it was still moving about, but not so violently. With the shed lighted, the comforting bulk of my father on one side and Wilfred still holding my hand tightly on the other, I was no longer afraid. The creature itself did not now look so fearsome. Its opening and closing mouth and slight gasping noises made me, in a childish way, only dreadfully sorry for it, and guilty that I had brought all this about. As I looked at my fish, now fighting to live, I could not get out of my thoughts the blows that had been hammered on its head when we had got it into the boat. . . . I was instantly consumed with a desire to get it back into the sea and let it live again.

The fisherman at first was dubious, but perhaps something in my passionate appeal to my father may have moved him, or more likely he saw in this a permanent and happy ending to the whole affair. The aid of another boatman was secured and, all of us helping, we set off through the darkening village street on the haul back to the sea. It was quite dark when we reached the jetty, but we could just see to slide the fish off the end into deep water. After the water settled, we could make out the ghostly grey gleam of it just under the surface as it rolled in the current. In launching it, while removing the heavier line, they had forgotten to take off the light line that had been knotted around its tail for my benefit.

The next morning fishermen in the bay reported that the fish had been seen near the surface swimming weakly, but most certainly alive, the piece of line still attached, making identity absolutely certain. Local interest had been aroused over the little English boy's catch, and the amazing fact that it had recovered life after having been apparently killed in the boat and then kept out of the water for over nine hours revived the excitement, and the little boy's fish became a local legend and something of a mascot. It was never molested and was watched with great keenness. I was to see it three or four times, swimming more strongly each time. It remained in the bay, cruising near the surface. Some injury it had been dealt by us may have caused this. Altogether it was sighted, but at longer intervals each time, over a period of eleven months, after which it was not seen again.

The interest in the episode sustained itself in the village, as such trivialities sometimes will in small communities. We were to know this because after we had returned home the fisherman got his wife to write to us from time to time. We were told the episode even reached the length of being commented upon in the local press, although we never saw a cutting.

Before our holidays finished, a curious and rather unpleasant experience befell us, a triviality notable only for its isolation. I say isolation purposely, for never in the whole of our family life, either before or since, did anything of a similar character ever brush us. It was something, too, which affected us all in exactly the same way, and this in itself is noticeable, so rarely did we react with such similarity; again, it was something which happened while we were all with one another. It was at the very end of our time in Ireland and my father, who was extremely fond of having his whole family together and about him—especially if it was to mark something such as this, the end of our holiday—had with one of his rare shows of determination insisted that we all walk for a few hours together. At the back of his thoughts in his own rather secretive imaginative mind he did, I think, want to make a picture for himself of us all in some happy connection, so that he could carry back with him to the smoke and dirt of Birkenhead an image that would perhaps give him courage to face the twelve months of anxiety and the constant irritation of uncongenial work which he knew inevitably must pass before another holiday took place.

This last walk together in Ireland which he had proposed started quite happily, perhaps because we were all a little quiet and sorry that our holiday was over. My father chose a direction with which none of us had so far become familiar. After some time we came to the opening of a narrow lane and following this up we found it brought us to the broken-down entrance gates of a forbidding looking avenue bordered on each side by dense woods. The drive itself was obviously in disuse and heavily overgrown. We walked into this place in quite good spirits until we got some little distance up. It was immensely long and dark; the trees meeting overhead roofed it so that the effect was of a rather dark tunnel. The weather which had been bright with sunshine suddenly changed and became theatrical— great dark clouds must have swept up swiftly and covered the sun, huge drops of cold rain came down, pattering on the foliage with a disagreeable tattoo. Inside our avenue it suddenly became very dark, a bleak feeling seized hold of us all and we became very silent though not fearful at all, and continued on our way, but not very happily—

at least I certainly was not, I was disliking it all more and more the further in we penetrated.

It was I who caused the first feeling—not I think of alarm but more a sensation of something strange that caused a curious apprehension to pulse through us all. I brought this about by calling out in a stifled voice that I had seen something large and animal-like moving along a branch high up in one of the trees. Curiously enough, my rather frightened ejaculation was accepted by the others as something almost expected and not with the derision that would have been normal for an outburst of mine like this. Wilfred, following my pointing finger, confirmed me, and almost immediately my father did the same. We all saw it move again, then freeze into immobility as if conscious of our concentrated stares. Horrid cold prickles were running up and down my back, which made me long to run and get away from this strangeness, and Wilfred was trembling and almost as frightened as I was. I remember we were all instantly frozen into a horrid still silence, which we could not break, and we recalled afterwards that we were all of us holding our breath. It was not until we heard the muffled roar of heavy rain emptying itself from a burst cloud that any movement by ourselves released our paralysis. The violence of the downpour broke our tension and in itself made a curtain between us and what we had seen in the tree. We were uneasy and could not speak; instead, we only stared in the direction of the tree. When the rain stopped, the curtain lifted; what we thought we had seen was no longer there, but the space where it had been was frighteningly clear. . . . My father, coming to himself, immediately took charge and with forced hilarity tried to break the spell and cheer us all up with light-hearted explanations of the tricks light and shade could play in trees and how deceptive these could be.

My mother was now quite desperate to get out of this dark wood and return to the friendly village, but my father would have none of it. The rain had now stopped and he was absolutely determined to find out what was at the end of the drive. We children were not now actually frightened, but an apprehension and chill oppressiveness had settled on us all. This was emphasized by our surroundings of thickly growing woods which gave us a trapped feeling as we went deeper into the increasing narrowness of the avenue; we were, we thought, getting shut in under this dismal dripping canopy. The water from the cloudburst was now rising up from the warm earth in spirals of pearly coloured vapour which twisted and turned in slow convolutions among the trees and undergrowth. We continued walking along this seemingly endless tunnel, but after some little time it seemed to grow lighter, the trees were becoming thinner and now and again there were open spaces that had only brushwood and no trees. Soon after this the drive, which was dwindling to little more than a rough track, took a sharp right-hand bend and shortly afterwards another—this time to the left. After we had rounded this last curve, we came into open bare-looking ground and were immediately faced with what appeared to be a sheet of water. It was separated from us by about thirty yards of stony foreshore. It did not somehow quite look like real water; instead, it had the metallic sheen of polished gunmetal. The whole effect had the eerie quality of a mirage. This was accentuated by a strange high wall of mist which cut across the water in a perfectly straight line. In this way every bit of background was obliterated and, by some curious trick, it seemed that behind this mist there was just nothing at all. The effect was of utter unreality. This dreamlike unrealness gave it a weird mystery and some menacing threat of danger that produced in us all a sensation of being warned. So strong was this feeling that we all closed up together and then remained motionless; we did not speak, but just stood and stared. I am certain that we remained in this trance-like state for several minutes until my father, shaking himself a little, spoke to us (his voice, I remember, was not quite firm), telling us that this nonsense of being frightened of nothing had gone quite far enough, and throwing some jocular remark that had a merry challenge in it, he started off towards the water. The rest of us were instinctively holding hands and, still under an inexplicable spell of some sort, followed along just behind him. We had perhaps gone half-way when we realized that the water and the wall of mist were receding from us at exactly the same pace that we ourselves were moving. The strangeness of this stopped my father—immediately the water and the mist became stationary again, only now the whole scene had taken on a transcendent appearance as if it was not really there at all but superimposed over the rough open space. . . . My father was anxious now, and my mother and Wilfred were trembling violently; we younger ones were, I think, more unhappy than frightened. It was darkening now and there was a chill in the air.

My father advanced once more and the same thing happened—the water and the mist again went back, only this time the normal background of trees and sedgy grass seemed in a horrid way to be coming through as if they were real and solid and the water and the mist were nebulous. This was too much for my mother and, swinging around, she turned to get away from it. It was as she turned that for the first and only time in my life I heard her give a stifled scream. This spun us all around to see, standing ten yards or so from us, the shadowy figure of a tall man. This strange figure seemed to radiate the same cold incandescent quality that even now was permeating the hallucinatory lake. For some inexplicable reason the whole attitude of this illusionary being diffused a mute declaration of his intention to do harm to us and this, I know, gave us all a quite unreasonable feeling of desperate insecurity.

My father must have recovered himself and at once addressed this sinister looking person, I have no doubt with some apology for our trespass if we were committing one. The sound of my father's voice had the unexpected effect of contorting the man into a frenzy of fury, and he raised the heavy stick he was carrying with such ferocious intent that attack from him seemed unavoidable. The surprise perhaps silenced my father and immediately the figure relaxed to its original stationary position. After a minute of bemused silence my father tried again, only to produce the same silent paroxysm. Perhaps it was the unnatural muteness more than the gesticulating that created the cold fear that now held all of us except my father. The rest of us were motionless and speechless, but he was now very angry and belligerent and advanced upon this thing or man, with the astonishing effect of causing it to walk backwards away from him, keeping an unvarying distance. It seemed as though the two of them were synchronized, every hesitation or movement of my father was repeated in a backward direction by the figure who still faced us. If my father retreated the figure came forward. This marionette movement continued backwards and forwards until my father, his quick temper rising, strode forward with real determination until he came to the very edge of the wood. . . . It was now that my mother's despairing voice cried out so urgently, 'Tom, Tom, come back, come back.'

At this instant the figure, which had been clearly there until now, was suddenly not there any longer. . . . Our tightness left us, and freedom once again was all about us.

My father we could see was standing motionless. It was something in my mother's voice which seemed to awaken some awareness in him, so that he turned about sharply and then walked slowly and tiredly back to us. We were a very subdued family by now and my father was unusually silent. To add to our depression, darkness was falling more quickly than usual. Although still preoccupied, my father with great vigour hustled us together and taking a direction right away from the place, herded us along at a tremendous pace. As he turned us away we all looked back towards the lake. It was no longer there. He had picked up both Colin and Mary, carrying them one under each arm, and my mother had Wilfred and me by the hand. Striding just ahead of us he forced his way through everything until we came to a road—for once my mother had not protested against his rushing haste.

Once on the road he collected himself again and, bustling us along with much cheerfulness, did his best to raise our spirits. We younger ones responded quite well, but Wilfred—very quiet, sombre, and absorbed with his own thoughts—seemed unable to do so. I can remember trudging along for what seemed endless miles and then being lifted into some sort of vehicle; after that I cannot remember anything until I woke up in our cottage rooms.

We were, I think, a resilient family. I recall so well while we were having supper with what gaiety we children chattered in our childish way, and how merrily my father made fun out of the strange happenings. Wilfred was in high spirits and was eagerly leading our excited little arguments. In this way all the horridness of the wretched afternoon seemed to melt away and instead took on the brilliant lustre of adventure safely passed, in which we had all played most splendid parts. With immense enjoyment we were vying with each other to claim for ourselves special importance. In the warm cosiness of the fire-lit cottage room, pervaded as it was with the bright cheerfulness of my mother and father, menace could not touch us . . . in retrospect we could feel no threat. . . . Instead, as our excited babblings embroidered themselves, we began to feel brave as lions.

Down the years it was to turn itself into a fine family legend, to be frequently talked about—but only amongst ourselves . . . we would never speak of it to anyone else. We were still chattering and quarrelling happily when the fisherman and his wife in their customary way came to our room to wish us good night. After a few preliminaries my father and mother began to ask some questions and commenced to recount some of our peculiar experiences. The change in them both was immediate and astounding—their friendliness was wiped away, their faces hardened, and they gazed at us with such frigidity that it became very near to incivility, muttering to one another in a most furtive way. Surprised, my father, realizing that their whole manner forbade any discussion, stopped abruptly. After an awkward silence they relented a little, and both of them together begged him not to speak of it to anyone at all, and to see that we children did not do so either, and in a somewhat peremptory tone implored him to forget all about it entirely. After another long and difficult silence, during which they stared from one to another of us with looks that were full of curiosity and conjecture, they turned about suddenly and without any of their usual courteous ceremony, left the room.

Early the next morning we started our homeward journey to Birkenhead.

3. *Ships, Sea and the Docks*

The excitement of the sea and of ships had always been part of the fabric of my life and had been instilled in me by my father's enthusiasm and, living as we did in a town that was also a seaport, he soon found opportunities for making contact with ships and sailors. This gave him great delight, both for the immediate interest it offered and for the memories it brought back of his early, more adventurous days.

When he and my mother were still at Plas Wilmot he had built, especially for Wilfred, the S.S. *Susan*, the perfect replica of a sea-going ship—three feet in length. The steering system was exact and could be set to steer a course; the steering-wheel itself, carved in one piece from the lid of a cigar box, was masterly in execution; the life-boats were gems in themselves, complete with minute—but removable—canvas covers, and could be correctly lowered to the water-line by working davits. It was properly equipped with regulation navigation lights, binnacle, and real compass; even the skylights were glazed with real glass. Fitted into the ship were real boilers with furnaces fired by methylated spirit and cotton wool for fuel, which drove the engine geared to the propeller shaft. The foghorn fitted to the foremast funnel was operated from the bridge by lanyard.

This enthusiasm of his for the sea was one of the earliest bonds between us and was perhaps first created by his possession of the seamen's 'Certificate of Discharge'. This he had been given when leaving the *Benalder* on which he had worked his passage to India and he treasured it all his life. It was, I know, one of his most prized possessions. During the dullness of his later life it became emblematic of early adventures, and a signal mark to him of real manhood . . . he had at least once been a sailor before the mast. I so well remember when I was about five years old one day finding ourselves alone together in the house, he, having with enormous solemnity first of all bound me to secrecy, showed me this certificate and told me the story of his voyage, exaggerating the terrible storms, near shipwreck, and the barefoot work about the decks and up aloft, painting all the time a gruesome picture of the dark fo'c'sle, the decomposing food, and the strangely dangerous sailors who were his companions. In my imagination it became a ritual between us, so that all rites had to be observed: we must be alone in the house, the key must be produced with drama and the removal of the papers must be done with mystery. This taking out of the certificate became one of my greatest excitements: we never grew tired of looking at it, and each time the story was a little more embellished. On very special occasions I was allowed to hold it. The secrecy was genuine, my father was reserved and often shy with his family, and I think he felt my mother might look askance at this reminder of sea-fever.

By the time I was of an age when I could be taken about, my father had contrived to get authorized access to the ships in dock or in the river, and very often trips by launch up the Mersey to ships at anchor. In such surroundings he would seem completely in place, for his general appearance was very typically seamanlike. His short stocky figure with the breadth of shoulder and deep chest gave him a rather savage bearing resembling a small but uncertain bull. The effect was one of physical toughness and strength. His dress, too, quite accidentally seemed to conform, for he always wore dark blue serge suits with white shirts and stiff white collars and dark ties, which seemed to be the universal shore-going rig of masters and mates, more especially from the sailing ships and cargo steamers. The liner captains were, except to very close observers, indistinguishable from ordinary professional civilians. The build of his face and head, with its brickish red complexion, the general weather-beaten look, and the network of fine lines and wrinkles that surrounded the eyes, seemed to me to suggest the sea.

After much priming as to the treats in store for me, and having made a few trial trips, he told me one day—with a flatteringly conspiratorial air—that from now on I was always to go with him on these adventures. I was overwhelmed with joy, for already some of the romance of it was beginning to prickle in me. To begin with, these outings were not quite the success we had hoped for. At first I was rather overawed. The immense ships looming up above me so threateningly, the ceaseless clang of steel on empty steel from the riveters' hammers, the enormous gantries rearing upwards like one-armed giants, the ships' derricks loading and unloading and swinging out their huge slings of cargo—aiming them, as it seemed to me, straight for us—the constant avoidance of falling over the great steel and hemp hawsers, that stretched like snakes from ship to quay-side, the throngs of dock labourers and roaring stevedores, and the seamen themselves, these the gentlest and quietest of all—and of so many colours from coal black through the browns and yellows to the whites—all this was perhaps overwhelming for so small a boy, but I soon came to enjoy it all. What really did frighten me was having to walk with my father along the narrow quay-sides which surrounded the docks. He persisted in walking as near as possible to the edge, which always gave me the feeling that sooner or later against my own volition these hungry-looking dock-basins would, with some dark power they seemed to exert, suck me down into their depths. This horrible feeling was especially strong when we stood on the bare unguarded lip of the deep graving docks to watch the shipyard workers crawling about like ants underneath the ships. My father delighted in doing this and always forced me to do the same. He would seek out all the narrowest gangways and unrailed planks from ship-side to quay and make me walk or stand with him. I was able to become accustomed to this, but the feeling was always strong enough to spoil what would otherwise have been perfection. I was never quite able to lose this curious floating, almost light-headed, feeling when walking along a narrow gangway, even after I had been at sea for years. My father's favourite place to stand was on the narrow two-foot sluice-gates, for choice when the rope life-lines had been removed just prior to flooding, so that we had cold, angry-looking water a few feet below us on one side and twenty feet or more of yawning stone depths of emptiness on the other.

Once on board a ship I lost all this unpleasant feeling and would climb up and down ladders and balance on guard rails and bulwarks with dangerous facility, and as we spent most of our time actually in the ships I was able to forget it. My father would talk away by the hour to the officers and men. Hospitality was always offered, cups of black syrupy tea, gritty cocoa, or weak coffee for me, and, after much delving about in lockers and under bunk mattresses, fascinating bottles were produced for my father.

There is one ship I remember very vividly. She was a smallish three-masted barque with a crew who could hardly speak any

English. She was, I think, Norwegian or Swedish, and was laid up for months, probably for re-rigging or just lack of cargo, and occupied a berth in what, to my childish mind, appeared to be the countryside. Anyway, there were fields near. She was probably in some riverside creek. It used to be a long and tiring business getting to her, but it was well worth it, and although communication, owing to language difficulties, should have been impossible, it never proved so.

With smiles, nods and gestures and great bursts of roaring laughter and occasional English words, we seemed to understand one another perfectly and, to complete a fairy-tale picture in my mind, this ship carried as cook a huge kindly Negro who made special pastries for me. The captain, a large yellow-haired man, took his wife with him on all his voyages, as was not unusual in that type of vessel. She, too, was fair-haired and handsomely built. They appeared quite old to me, but were probably very young. Anyhow, between them with their chief and second mate, the tea parties they made for us in the cuddy were very happy and gay.

My father sometimes made an effort to bring the atmosphere of the sea into his own home. There was the never-forgotten occasion when he insisted upon inviting four lascar seamen whom he had met through befriending them when they had somehow missed their ship. They were just ordinary seamen from some steamer in the India trade. It was a heaven-sent opportunity for him to practise his Hindustani—all his life he maintained his fluency in this.

An evening was arranged and my mother was duly instructed to prepare a special curry, the recipe of which he had brought home from Bombay. The occasion when he did bring these Indians home created something of a stir in the road where we lived. For some reason, not one of them would walk abreast with my father, but insisted on shuffling along behind him, in single file with their flimsy slippers clipping and slapping on the pavement as they moved along. Following closely behind them came the young street rabble, shouting and calling out insults. The Indians, like my father, remained stoical and impassive. Ceremonial was gone through before entering our home, slippers were carefully removed and the beautifully ornamented round silk caps retained on their heads. They were perfect guests, appreciative and complimentary and delightfully courteous. They enjoyed the food immensely and ate entirely with their fingers. Knowing from my father their national weakness for sweetmeats, my mother had placed four or five pounds of home-made treacle toffee on the table. The sight of this seemed to have a mesmeric effect on them in a most extraordinary way; at the expense of the other carefully prepared dishes, they could not stop eating it, and although they did this with restraint and dignity, they finished every bit.

Perhaps their nicest touch of all was the trouble they had taken previously to find out from my father how many children he had; all of the four Indians had prepared a separate little gift for each of us, carefully wrapped in Indian tissue paper and tied with tinsel thread. My mother was presented with glass trinkets and my father with a bundle of cheroots. All were tendered in the most graceful manner with low bows and spoken benedictions. Altogether the evening was a success, although my mother did not give the proceedings quite her full approval. We children were completely fascinated with these brown seamen, especially with their dark skins and, to us, curious garb, and most of all by the eight bare feet so carefully arranged underneath the table.

4. *Wilfred*

In these early years the gap in age between Wilfred and us other three was very noticeable, being accentuated by Mary's extreme smallness of stature and her delicacy which always made her appear younger than I, so that the four years and a half between Wilfred and me came to be accepted as the demarcation between Wilfred as the eldest and responsible child and us three as the small children, always in need of care. This demarcation was to remain in a lessening degree until Wilfred left home. Owing to my mother's delicacy and my father's very long hours of work away from home this very often threw undue responsibility—for so young a boy—upon Wilfred, and did account in great measure for his early gravity, and made him mature beyond his years. My mother encouraged this, with her indifferent health she had little choice, which meant that in the beginning Wilfred was very often in charge of us three.

This often involved Wilfred in incidents which, at the age of ten, were more than he could manage. Once, for example, when having been told to keep Mary and me (Colin was ill) well out of the way one wet morning, he took us to a green hill some distance outside Birkenhead to which we occasionally went. I suppose to amuse us—it could not have been for safety, for we did not always use them—he made some reins out of thin clothes lines, and at the beginning of the day made great play for us by driving us tandem or abreast, and invented situations and destinations for us to bring reality and entertainment into the games. But these reins caused Wilfred the biggest fright and upset he had so far experienced. Wilfred had harnessed me up, and by some fluky mischance had unknowingly tied the rein in a self-tightening knot. Very soon this began to tighten on my arm most painfully and I called out in distress to Wilfred who struggled to release the tightening band, but the wet was shrinking and stiffening the cord. It became too strong for his small fingers and the more he struggled the tighter it became. I remember Wilfred calling out frantically for help, but there was no one in sight so he trotted us down to some nearby roads and houses and as soon as he saw a woman he called out to her. She ran up to us, but in trying to release my arm only made the cord still tighter. My arm was now swelling painfully and growing cold, but she must have been sensible, for she hastened away and soon came back with a rough-looking man who managed to cut the cord with his pocket-knife. Wilfred was almost frantic with anxiety and remorse. No sooner had the man done this than he turned on the small Wilfred in a most threatening and abusive manner, accusing him of deliberate cruelty to his small brother and threatening to thrash him there and then. This frightened us all badly. Mary and I closed up with Wilfred and piped up in shrill defence of him. The man made a grab at Wilfred, but the woman intervened and the man turned revilingly upon her. Wilfred, gathering us both by the hand, ran us safely out of sight. I expect the man was drunk. The unpleasantness, together with his acute concern about having damaged his charge, had upset and unnerved Wilfred and he took us home as fast as he could.

Being so frequently in sole charge of us was also the beginning, I think, of a fixed feeling in Wilfred's own mind that he really belonged to and shared the responsibility of the parental side. In this way I always think Wilfred was denied, if not his boyhood, at least his boyishness. In later years as he became more and more preoccupied with his reading, this characteristic became even more pronounced, so that his quiet gravity was very noticeable even outside the family.

A picture of Wilfred remains in my mind which characterized his bearing at this time. The occasion was our move from Birkenhead to Shrewsbury when we were awaiting the cab which was to take us to our new home. He was hunched up in a corner deep in some book or other, seemingly impervious to the fretted tempers snapping round him. He was dressed in a Norfolk knickerbocker suit, much in vogue among schoolboys at that period, of some brownish material, with stockings and boots, and a narrow white stiff collar with a stringy looking tie that would never keep closed up to the collar itself. His very dark brown hair was falling untidily over his forehead: it badly needed cutting. A source of irritation to my father—of which we three boys were all guilty—was our aversion to visiting the barber often enough to satisfy him. Wilfred had slung over his shoulders his school satchel containing his current exercise and text books from which he refused to be parted. In his hand was the book he was reading, and stuffed into his pockets were other books. He seemed unconcerned and calmly indifferent to what was going on around him, and only raised his head to admonish one of us if he thought we were making things too difficult for my mother.

Wilfred's maturity not only showed up but most markedly betrayed my own immaturity and natural boyishness. One effect of this was the ready acceptance of me as the rather commonplace child of the family, a relegation which was to hang over me for a great many years. It was something which often not only made me childishly angry but set up a harmless sort of hostility between me and Wilfred. It must be admitted that even at this early age my parents had made up their minds that I was a child not only of little promise but of some stupidity. Curiously enough Wilfred himself was not guiltless of this attitude and even abetted it, albeit unconsciously, for his scholarly seriousness came not from any selfish attitude or any desire to seek greater opportunities for himself at our expense. It was something else, something so violently inherent in him that it was altogether outside his own control. He was so obsessed—there is no other word—with the necessity to equip himself scholastically that he was utterly unaware of any unfairness. . . . This is, I think, extremely interesting, showing as it does that even at this early age he was possessed by the urgency—perhaps inseparable from creative artists —to develop, at any cost, his dormant powers of creation, as yet only instinctively realized. Separated from this creative singleness, he could be made to appear as ordinarily selfish, self-centred and, for his age, unnaturally absorbed with maturity and his own future, and in this way might appear to be really priggish, which he never was. But to represent Wilfred as an average-type schoolboy, who later on developed a literary bent, would convey a great falsity.

5. Schools

When it became necessary to consider to what school I should go when I left the preparatory school I had been attending, Wilfred was firmly established in the lower half of Birkenhead Senior School as a very favourite pupil, so much so that it was openly discussed in front of me whether or not, if I was sent to the school, I should jeopardize his chances in any way. Certainly, we were altogether different in our approach to school: while my own presence in the Birkenhead Institute created from the start minor upsets both in school and at home, Wilfred's own unbroken seven years there were of absolute tranquillity.

An incident occurred during my first term at the main school which was probably the deciding factor in causing my parents not to keep me there. I had made friends while at the preparatory school with a boy named Matheson; he too had been sent to the main school. During break one afternoon I was walking across the playground and, noticing an unusual crowd of boys in a cluster, I ran up to investigate and found Matheson being set upon by a bunch of senior boys. I immediately joined in the scuffle and very soon, with Matheson, was getting the worst of it. A stinging blow from one of the seniors so hurt me and infuriated me that I lost my temper completely: all fear of being hurt left me and I lashed out with such good effect and with such—to the senior boys—obviously bad-tempered dangerousness that what had started as probably only unpleasantly rough horse-play had now developed into a vicious and rather dangerous mêlée. Fortunately, a master came along and with some difficulty broke up the fight. We were all bruised and bloody. The master reported the happening to the Head, and even before I could clear myself of mud and blood I was taken before him and, to use his own words, was asked for an explanation of my unprovoked assault on half the school. As I had no idea of the meaning of the word 'assault'—I could only think of table salt—I was rather nonplussed and remained silent. After a penetrating stare at me, his eyes twinkling pleasantly, he delivered some sort of homily, telling me I was to remember that the Institute was not a training ground for prize-fighters, and closed the matter by pushing me through his door in a friendly way.

It was perhaps unfortunate that Wilfred gave a different version to them at home. An explanation of my condition, for I was quite badly knocked about, was necessary, and Wilfred was very angry with me, and was convinced I had seriously disgraced him. Undoubtedly the episode set my parents wondering if it was worth expending the fees on me in order to keep me at this school. In reality, of course, it was the difficulty of finding the money that decided them, but I think they found it easier to take me away after I had myself supplied this other black mark. However it was, at the end of that term I was taken away from the school, but not before I had earned the nickname of 'The Birkenhead Bullfighter', a nickname which was to follow me around all my various schools and, by a curious coincidence, even to the schools in another county.

It was now decided that I should attend a free Church School of some sort in Birkenhead, and I well remember my father taking me out one dark and rainy evening, this time not so much to see the school but more to be interviewed and approved by the master conducting it. We arrived wet and I was shivering with cold. After climbing a flight of outside steps which were vaguely lighted by a distant street lamp, my father pulled a jangling bell and we were admitted by a mouldy draggled-looking individual who proved to be the master. We had entered by a door immediately into the class-room. This was a horrible room, long and narrow and lighted by a single bare gas jet which forked up spasmodically to a dim light, dying between the forks to almost nothing. The room, of course, contained the usual desks with yellow wooden tops and cast-iron legs. These in the flickering light appeared to me to be jumping about in a most eerie way, and the whole atmosphere was pervaded with a cold sour smell so strong that it seemed almost visible to me, and I felt if I opened my hand and then closed it again I would be able to imprison it.

The dirty, unkempt individual kept up a desultory conversation with my father, occasionally asking me some educational question and taking not the least notice of my answers. The feeble conversation soon died away to a lethargic silence, and my father took his leave. They must somehow have arranged for me to go to the school, for after we had stumbled down the steps and regained the street my father told me that I would be starting there on the following Monday, after which we relapsed into a mutual damp dismay and misery, and, with our hands in our pockets, trudged silently home.

My recollection of this school is rather blurred and vague, probably because it was marked with little incident. The other pupils, coming as they did from some of the poorest homes in Birkenhead, were ragged and dirty, always with running noses and often with running sores. In this place nothing mattered. The master in charge sat at his desk, scanning a piece of newspaper in a dejected and uninterested manner. I can only suppose that his utter indifference to what we did was so genuine that it made no fun for us to be unruly, so that apart from wandering around the classroom, which we all did freely, I can remember no disorder at all. We were all cold and hungry and I suspect the general physical condition of the school was so low that energy was easily absorbed by merely sitting and vacantly staring. Something of the condition of the place must have got through to my father and I was whisked away from it very suddenly. It was decided after this that I should remain at home, so for a time no other school was sought for me. However, whenever possible my mother gave me some instruction.

It must have been in the winter of 1906–7 that we moved to Shrewsbury, when my father was appointed to a more responsible post. I myself was glad and excited at the thought of leaving Birkenhead and its misery of dirty streets and the gloom and horridness of our dark and dismal little house; and above all I wanted to be free of the anxiety ever present in my journeyings alone through the streets, for I was always liable to attack from the small and large ruffians who inhabited our neighbourhood. I had early developed a technique for dealing with attacks—singly or in pairs—by these boys of my own age, for I had found out that a rush towards them with an attacking blow or two evaporated their aggressiveness in a most satisfying way, and the ensuing struggle was merely a face-saving scuffle which would end by one side or other seizing a cap or school satchel and flinging it into a garden or the road, after which we would each be glad to go our ways. But the marauding gangs of bigger boys who lay in wait for small defenceless boys were dangerous, as I had found out when I tried out my early technique on one of these bands. The six or seven bullies would smother the victim, three or four holding him powerless and the remainder raining blows until blood flowed—nothing but blood satisfied them. By violent struggling, biting, kicking, and butting, it was sometimes possible to hurt one or two of them and make an escape, but being caught nearly always meant a really bad fight. Getting mixed up with these gangs was largely my own fault, through my incurable liking for walking about alone and this practice of exploring strange streets.

To these quick-witted sharp-eyed little Birkenhead boys this habit was enough to mark me down. I was beginning to dread these disgusting encounters and they were by now a spoliation of the fleeting moments of happiness I had been able to snatch in my journeyings through the miserable streets. In my childish way I had thought all this to be a local unpleasantness and that a move away from it would leave it all behind. But at first my experiences in Shrewsbury were not to be very different, particularly as regards schools.

While we were settling into our new home, the problem of schools for us children came up and much discussion and some argument floated about perpetually between my mother and father. A great deal of it was in front of us and, I have no doubt, some more when we were sleeping. Once again Wilfred, being the eldest, was the subject of most of the discussion and argument, but it was eventually decided that as he could so safely be left to pursue his own studies the need for finding a school for him was not immediately urgent, and that it would be better to wait rather than risk sending him to a wrong one, until they knew a little more about what could be found for him. My father's natural affection for Wilfred caused him to keep seeking the right setting—within his means—for Wilfred. This eventually led to his discovery of what was known as the Technical School in Shrewsbury. There were, I believe, one or two formalities to be complied with or got over, which may have been something to do with age of entry. It was of course a fee-paying school and, although these to my father were considerable, they were within his means. The upshot was that a further interview was arranged at which Wilfred was to be present. If this went satisfactorily he would be able to start his studies there at once.

This meeting was thoroughly successful and both my father and Wilfred returned from it pleased and happy. Wilfred was unusually jubilant at the prospect of once again commencing organized work, and he indulged in one of his moods of buoyant fluency, amusing us all with his description of the evening. My father joined in and contributed to the fun. Wilfred and I were sharing a bedroom and when he came up to bed that night he at once set about sorting and arranging his text and exercise books until he had them to his satisfaction (for he was to begin at the Technical School in a few days), after which he regaled me with choice bits about his plans and hopes for the new school and persisted in reading long stanzas of poetry. But I was sleepy and more than a little envious of the care and trouble that was being devoted to him to ensure his ease of learning, for I had been given much shorter shrift and had been dismissed as not being of sufficient promise and ability to warrant unnecessary expense, and so it had been decided that a free board school was the solution for me.

My beginning at this board school had not been happy, for my entry was made conspicuous by my being a new boy arriving after term had begun and, also, in consequence of having lost my way, by being late on the first morning. At break-time the junior boys ganged up, and mobbed and mauled me. But because I had to re-appear in school, it was confined to disarrangement of tie and cap and hair and rolling in the dirty playground, and blood-chilling threats and promises of what would happen to me when we were finally let out of school at four o'clock.

When school for the day ended we were spewed out of the class-room in a howling, yelling crowd. I found myself hemmed in on all sides by jeering boys, big and small, and my secret hope that fleetness might save me disappeared. Once outside, I was carried along to some waste ground and a concerted attack on me began. I was soon taking a bad bruising and I began bleeding profusely, but I suppose I must have made some resistance, for I found myself temporarily with a clear space round me, and it was then that uncontrollable rage and some inspiration once again helped me. In a flash I had picked up a large quarry stone and hurled it with all my diminishing strength straight in the face of one of the big boys. Luckily for him, and for me, my aim was low and the stone struck him in the ribs. Had it hit him in the face it would have laid his cheek wide open. As it was, it sent him down gasping and twisting in horrid pain. The effect was miraculous and after a few seconds of frightened quietness, all the boys, except two bigger ones, fled in all directions. The two remaining boys and myself helped the smitten boy to his feet and he became disgustingly sick, but otherwise he seemed all right. My anger had subsided now, and fear at what I had done gripped me. I was glad when the two big boys ordered me to get off home quickly. On my way home I stopped by the river bank and, with my handker-chief, sponged off what I could of the mud and blood, and straightened up my clothes and combed through my hair with my fingers, for I did not expect sympathy, let alone understanding, of what had been happening to me, and could only hope that by preen-ing myself I could disguise the seriousness of it and so lessen the blame and scolding which my appearance was bound to bring upon me.

When I arrived home my dishevelment did cause some consternation, but when it was found that there was no serious hurt to me, the concern switched—as it so often did—from alarm to recrimination. My mother and Wilfred, after extracting from me what had happened, were disinclined to believe my story; instead, they were both comfortably certain that it was only my own stupidity and ill-behaviour that had brought my troubles upon me. Perhaps from a feeling that I could not stand having any more unjust guilt thrust upon me, I said no word of the final stone-throwing action. Later, Mary tried to soothe and comfort me and administered first aid to my cuts and swollen nose and gave me all her stored-up chocolate. I could not be comforted, though, for I was tired and very frightened, not of the future but of what I had done by throwing the stone at the boy. The guilt of it nagged at me and I longed for somebody to unburden myself to and to share my secret misgivings.

I still had a hope that my father when he came home would let me talk to him and that I should be able to tell him everything and be believed. I was sent to bed early and my father came home late and I expect very tired, and when he did come up to see me it was only because my mother sent him up to give me a serious talking to and threats of punishments if I did not mend my ways. But he was weary himself and in need of his evening meal; he seemed elusive and far away and could not help me and, after a few stereotyped phrases about trying to be good in the future, left me and went downstairs. This to me was the final heartbreak after the long and bitter day, for my own family had now succeeded in doing what the masters and boys in the whole of this first day at the school had failed to do—brought a lump into my throat which I could not force back, so that tears brimmed into my eyes.

I went back to the school next day and to my relieved surprise found myself left entirely alone. This of course was not due to ostracism, which in better class schools would have come about through my unorthodox and dangerous rock-throwing. The only known criteria there were bodily strength, lying, and low strategy. It was quite simply catch-as-catch can, all-in, and nothing barred. In this way my unpremeditated violence in hurling the rock, although an act of desperation on my part, was an inspired one—this was something that they could understand, and out of this understanding came the realization that it could be dangerous to molest me. In this way I was able to maintain my aloofness and, when my previous nickname of the Birkenhead Bullfighter caught up with me, the illusion that I was dangerous was built up even more strongly, which suited me very well.

I found these boys even less pleasant than the tough, stringy little Birkenheadites who at least were alert and could think and act for themselves. In comparison, these Shropshire boys seemed fatter and heavier and altogether more bovine and stupid and what ruminations came to them seemed foul and beastly after the Birkenhead boys' brighter, cleaner, and harder evilness.

Of all the hundreds of boys in the school I can only recall one individual, the rest I can remember only as a belligerent and noisy mob that I could not like. It must have been near the end of my time in this school and I would have been about eleven years old. This boy was only important to me because it was through him that I first became—in a way I could recognize—aware of compassion and pity and, perhaps more important, alive to the knowledge of the power that was born with the possession of this understanding over the person to whom the sympathy was shown. Until now I had, I expect, been only occupied with my own reactions and my own struggles to maintain some semblance of coherence in what was happening about me. This boy changed all this in a marked way. He was considerably older than I, tall and very delicate-looking and the idol of a doting mother: so much so that he became literally a figure of fun in the school, to such an extent that his passage through it was fairly easy—he experienced very little physical violence, for he seemed only able to evoke absolute contempt from the other boys and was merely the object of derisive and ribald mockery. It was most likely this, to me, extraordinary capability of accepting so many foul insults without resentment that made me first notice him, and his degraded helplessness was so immense that in some way it brought to me this realization of extreme pathos so that I felt drawn to behave with kindness towards him. His gratitude was appalling and poured over me with such avid hunger that his lack of restraint overwhelmed me. He attached himself to me with a limpet-like eagerness which I found embarrassing. When I attempted to discourage him the abject hurt which came into his eyes forced me to relent.

His mother overdressed him atrociously, and I remember with a pang when he appeared in the most frightful pair of bright yellow boots. These wretched boots were too much for my newly born sense of sympathy, so that I was ready to spurn both them and him, but he forestalled me by drawing my attention to the atrocities with such genuine pride and pleasure that my hardening heart melted and instead I outshone him in my admiration and simulated envy. Once again his gratitude and obvious pleasure were so inordinate that I had a most uncomfortable feeling of responsibility towards him and a quite puzzling sensation of power, and began to see that by manipulating words and assuming attitudes—which were false—it was possible to control reactions, especially happiness. The boy himself was unimportant to me at the time; it is only when I look back that I can see that he was the vehicle through which came to me the awakening of a receptiveness which could be stabbed by pity, and an awareness that to encounter pathos could scorch. Our relations never developed into friendship, his own tragic humility prevented this happening, yet he remains the only boy that I can remember anything at all about.

I suppose I must have learnt something, but it could not have been much. As far as the lessons themselves went, I soon discovered that if I sat quietly and did not fidget little notice was taken of me and it did not seem to matter whether I paid attention or not. I found this to my liking because I could safely think of other things. Now and again my interest was caught but never held. Any attempt to seek enlightenment was quite obviously discouraged; a quiet well-ordered classroom was the only concern.

But after a serious illness which meant that later on I had to have my tonsils removed (at home and without a proper anaesthetic), my resilience was lessened and I came to hate the school even more and became difficult and intractable. The smell of improperly washed bodies bothered me; the way we were all squashed up together in bodily contact during class-time made me feel sick so that I elbowed and fought for space around me, causing innumerable fracas and bringing anger down upon me from the masters. I was becoming a trouble-maker and did not mind, for the boredom of sitting through the school hours without any interest was making me difficult and sometimes mutinous. After an exchange of letters between my father and the school I left and was sent to another free school. Here the boys were more agreeable and I made a number of temporary friends and began to take an interest in the work, especially in the drawing classes. But my stay was short and my exit dramatic.

After a term or so I discovered to my dismay that I had irretrievably aroused not only antagonism but violent dislike in the headmaster. As far as I can recall he was the one and only master, the classes being shared by his wife and daughter. I had already seen how easily he could work up a dislike for the whole school and a fanatical hatred for individual boys. He liked selecting one or two of the less promising boys on whose heads he vented his ill-humour and sarcastic malice. He revelled in scheming to get these unfortunate victims in compromising positions and predicaments and would derive abominable joy from watching them try to extricate themselves.

I cannot remember just how long I survived in this school. It may have been two or three terms or most probably even less before the inevitable and, as it happened, the final storm burst about me. He had for some time been bullying and selecting me for his butt and was persistently finding fault and flashing out poisonous gibes to incite me. Eventually, by odious machinations and taking advantage of my bewilderment, he so contrived that I should stand apparently guilty of downright lying. I resented this fiercely and so added further to his real or simulated rage. I was called out in front of the school and ordered to take six strokes of the cane on the hand. I walked up to his desk and when ordered to hold out my hand I refused to do so. Seizing my arm, he attempted to extend it by force, but I wrenched it free, pushing him away at the same time; with this he lost all control and set about beating me with the stick about my neck and shoulders. I was tigerish now with anger and I warded off his savage blows with a fury and determination that enraged him to insensate fury; but I was frightened too, for he was big and dangerous-looking. I dodged around his desk and picking up a pile of heavy books I was just prepared to hurl them at his head when with a sort of grunting noise he lunged at me, overturning the desk as he came. He must have lost balance in his rush towards me, for he spread-eagled over the falling desk, knocking the breath out of himself, which was very lucky for me. The crash of the falling desk and the general uproar in the classroom, which was beside itself at the unpleasant spectacle, brought his wife and daughter on the scene and they took the lunatic in hand and restored quietness. Brandy and water was brought for him by his wife, for he was now in a state of emotional frenzy. The daughter seized me and for safety shepherded me from the classroom into the street, telling me to go home.

When the schoolmaster's daughter hurried me out of school I took my time going home; I was feeling rather wretched; the splendid glow I had felt in defying the crazy man had evaporated and now I only felt small and deflated. I did not see how I could explain what had happened when I got home; I knew I should never be able to do so. I knew that this was the end of this school for me and drearily wondered what was to come next. I cheered up a lot when I remembered that I had a drawing that I had started and would now be able to finish.

When I got home I told my mother and Wilfred—who was at home with a cold—that I didn't like this school any more and had tried to throw some books at the headmaster. Eventually, under persuasion I tried to give my version, but I did not seem to be able to put it very well and before I had finished I was confused myself as to just how it had all come about, so that my mother thought I was prevaricating again and she was upset, too, at the thought of further trouble over me. Wilfred tried to give me a wry grin, which was nice, but it did not comfort me much, for I had the feeling that he thought I was being quite impossible. The whole thing was then deferred for my father to sort out and settle when he returned in the evening. He, too, showed nothing but annoyance with me until I came to where I had been set about with the stick. After he had satisfied himself about this he left me and went straight to the school-house. What exactly transpired there I never quite knew. But the man was, I think, too clever for my father's rather direct simplicity and by adroit misrepresentation extricated himself; and after some discussion it was decided that I should not return to the school. I was undoubtedly sacked.

A week after this I was sent off to another board school. I found it tucked away behind one of the main streets and it had to be approached through a slummy alleyway which smelled most abominably in the summer-time. My settling in here was almost precisely similar to what had gone before. There was the same struggle to prevent submersion, which, if not effected, meant perpetual bullying by the bigger boys, with the usual wrestling and struggling with the occasional more serious bouts of real fighting. Sometimes the bigger louts would gang up and give us smaller ones some bad maulings, but on the whole I held my own somehow and retained my independence throughout. The boys were lower in type than the contingent in my first board school in Birkenhead. The school was known as the poorest in the district and generally possessed a bad reputation.

The teaching was carried out a little differently. The classes were smaller and I seem to remember that I got on quite well in a negative sort of way. There was one youngish man who became very intrigued with my ability to draw. My efficiency in this was actually very much in advance of my age and I was deriving intense interest from it. I am sure he was not interested in art at all, yet he took a curious pride in my efforts and would bring various objects from his rooms for me to draw. He would show these sketches to the other masters with great pride.

This was to be my last school in the ordinary sense. Soon after this, and when I was eleven years old, I decided not only to get myself out of this time-wasting place with its unpleasant associations but to finish with ordinary schools altogether. I did not at all see how I was going to be able to do this, yet I was curiously confident that somehow I would bring it about.

However, before this happened I was to spend some time yet in this school. I was by now well into the dreary routine and by practising a technique of using the school hours to plan what I would do with my free ones I managed to avoid any further major incidents. My conviction that I would be able to get myself out of it gave me a hopeful feeling and with this to look forward to I expect I gave the impression at home that I was at last settled.

Although I was absorbing some very rudimentary knowledge—I believe this process was known and currently spoken of as the three Rs—in any true sense I was learning nothing and disliking the foul-smelling little school more and more. I would sit through the boring school hours in a state of numbed futility and somehow get through the four walks to and fro to morning and afternoon school. In the summer they seemed hot and wearying and in the winter cold and wet. It was possibly a two-mile walk to the school. I was becoming more and more absorbed in my own private pursuits at home. Drawing and painting took the foremost place and I was learning to relegate the school and its unpleasant associations to a background which had to be endured. By shutting down my thoughts about it I could largely obliterate the unliked hours, which was good for my drawing and my childish attempts at carving, but very bad for my three Rs. But even so this abominable school was never entirely negatived and its lewd and physically dirty atmosphere still loomed too large for my childish liking and endurance.

My hatred of this place was becoming acute and rather forlornly hopeless, for I knew now that there was no hope of my family reprieving me from it. It was by accident that I discovered an escape and set about securing this for myself. This was a diversion that was soon to overshadow the effects of the bad schools so that they no longer mattered to me at all, and eventually to sever me so decisively that I was able to free myself and finally force my way out of the school altogether, leaving it to its odorous fate with immense satisfaction and gladness. My partial escape happened quite soon, although my ultimate severance was to take another year or so.

It happened one summer afternoon when I was loitering rather lazily home from school that, in passing Wilfred's school, I saw that a notice board which had always stood near the main entrance was freshly painted and varnished. The cream-coloured background and cerulean lettering held my attention and I went idly up to it to study the information displayed. It contained notices about the School of Art, and my interest became riveted; I stretched to tiptoe the better to take it in, and my heart began to beat hard with excitement when I found they were beginning evening art classes on Mondays, Wednesdays, and Fridays. All at once an irresistible desire overcame me to attend these classes as soon as possible, and with it a clear picture of what my action must be in order to succeed. I knew that to propose it at home would receive sympathetic non-attention and my project would be added to the long list of things that might be done when I was older. As I stood peering at the board I knew what I must do, though I quailed at the demand, for I was not a bold little boy, especially not in thrusting myself into strange buildings or houses or meeting strange people; so before my resolve could weaken I had opened the iron gates and rung the bell of the main door. By this time my heart was thudding painfully and my throat and my mouth were dry. The door was opened by the janitor and I stuttered out my request to see the head of the Art School. Years of contact with boys had made him soured and sceptical; his appearance was forbidding and he gruffly tried to send me away, but my anxiety was mounting and with it an incoherent determination. My appearance and eagerness must, I think, have conveyed a sense of urgency and I was reluctantly admitted. In a surprisingly short time I was ushered into the Principal's studio-office.

A small-made man with brilliant merry brown eyes came forward and after an astonished stare at his small visitor immediately set about making me feel comfortable. He did this by fussing about and chuckling to himself most infectiously. Very soon he invited me to look at a water-colour he was working on, and friendship between us was immediate. My nervousness disappeared. It was not until this happened that he inquired how he could help me. I told him my

story and he was intrigued with it and at once became my avowed
ally. He demurred a little about age, but I knew it was all right, and
he progressed to fees. Here he felt he could hardly conclude negotiations without consulting my father who, I must remember, knew
nothing about this idea; but comforted me with an audible quip to
himself which sounded like 'small boys small fees', followed by more
merriment. He was much given to these—always kindly—asides.
After showing me some of the school he made a final suggestion that
I should bring my father to see him one evening to try to fix things
up. He ushered me out, escorting me through the door with some
ceremony. All the way home my heart sang with happiness at the
thought of the evening classes that might lie before me.

A few evenings later, my father and I went along to see Mr.
Weaver. After some hesitation on my father's side and some discussion by Mr. Weaver about how the problem of my age was to be got
over, it was decided that something could be done. Mr. Weaver was
extremely adept at arranging things; he said he would manage it
somehow and the fees too, and suggested I might start next term,
but this did not suit me at all and I begged to start at once. After
more hesitation, this time on Mr. Weaver's part, he said with a
chuckle that he would fix this as well and that I might present myself
the following Monday evening. On the way home my father was
thoughtful and quiet; I was exhilarated and triumphant. At bedtime
that evening as I went to kiss my father good night, he told me that
he would call me at six o'clock in the morning and we would start
building a model ship.

My father's thoughtfulness on the walk home was brought about
by the realization that here was yet another son of his pursuing the
arts, and a lessening of the chance—perhaps a serious one—of
getting me started on a sea-going career. This School of Art nonsense
could be a serious menace; to offset it he must get me interested
in building a ship. My childish enthusiasm for drawing and painting,
culminating in my impetuous attack upon the School of Art, must
have made him wonder if he must not again prepare for further
disappointment.

The almost astonishing thing about this deep wish of my father's
was not the desire itself, but in the fact that it never took really
definite form in the way of action of any sort. It became almost
secretive and was referred to obliquely and never put before Wilfred
or myself with its advantages and disadvantages openly laid out for
our inspection. In Wilfred's case, he was so undeniably unsuitable

that this was understandable; in my own case less so. This trait of his was the commencement of a future fatal inability in my father to help and advise his sons by placing before them through his own experience and greater knowledge of the world any definite results that would be likely to follow certain defined actions.

The boat-building began, as my father had suggested it should, the next morning. This model boat-building was to be quite a part of our lives for several years to come, especially for my father and me. Wilfred never took any part in it, but Colin and Mary, although not doing much of the practical work, were always keenly interested in our efforts and would always want to be with us when we were working, content to watch and be useful in handing us things. The fashioning and shaping appealed strongly to me and one of my efforts was a full-rigged, four-masted ship completely clothed up to skysails and stunning sails, with all running parts free and all spars and booms properly made. My mother made her suit of sails, some thirty in all, out of linen to my paper patterns, beautifully made with reefing lines and bolt holes, all eyeletted. Great care was taken in selecting the small log of yellow pine, which we were able to buy from a friendly builder, from which the hull was hollow carved, and afterwards decked over. I would work hard with paint and sandpaper on the outside of the hull to get a perfect finish, filling all the grain of the wood until it gleamed like satin. The moulding of lead for the keels was rather a ritual and much looked forward to, as it meant bringing old pieces of lead piping to boiling-point in a saucepan on the gas stove, then skimming the dross from the boiling liquid and casting the refined molten metal into a carefully prepared clay mould. This operation was pleasantly dangerous as the bubbling, spitting lead could be vicious. Often four or five recastings had to be done before the exact size and weight could be obtained. Already the craftsman's lure of seeking perfection and discounting time or labour was seizing hold of me. The moment of completion was always the least rewarding of all. This ship I had built, I launched and christened—with proper ceremony—the *Mary Millard* in honour of Mary.

As at Birkenhead I was often my father's companion on expeditions. These, on account of our schools and his work, had to be fitted into the early mornings or the evenings. The early morning was his favourite time; in the evenings he was sometimes jaded and irritable.

At first these early mornings did not seem much fun and I did not much like being got up at half-past five or earlier—especially if Wilfred had kept me awake the night before—and the washing in cold water which my father insisted upon was a shivery business; but the hot tea and nice thick piece of bread and butter that he would have ready downstairs made it almost worth while.

After the tea and bread and butter, we would steal quietly out of the house and set off for the fields and river which were no distance away. My father took great pains and interest in pointing out to me the birds in the air, the fish in the river, and the crops growing out of the fields, about all of which he had considerable knowledge stored up from his boyhood. These excursions were not a daily practice and although I rebelled about getting up when the morning came, the nights when I went to bed with his promise of an early morning were my happy ones, and I would fall asleep thinking of the new delights we might find in the morning. My father was good, too, at helping me to get up and if I was very sleepy would lift me out of bed whole-sale and, standing me up at the bedroom basin, would start me sponging my face.

The river was always a source of interest and we came to know the swims of the roach and where the fat, coarse chubb lazed just underneath the surface. The big, cruel-looking pike lying so cunningly dangerous in the waving reed beds and the flashing little jack were all looked for and noted for other days. Sometimes a lovely speckled trout would be found sucking down with greedy selectiveness the mayflies as they floated down the river.

The country around was heavy with uncut hedges and small clumps of bush and trees, and in the nesting season my father would find—and mark down for watching—many different kinds of birds' nests and was always seeking to add new species to our list. In the breeding season we would go out almost daily and if a nest was expected to hatch out, would return in the evening to mark progress. Sometimes we would take one particular nest for watching and, hiding ourselves in the bushes nearby, would stand motionless for long periods watching the parent birds rearing their young. Other times on warm sunny mornings we would walk straight down to the river. I enjoyed splashing about in the water and swimming short distances in deep water with my father, but I always felt a little weak and hungry when I came out and the walk home seemed rather long. On lucky days my father would fish out a bar of chocolate from his pocket or sometimes just a dry crust of bread. If he did not produce anything, I would not dream of asking for it or even reminding him but would trudge along by his side contentedly disappointed. Once home, he would revert to his nervous manner and would be brusque and cross again and storm up and down if breakfast was not ready— as it never was until Mary grew a little older and bigger—and he would be fantastically cross with Wilfred, shouting at him with angry disgust for not being dressed or, as it mostly happened, not even yet out of bed; I myself had only to make one slip or be negligent in manners to bring a tirade down upon my head.

It was sometimes hard to believe that this stormily petulant person was the same gentle man who a few hours earlier had so skilfully widened a nest without damage so that I might watch a minute baby wren peck its way out of its tiny egg shell. If he was in a particularly irate mood Wilfred would take care not to appear at all until he had stormed out of the house on the way to his office, which meant that Wilfred only had time to drink some tea, usually on the stairs as my mother met him half-way up with it, taking it to him so that he could be hurried away by her and get to school without being late.

6. *Uffington*

I was now, at the age of ten, turning more and more to Colin for companionship, and as he responded so warmly and co-operated so loyally in the various schemes we devised between us for our own entertainment we became, for the next few years until I went to sea, quite inseparable. One of these plans which we were so often to carry out together was the spending of our Saturdays—on which day we neither of us went to school—away from home, taking our lunch and tea with us, carried in our school satchels.

It was during one of these days that we discovered my lovely village of Uffington. The day we found it we could not penetrate into it, for between us and it lay the river. I had not on this day the pennies necessary to use the ferry. But we resolved there and then to save up our weekly pocket money—at this time Wilfred had 6d., Mary 3d., and Colin and I 1d. each—and worked out that we could do it in two weeks' time.

I had fallen in love with the look of the village from my side of the river, but I was not impatient and enjoyed the thought of the tantalizing wait at the end of which I knew with absolute certitude that I would not be disappointed. Before we got home again I had

sworn Colin to secrecy about it, for I did not want to be given the
extra pennies, which would have been instantly forthcoming if I had
explained what they were for. This might have meant being taken to it.
I did not want this to happen. I wanted to find it myself and so in my
mind possess it. I had infected Colin with my enthusiasm to penetrate
into and explore this place by ourselves. Two weeks later, this time
with our ferry-fare pennies, we started off early and, very pleased
about our prospect for the day, we trudged along steadily until we
came to the river bank and the ferry. This had to be hailed from our
side of the water and we enjoyed piping our calls in unison to attract
the ferryman's attention. This was never easy to do, but eventually
we saw him emerge from his cottage, lumber slowly down to the
landing steps and, throwing out the securing chain, push off towards
us. These boats were long, flat-bottomed, heavy, punt-like contrap-
tions and were propelled across the river by the ferryman hauling
hand over hand on a light wire hawser that was stretched tautly from
one bank to the other, the one side of the punt being fitted with
two iron stanchions mounted with steel rollers clipped securely
but freely around the suspended wire. Normally, it was a simple
operation, but when the river was running fast with heavy flood
water, it needed great skill and long experience to manœuvre the
clumsy craft safely across.

Colin and I, arriving on the other side, felt the day had started
splendidly when the kind boatman told us that as we were so small
he would only charge us a halfpenny each, which left us with an
extra penny each to spend. Both full of expectation about the newly
found village, we climbed up the steep and narrow alder-lined path,
past the ferry cottage and so into the dusty village square, around
which the cottages and farm buildings leaned and nestled so warmly.
We were enchanted with it all and wandered around happily, now
and again exchanging polite words with the men and women who
slowly moved about their business. They welcomed our staring
interest with kindly regard.

Our bewitchment was completed when the immense black water-
mill wheel with thunderous clankings and muffled inner clangings and
groanings commenced ponderously turning its creaking bulk. With
its first half-turn it drove out in mock alarm hundreds of gaily
coloured pigeons from the whitewashed cobweb-encrusted lofts. The
birds wheeled and tumbled and spiralled above and about our heads
in lovely confusion of black and white, blue-grey, and blue and slate,
their backs and wings glistening in the sunlight.

Rather dizzily, from watching the churning cascading wheel and the rapid whirring of the birds about us, we made our way out of the village to find a quiet field in which to lie on our tummies and eat our lunch. After our meal, which Colin and I ate as we always did with such hungry happiness, we wandered back towards the village. On the way we found a pump at which we stopped and after drinking from our cupped hands, took it in turn to pump water over each other's heads, for the sun was blazing down. We found another lane leading out past the back of the mill-house, which we saw to our delight led us to a hump-backed brick-built little bridge that carried the lane over a canal. The strip of water, fringed on either side with bulrushes, lay sleeping with glassy stillness.

We had not expected this surprise and at once made our way down to the towpath that we might look at the canal itself more closely. We soon found a narrow cutting which curved steeply down to the water level. One side of this constricted passageway was lined with the minute village shops, placed here no doubt to attract the custom of the passing narrow boats and the bargee families they always housed. The windows of these very small shops were so low that their uppermost panes of thick green bubbly glass only reached our eye-level, so that even we small boys had to stoop to see what was mistily displayed behind them. In the few summers to follow we were to come to know these small shops and their owners very well and to spend many pennies with them. We started then and there by investing a halfpenny each in pear drops and acid drops which we ate alternately and with precise exactitude from each other's paper bag until they were all finished, when we blew up the bags and burst them.

We were getting tired now and I thought it must be time to be going home, for I remembered the long way we had to walk after we had crossed the river again. But there was still one more unexpected happening waiting for us. I had noticed the tiny church with its little exposed bells and on the way back looked for it again, but this time it was not the church which caught my attention but the garden adjoining it. I was astonished at the massed array of colour that seemed to flow along in such dazzling brilliance. It was most likely my first look at a really beautiful summer border. It was certainly my first conscious appreciation of one and I remained just mutely staring. Presently, unseen by me, a gentle hand was laid on my shoulder and a quiet voice asked me what I was looking at. With some trepidation I replied as politely as I could, I suppose saying

something about liking the flowers. Whereupon, brushing aside our
rather shyly uttered excuses, an old clergyman ushered us into his
garden and, escorting us around, showed us all of it with great kindli-
ness. He disappeared into the house and came out with two glasses
of milk which we drank gratefully and after pressing slices of cake
into our hands allowed us to express our rather timid thanks and
sent us on our way to the ferry. Fortified with the milk and cake and
the pleasant feeling of good-will the kindly vicar had inspired in us,
the way home did not seem so long. I was day-dreaming too of
paint-boxes and sketching easels, so that I did not notice the miles.
I was enchanted to have found this village for myself: there was an
exact rightness about it that in a curious way supplied a need in me
—perhaps it was the sun-warmed peacefulness of the crumbling
brick and tiled cottages, the farm smells, and the undertones of quiet
sounds that drifted through the air from beasts and birds mingling
with the muted vibrations that came from the noise of pails and
country tools being used in farmyard and cottage garden.

A happy outcome of the finding of Uffington was an escape for me
from having to go to the dreary town churches on Sunday mornings.
My father suddenly thought how nice it would be if we went instead
to this little village church. I liked this idea tremendously and
abetted him in every way, for besides the church service, which I
thought must—in my village—be much easier to sit through than
in any other church, there was the lure of the walk through the fields in
the early freshness of the mornings, and of course the ferry crossings.

At first my father would take one or two of us with him. By starting
very early we had time to loiter slowly along the riverside watching
the fish—of this my father never tired. These were the only church-
goings that I ever enjoyed or looked forward to. This was not
altogether due to the interest of the country walk, for during the
service itself I was never restless or bored; instead, an awareness of
tranquil spirituality seemed to descend upon me that in some way
enveloped me with a feeling of protection. Inside the friendly little
building I felt secure from anything disagreeable. During the
morning services I enjoyed the musty warm smell that was driven
out of the stone walls by the hot sunshine that burned its way
through from the outside. I loved the shaft of transparent golden
light that blazed through the square made by the always open door.
All around me were splashes of blue and green, rose and amber, that
filtered through the stained glass in rainbow beams to make

suspended pools of warmth that glowed under the dark arched roof. The sparrows and finches flew in and out as they wished; swallows also would dart in, inspect the interior, flash around with a perfection of speed and timing, and not finding what they wanted glance their way out again. The murmur of the countryside with its creaking activity mingled with the drone of the prayers and made me languorously happy. On still days if I listened hard I could hear the rustle of the fantails in the mill lofts. After church we would walk through the quiet village to the little canal bridge, here to lean over the parapet watching and waiting to see the dragonflies as they skimmed the dark water. These were the mornings.

The evenings would be different, for then the summer night would let fall enchantment over all of us. If my mother was feeling well and able for the walk, the six of us would set out to walk through the lanes and over the fields and across the river to enjoy the quietness of the evening service in the church. On these occasions an instinctive unity joined us closely together. It may have been the peacefulness of the lovely summer evenings that gave us all this sense of well-being, or—and I think this more likely—the influence of my father and mother who with gentle restraint would bring about an atmosphere which unified us all. Their effort may have been an unconscious one as a concession to the spiritual and religious character which marked the setting forth on our simple occasion. Whatever it was, it always gave me uplifting surges and made me purely happy, for in spite of my childish exasperations and rebellious disregard I loved my family in a way I found impossible to explain and was never more consciously happy than when this unexpected wave of unity swept over us.

The return journeys home were always to me the most beautiful time, especially when darkness was falling. We would file out quietly and solemnly from the tiny church and, after an exchange of simple benedictions from the vicar, wind our way through the darkening village until we came to the opening at the top of the narrow root-strewn, tortuous path leading down to the river, when we would all join hands for mutual safety in our descent to the ferry. The river, as we crossed, would look black and satiny and very deep, but gave us assurance of its friendliness in musical clucks and swirling gurgles in answer to the caressing pushings of the ferry's flat square bows. Safely out from the ferry, the long walk through the water meadows commenced, and in the almost and yet not quite darkness of summer this was mysterious and full of delight. In the fields the fragrance of the beast-smells mingled with the crushed buttercups seemed powerful and somehow urgent. The great beasts themselves were dotted about across our path and others could be seen as dark hillocks lying with all four legs neatly tucked under them, the wide white blazes that marked their great heads glowing like ghostly little lamps. On still nights we could hear the rhythm of their grinding ruminations. Now and again we would disturb one. With slow movements of mild reproof it would rise awkwardly and with staggering gait turn towards us and, opening its nostrils, blow out twin winds of scented globuled air that, wafting and misted to whiteness by the chilling air, would roll buoyantly along the top of the layer of mist that lay like cotton-wool just above the dew-drenched grasses, until they mingled and were lost.

On one of these summer-night returns from Uffington church, when we were walking through the last of the meadows before we reached the lane, I had fallen back behind the others as I was sometimes wont to do—I was fond of slowly dragging my feet through the cool wetness of the grass. When I was climbing over the stile leading into the lane I noticed in the half-darkness that my boots looked strange, and peering more closely I saw that they were completely covered with buttercup petals; in the darkness they glowed like gold. I was immediately intrigued with this and called out to the others that I had feet of gold, but they were a long way up the lane, the mist was muffling my voice, and they could not hear me properly, so I did not persist and presently heard Wilfred walking back to see what I was calling to them about. When Wilfred reached me he too was fascinated with the strange luminous effect. While we were still looking at them we heard my father's footsteps turn and come towards us. He was softly calling out as he came to ask if we were all right and I was just about to call back through the darkness when Wilfred gently pressed my arm for silence—hesitated a moment and then called quietly back, 'Harold's boots are blessed with gold.' There was a silence after this, my father did not hear, or if he did, could not make anything of it, but called back telling us to hurry and not dawdle so much. . . . We heard the rap of his brisk footsteps as he turned again to rejoin the others. . . . Wilfred and I followed on, but with every step my boots lost some of our flush of gold. . . .

Six or seven years later, in very different circumstances, Wilfred was to write the lines in *Spring Offensive*:

> And the far valley behind, where the buttercup
> Had blessed with gold their slow boots coming up.

7. *Art School*

On the Monday evening that I was to attend my first night class at the Art School I asked my mother for permission to wear better clothes than I always wore to go to school, and on this first evening I had taken special care of my appearance and set off feeling pleased and happy. I had no real qualms, except for twinges of natural nervousness about entering yet another school. For one thing it was my own special find and I knew I had no need to continue unless I liked doing so, and I was firmly convinced that it would be all I expected and not in the least like any of the other schools I had been to. How right I was. As I had thought, there was no new-boy nonsense and I was accepted with warmth and friendliness and, best of all, without any exhibition of curiosity. Some of the students seemed very old to me. The youngest must have been six years older than I was. I was set a freehand drawing test and I was soon absorbed and interested. I was surprised when nine-thirty came. I did not think that the time could possibly have passed so quickly. I was told to remain behind until the other students had gone when Mr. Weaver and the other teachers would assess my test work. I was happy about this as I knew that I had been drawing very well. It must anyway have been satisfactory, for Mr. Weaver ordered primary instruction to be cut out so that I could go straight into advanced work. I was particularly pleased and excited about this, so that when I set off in the dark for the walk home I had a nice springy feeling in my legs and I was looking forward very much to the specially nice supper my mother had promised to have ready for me, and very much hoping it would be pork pie.

I detested my ordinary school more than ever, but this was not to last very much longer; indeed, it could not, as incidents were piling up against me in the school. These happenings were of a negative rather than of a positive nature and were the direct outcome of my aloof disregard of the school and all it contained. Since I had found my School of Art I had become genuinely remote, unconcerned, and careless as to what did or did not happen during school hours. This annoyed both the other boys and the masters, and particularly the Headmaster; my conduct appeared to throw him into frenzied infuriation. It was during one of these states that he accused me of disdain and contempt of the school and all to do with it. My simple but polite whole-hearted agreement with him nearly engulfed him in apoplexy. I had made up my mind to forestall more trouble by bringing about a plan I had for some time had in mind. I would take myself out of this sort of school altogether, and get myself installed as a full-time day student in the School of Art. I knew this would not be easy to bring about, but I was quite determined to break away from all day schools. Instead, I would go on with my painting, and do nothing else. I had faith in Mr. Weaver's power to arrange everything. My age, of course, proved a difficulty, and at first Mr. Weaver was not hopeful of being able to accept me as a whole-time student. However, my eagerness impressed him so that after some deliberation he gaily announced that he would manage it somehow, if I could get agreement from my parents. I lost no time in putting forward my proposal at home, and, after the first surprise, it met with less opposition than I had believed possible. They were genuinely worried about having to keep me in the wretched board school. Considerable argument and changes of mind ensued, but in the end, as I was making so little progress where I was and as no alternative of education seemed available, it was agreed in desperation to let me have my way.

These School of Art days were lovely ones for me. Both summer and winter held their different attractions. I became particularly fond of mid-winter afternoons and evenings, and although the walk from home to the school would often be wet and bitterly cold, I would battle along against the driving rain or snow cheerfully enough, well knowing that once inside the swing doors I should be enveloped in the warmth and would feel the friendliness of the yellow-lighted but rather dim painting rooms and the even darker corridors. I was becoming sensitive to my materials and developed a passionate love of them. I could gloat over a piece of chosen Whatman paper and feast my mind with how much I would stretch it with such care on the drawing-board, giving it the exact amount of wetting necessary, so that when a marginal dry inch all round was glued to the board the sponged centre part would have the right amount of shrinkage left in it to dry itself back taut and unshrinkable, and not too much to make a split. My mind was always envisaging tubes of gorgeously coloured paint and red sable brushes that could only be drawn to a beautiful point with the lips and saliva—I saved all my weekly pennies to purchase some of these things, always insufficient, but the thrill of anticipated purchase remained powerful. The work, materials, and the building itself, of this Art School all invested me with a happy sense of fulfilment and worthwhileness that has never been easy to recapture.

It appeared that Mr. Weaver, finding out that I had an elder brother in the other department of the school, had sought Wilfred out and in his impetuous way had at once started talking enthusiastically about me. Wilfred was genuinely surprised over Mr. Weaver's praise of me and deeply impressed, the more so because this aspect of me was so novel to him that it really did strike him as extraordinary that merit of any sort should be found in me and proclaimed so vehemently. He recounted the conversation with all its extravagance to the rest of the family and my prestige ballooned up accordingly.

In the summer after school and in the holidays I would set off into the country, my mother packing me some food and a bottle of water. Sometimes I would walk, sometimes I would use my father's cheap railway facilities and travel this way ten or twelve miles into new country. As I grew a little older I ventured further, often over the border into Wales. One occasion I remember particularly. I had set off very early to get in a good day's painting of the mellowed red brick hump-backed little bridge that spanned the canal outside Uffington. I had previously found a position from which I could bring in the bridge, a wooded blue distant hill behind it, the canal itself, and its neighbouring broken-tiled cottages, all of which it seemed to me would compose itself—with a little justified manipulation—into a most pleasing picture. I became certain of this when, arriving at my selected spot, I found moored on my side of the bridge a fine long, low canal boat, all newly painted in reds, blues, and yellows, the blue of its hull and the red of its ribbing reflecting beautifully in the still greeny water. This was a good day, and my pencil and brush seemed possessed by a flukey aptness, so that the picture finished itself almost without help and by four o'clock I felt if I worked any more on it I would only spoil it. As I was collecting my things together to go home, the bargeman and his wife who, I had noticed, had been watching me off and on all day, but always from a mannerly distance, hurried up to me and asked if I had been painting their boat and, if so, might they see what I had done. They were greatly taken with it, and after admiring it for a long time walked away a little distance and conferred together, after which they came back and asked if they could buy the picture from me. When I told them 'no'—for I felt it was the best thing I had yet done, and I could not bear the thought of parting with it so soon—they were greatly disappointed and after a little more persuasion to make sure I meant it, their good manners preventing them from further insistence, they asked me instead to come aboard their narrow boat and have some tea. I was very pleased and went eagerly, for I had been wanting to see the barge at close quarters all day.

I wished very much that I could bring myself to give them the drawing and began to feel uncomfortable about it. It was while they were plying me with strong tea and delicious thick bread and butter and jam, that the idea occurred to me that I might quite well be able to do another one straight away for them. I hurried away without saying to them what I was thinking, and setting up my spare board, started another drawing. My enthusiasm, this time with my idea, now carried me along and in two hours or so I had a fair replica. I knew it was not as good as my first one but, sensing their real interest, I had been careful with the boat and stressed some extra details—which when I again boarded the narrow boat to present it to them they were delightfully quick to notice. There followed some embarrassed fumbling with silver by the man, but I had thought of this and decided that to take any money for it now would somehow spoil my idea. It seemed altogether out of place and displeasing to do so, especially after the splendid tea and the kindness they had shown me in spite of their first disappointment. I was able to refuse payment without any offence and instead they showed me the place of honour where it would hang after they got a frame for it, which they meant to do in Gloucester. It was getting very late for me now, so I took my leave, during which they both shook hands with me very solemnly and grown-uply.

8. *Holiday Interludes*

We were to have one more holiday together, probably our last as a complete family unit, before our childhood came to an end and family dispersal began.

This we spent in Scotland with the grown-up family of a childhood friend of my mother. When we arrived it was obvious from the very start that the whole family was determined to make this holiday a tremendous success. Bicycles had been hired for us children, fishing arrangements made, and various sporting activities planned and excursions organized. Two incidents I recall particularly vividly which arose from one of these planned excursions, though nearly all we did that holiday was memorable.

We were, at least Colin and I were, experienced cyclists. Actually we were something of trick-riders, and could make bicycles do the maddest evolutions. Wilfred had been riding for a long time, sharing my father's machine; he was much more prosaic about it and looked upon it only as a quicker and easier means of getting about than walking, and not as Colin and I did as an end in itself for thrilling pleasure. However, this over-confidence of mine when riding a bicycle was to lead me into further depths of knowledge, this time to an awareness that it was possible that I myself could cease to live. I had so far accepted death in others as something normal, but I could not in any way believe the idea that I myself could be extinguished.

It was almost at the end of our time in Scotland that we were invited by some people we had met to go over and spend the afternoon with them. We had met them by chance when out fishing. They, too, were from the south and had taken for a few weeks a large, lovely old house, part of which was still being used as a farmhouse. This was some little distance away, so my father engaged a horse-carriage to take us there. To leave more room in the carriage and for the sake of the horse, for it was hilly country, it was decided that Wilfred and I should bicycle there.

Wilfred was in a cantankerous mood, because he did not really want to come with us at all but had been prevailed upon to do so. Because of this the start of our long bicycle ride was not a good one. Under the best of circumstances, mostly because of our difference in age, we did not make a satisfactory cycling pair, our ideas upon the proper use of a bicycle being so hopelessly opposite. I was inclined to sudden dashes at the fullest possible speed I could obtain, and to abrupt brakings to bring about skids which made the road surface fly, sometimes into Wilfred's face. This he considered brainless and unedifying, as indeed it was. When my wild cavorting which took place so irritatingly close to him resulted in a collision—as it sometimes did—his furious crossness would burst upon me. He would demand my attention and, dismounting, discourse with wholly ridiculous long words and absurdly erudite phrases upon my silly behaviour, with appeals to be more circumspect. Sometimes during these tirades there would be a mischievous gleam in his eyes, and he would end them with a sudden mounting of his bike and a quick chase of me and a complete turning of the tables. I enjoyed these flashes of fun immensely; much of my baiting I only did to bring them about. When they could be prized out of him, he would match any of us in fun and senseless hilarity and when this happened our high spirits would roar and soar to heights of exuberant, irresponsible happiness. If the gleam wasn't in his eyes, but only the dark sombreness of his introverted thoughts burning gloweringly, it was better to leave him alone. On this special afternoon I could see little signs of a gleam and our first collision brought forth a vituperative harangue, the theme of which was his misfortune in being forced into the company of such a moron as myself—a newly discovered and pet word of his at this time which he liked to air at every opportunity. We gave him many of these. . . .

Seeing there was no hope of fun with him but only a certainty of continued provocation, I rode ahead as fast as I could so that I should be out of sight to do my acrobatic prancing alone, and also to try to think out just exactly what a 'moron' was. I finally decided it was a deep sea monster and wondered what it would be like to be living on the bottom of the sea. I had been cogitating amiably with myself like this, riding with my arms above my head or folded across my chest—a trick which particularly infuriated Wilfred, partly because he could not master it himself and partly through anxiety about the risk to me—when, swinging round a bend, I saw stretching down in front of me a gloriously long and steep hill, which promised at least a mile of high-speed free-wheeling. I had for a long time been wanting to test out my skill by riding down just such a hill without touching the handle-bars. My pique with Wilfred's scathing belittlement of me was mounting. It was this as much as anything which propelled me into my extreme foolishness. In a few seconds I was hurtling down the hill, my hands held away from the bars, and in no time I was rapidly developing a dangerously swinging wobble. By now my balance was so uncertain that I felt unable to regain my handle-bars, as I knew that to relax my intense effort of balancing would throw me off. A stone in the road settled this for me by swerving my front wheel so badly that instinctively I clutched the handles. After frantic seconds of uncontrolled rushes, which brought my heart like a live thing up into my throat, I found myself again with some control of balance, but the bicycle was bucking so badly, the front wheel lifting so violently at every unevenness in the roadway, that this small control became nightmarish and developed into a fantastic sea-saw between powerless loss of control and convulsive regain.

So swift had my acceleration become that I was now incapable of checking it in any way. This realization must have steadied me, for although the road hedges and telegraph poles appeared only as streaming grey ribbons which I seemed to be dividing into a lane-like tunnel as they streaked away from me on either side, I felt that they too, like the road, were solid walls. I was rushing through a grey tunnel with only enough room for me and my bicycle. Every moment my speed was increasing. It was now I think that an exhilarating sensation of irresponsibility came upon me, born out of the instinctive awareness that beyond retaining my seat I was not only helpless to do anything else but blessedly not required to make any other decision. The certainty of this in its very absoluteness was curiously comforting. I was, in later years, to experience this same feeling of isolated disassociation from actuality when sitting in aeroplanes I was piloting and about to crash.

It must have been when I was commencing to lose speed, and the bicycle began to rock and leap about once more, that fear in its stark horror again swept through me, so that I knew with appalling certainty that to fall now would be to cease to live and, with this, came a terrifying appreciation that to hit the road would break and smash my body. It was my first revelation of death and its possible connection with myself. It presented itself to me as a simple realization of my own vulnerability.

It was the opposing hill which finally slowed me down and another loose stone which tumbled me and the bicycle in a heap on the grass verge of the roadside. I scrambled up and felt I was trembling, not from fear or the tumble but from an ecstatic experiencing of triumph over danger. I felt sore and ached everywhere—I expect from the taut rigidity with which I had been steering. In spite of my reaction, I felt most of all an overwhelming sense of elation and a feeling of surprised relief at my escape from calamity, and with this feeling came another that in these exciting moments I had been lifted out of vague ignorance and put down inside the fringe of serious knowledge.

I was feeling lonely now and had an overpowering wish to talk to somebody about what had happened to me. Thinking of the Old Wolf trundling along behind so morosely, I set off back to meet him and tell him all about it. When I came up with him he sprang off his bicycle in great concern, for my appearance seemed to alarm him, and commenced to clean up my face with his handkerchief. Unknown to myself, I must have scratched my cheek in the brambles when tumbling off. Satisfied that my hurts were harmless, he at once accused me of falling off and continued a censorious gloating over his prediction coming true. A few moments later, my agitation and his intuition told him that something more than an ordinary fall had happened and he dropped his hectoring manner and tried, with gentleness, to draw me out, but it was too late now. My childish unreasonable expectation of immediate sympathy had fallen flat; in my disappointment I became silent, and when I did speak it was with bravado and airy dismissal. But Wilfred was smitten with compunction and was humbly placating to me. A warmth of unspoken understanding crept up between us and made us talk of other things with pleasure and happiness, so that we ceased provoking one another and the journey that had commenced with so much friction ended in an unusually affectionate vein as we both pedalled away in the brilliantly hot afternoon sunshine; I, now, with great circumspection and enormous care not to swerve too near Wilfred or in any way jeopardize his even and rather stately progress; he, on his part, being solicitous as to my continued bodily well-being, with grave exhortations to inform him immediately if strange pains or sensations attacked me.

Dismounting from our bikes at a discreet distance from the farmhouse, we sat in the shade of a tree—silent, now, and contented over our recent misunderstandings—to await the coming of the carriage with the others, so that we might all go up to the house together. Sitting there in the cool and peaceful shade of the tree with the golden heat running up to the edge of its pool of darkness gave me the not unpleasant feeling of being imprisoned in a patch of coolness. All around us the golden heat built itself into walls of shimmering brilliance that secluded Wilfred and me in a cage of blue shadows.

Wilfred shook me out of my remoteness by telling me that he could see the carriage coming. In a few moments everything was stir and bustle again as we all made our way down to the farmhouse. As soon as we passed through the garden gates I knew that I was going to enjoy this party. There was a warmness about everything, our gay welcome, the collection of young people who rushed to cluster around us in friendly interest; even the flagstones of the path were warm, I could feel them through my thin plimsolls with tingling pleasantness.

The garden, which seemed beautiful to me, was massed with colour and wandered about in an entrancing way in and out of the farm buildings, cowsheds, and barns so that the farm and garden intermingled with alluring unexpectedness. The heavily sweet beast smells from the byres and hayricks floated about, mixing with the headier and sharper scent of the flowers. The summery sounds of farm and garden—the distant rattle of a chain, the champing and shuffling of a horse, and the clank of a pail—blended with the drone and gentle buzzing of the garden and were interwoven with the tinkle of young laughter and the hum of clear and happy voices. All the chill and fear of my frightening ride down the hill was melted away, leaving only my perception and vivid awareness of living, over-heightened to a pitch of stimulation that made me feel airy and without weight. Among all this medley of scents and smells, sounds and warmth, laughter and mingled voices, a long trestle-table had been set for tea, the dappling gleam of its whiteness flirting with the shadows of its overhanging boughs.

There was in this gathering on this afternoon a young girl just out of childhood. I did not know who she was and have never known. At the time I only knew that she was a visitor from another country, probably from Norway or Sweden. Quite early in the afternoon she had attached herself to me, and shown me much attention and affectionate kindness together with a complete disregard of any grown-up condescension, which made me feel warm and happy. Her ingenuous and unreserved showing of her liking for me drew me strongly towards her. She took possession of me, sometimes holding me tightly by the hand, at others throwing her hot bare arm around my neck; I liked the friendliness of this although it made me tingle rather unaccountably. We explored the farm and animals and when we came to an open space we would with unspoken agreement release one another and, making a race of it, tear madly across the paddocks. To recover our breath and still our panting bodies we would seek the cool dark interiors of the great brick barns and, throwing ourselves down side by side on the hay, breathe ourselves back to ease and speech. Her English was good but not complete, and our amusement over it was gay and full of fun.

It was perhaps our perfect unreserve with one another which added mystery to delight; with her I found I had lost most of my shyness, and all my embarrassment. While close to her I had the extra-ordinary sensation that whatever I did or said was said or done with all the privacy of being alone, and somehow this gave me a strange feeling of affinity. So curiously strong was it that I had the sensation that I could say anything or do anything without the usual commit-ment that a second person would bring about. It gave me a lovely safe feeling and made me strangely sure of myself. We heard the tea bell ringing. Hungry and thirsty now, hand in hand and strangely happy, we wandered slowly back to the house.

We were late arriving in the garden for tea, but the two end seats had been left for us, so that when we took our places we faced each other across the narrow trestle. I remember so well how the late afternoon sun was pouring slanting rays of golden mote-charged loveliness over everything; even the starchily white tablecloth was palely yellow. Shimmering pools of lovely colour danced around the dishes of jam, deep yellow from the apricot, rich ruby from the raspberry, and pale purple from the blackcurrant; over it all hung the indefinable sharp smoky scent made from boiling water being poured over china tea, and the fragrance which only comes when out of doors in a garden full of sun-warmed flowers with hot sunshine blazing down.

It was when she jumped up and leaned over the table to ply me with jam that some of the mysteriously charged meaning of the afternoon came upon me, and with it a fulfilment of intensely awaited revelation. As I lifted my head to thank her I beheld her small body and knew that in seeing her thus I had for the first time become vividly conscious of an oppositeness to myself. Unknowingly absorbed, my eyes accepted the hard closeness and golden warmth of the small bosom. I did not immediately look away—indeed, I could not and did not want to. Instead, absorbed delight and slow awakening from what I beheld, for I felt no consciousness of guilt or wrong-doing, nor yet any sense of trespass towards her. This enthralled fraction of time held for me only freshly exposed knowledge and inviting beauty, which my wondering spellbound gaze could not refuse.

The cheerful clatter of the spoon hitting my plate to shake off the jam made me look up to meet her eyes, which I saw were gently smiling into mine; she did not withdraw immediately, but quivering slightly slowly drew away. Laughing and chattering together once more, we finished tea and springing up left the table. Strangely, we recognized in our crossed paths a completion which we must not disturb, silently we parted to lose each other; in the commotion and hubbub of dispersing guests and children this was not difficult. We never saw each other again.

9. *Problems of Wilfred's Future*

Wilfred had liked the Technical School and had established himself as a promising student. But now that he was sixteen or seventeen and was about to finish there, my father was becoming restive about his future. For some time there had been discussions about what Wilfred should do. It was an especially critical and trying time. The Shrewsbury Technical School, having brought him to matriculation point, would not be able to take him beyond it and, as far as this school was concerned, he was virtually finished with it, dependent of course on the result of the examination which was not yet known. He had sat for his matriculation at London University and had returned from the examination bitterly disappointed. He told us all rather dejectedly that he might as well have enjoyed himself these last months, following pleasanter pursuits, for all the good his months of application in preparation for the exam had proved to be. He was apprehensive about the result. His actual receiving of the news imprinted itself very vividly on my mind. I think my mother must have been away from home, otherwise it could not have fallen to my lot to deliver the fateful letter to him. As it was, I rushed up to his bedroom with the embossed and sealed letter—to find him, as usual, buried deep under the blankets, only the fringe of his dark hair showing from the top of his head and stupefied with over-tired sleep.

My excited shout about the news I bore stabbed him awake. He sprang up in bed and snatched the envelope from my hand and then commenced—again to use his own words—an ecstasy of fumbling, for he was trembling and shivering violently and his hands were all mixed up with the bedclothes and the envelope was obstinate and refused to open. At last he had the letter out and I shall always remember the few seconds of stillness, and then the long dragged out sigh of disappointment, despairing in its melancholy, and his inert slumping back on to the bed and the burrowing under the blankets. I asked him to tell me, but he would not answer or speak, so I left his room and went down to my father who was impatiently waiting for the news before going to his office. I was sent up again to make sure he had failed and, drawing away the sheets and blankets covering his head, gave him my father's message. Glaring fiercely at me he growled, 'Tell him I passed if he must know. He's not interested and doesn't care, and you go away. Go away—and leave me alone—only leave me alone, I tell you.' He would not speak to us all day, and refused to get up until just before my father was expected home at six o'clock. Later we learned that it was a good pass but not a brilliant one.

My father found it difficult to reconcile Wilfred's unnatural absorption in books with his apparent lack of design for his future.

He found it difficult to share my mother's utterly unfounded and
rather uncalculated optimistic view that everything would turn out
all right somehow. Wilfred, whose ambition was burning him up
inside, showed none of it outside, and any inquiry about what he
would like or intended to do would be met with a silent but somehow
confident stare; or if an answer was absolutely necessary, then it would
be an inaudible vague muttering about poetry and literature. . . .
This baffled my father completely, he could not understand where
with all his application to books Wilfred intended to go. . . . Poetry
and literature in our circumstances could not really be accepted as a
serious answer. Another disconcerting thing was that he showed no
desire for specific success; nothing else tempted him. I only once
heard him express with feeling any desire for a particular fulfilment
and this was very much in the literary realm. Any other prospect he
looked upon as expediency only . . . it might be used as a prop for his
writing. Gradually, however, the fact became accepted by all of us
that it must somehow be arranged for Wilfred to continue with his
studying and in some way be helped towards a literary or at least
scholastic career.

It was a big sacrifice and generous gesture on my father's side, for
his fear for all of us was still haunting him, and his instinctive distrust
of his own ability to help any of us materially bowed him down with
a heavy load of responsibility. His dearest wish was to see us all
started in some money-making capacity at the earliest possible
moment.

We were still occupying the same house that we had taken when
we first arrived in Shrewsbury. It had always been too small for us,
but now as we grew older it was becoming cramped. This in itself did
not matter especially, except that it made everything more difficult
for Wilfred and me, he to keep his books and papers together, and I
to find room for my home-made drawing-board and my large sheets
of paper. It meant that Wilfred had to work in the bedroom we were
sharing and I worked where best I could, but I was adaptable and
could usually fit myself into some corner or use one of the other's
bedrooms—anyhow I was in my School of Art for three evenings
a week. It would I suppose make a nice sentimental scene if I could
draw a picture of Wilfred and myself working away in the same
bedroom, he at his writing and reading and I at my drawing and
painting, but I could never work in the same room as Wilfred, nor
he with me; we both knew this and never disguised it from each

other. We both, I think, demanded our own stages and settings and having built these around ourselves refused to share them. This left our bedroom free for Wilfred in the evenings, and with the help of my mother he fitted up the only spare bit of room with an odd table and chair and a cupboard for his books to make a sort of study. He himself always designated this makeshift arrangement thus and, in each of our houses, this corner of whatever bedroom he was occupying came to be known to all of us as Wilfred's study. There was no heating of any sort in the bedrooms; the house was damp and sunless in the winter and very hot in the summer, so that for most of the year he had to work uncomfortably. Unlike Colin and me, who hated wearing thick or bulky clothes, especially in the house, he did not appear to mind this at all and would drape scarves and rugs over and around himself and wear mittens, which my mother had specially knitted for him, in his efforts to keep warm and so keep working. I do think, though, that much of this discomfort was an indirect satisfaction to him, and that the role of the struggling, ill, and striving student was a part which he had cast for himself; and he liked to think of himself playing this part. There was an element of self-infliction and almost a wish to endure bodily suffering in order to emulate the early days of great poets. There is no doubt at all that at this time Wilfred was very much preoccupied with envisaging himself in this somewhat romantic role, so that the prospect of enduring cold and hunger in some dilapidated attic—writing poetry— far from appalling him, had a strong appeal; but he did stipulate that the attic, if it came to this, must be in France. In his day- dreaming he never pictured himself suffering any privation in Eng- land; such a thought did appal him. It was something of this that made his freezing bedroom attractive to him, especially the necessity for piling on the clothes and blankets; this and working by candle- light—there was no other lighting—came near in his mind to a right setting for himself. The effect was perhaps a little spoilt by my mother's constant vigilance to see that he was moderately warm and her frequent ministering with hot cocoa drinks, but the swathing rugs and of course the very real cold helped the atmosphere he demanded.

Wilfred was toying with several ideas in a desultory and somewhat awkward way and was a little lost because at this time no career in itself made any definite appeal to him; for even at this age he was vaguely aware that all he really wanted was independence so that he could continue his reading and lever out of himself the creative poetic force which, uncertainly as yet, he knew to be in him. All that he could and did say was that he wanted independence from wage-earning for another five years, which would have brought him into his early twenties. Knowing this to be impossible, he could only look upon any suggested occupation as a means to an end, and never as an end in itself, and was only interested in a choice in so far as that choice would help him to decide the means which would be least adverse to his own determined goal of poetry and literature.

Some arrangement for him had to be thought of and worked out. Direct financial expenditure was so utterly out of the question that it never arose in my father's mind. We knew too well that the utmost he could manage was the negative help of enabling Wilfred to remain at home as a non-wage earner, thus allowing him to continue his reading for a degree and hoping—without perceiving how it could happen—that some sort of opportunity would present itself.

Through her connections with her church, my mother had been hoping that something might be done which would give Wilfred a chance of a scholarship, if any were available, or of some other means of getting him up to Oxford and eventually, as she hoped, into Holy Orders. It so happened that news came to my mother of a clergyman, a Mr. Wigan, who held the living of Dunsden, a small village in Oxfordshire, and who specialized in the preparation of young men destined for the Church. In return for tutoring and guidance, the students were expected to do some parish work partly as experience, and they were paid a token salary of five shillings a week.

At first glance, this did seem to Wilfred to be the answer to his problem, but in thinking it over he realized uncomfortably the real implication inherent in the proposal, for the vicar had promised him that, should everything work out as they hoped it would, he would do all in his power to help Wilfred to enter a university or by some means obtain his degree. This last, however, it must be understood, would be contingent upon Wilfred's implied willingness to enter the Church. Very early in the discussion Wilfred had tried to make it clear to Mr. Wigan that he felt no distinct vocational urge for the Church and was uncertain of himself in this direction. My mother's eagerness and possible emphasizing of his inclination towards Christianity and the Church, in earlier correspondence, had I think, given the vicar the impression that Wilfred would not be difficult to persuade. However, Wilfred made the vicar accept his view that any agreement must not morally bind him but should allow him at any time to change his mind.

That the two years at Dunsden held something of disappointment could not detract from the respite they provided for Wilfred from the need to earn a wage. As time went on Wilfred became more and more certain that an ecclesiastical vocation was not for him; with this and the vicar's unwilling realization that Wilfred was not going to be won for the Church, there came a lessening of tuition and guidance and a consequent increase in dreary parish work for Wilfred, and he became more and more disappointed. A pleasant enough sitting-room was provided for the two or three young men, but Wilfred, while getting on well enough with the others, did not mix awfully well. He found it quite impossible to work in the common room and consequently had to have recourse yet again to his bedroom. This was fireless and ill-lit, so once more he was back to working in discomfort and brought to bear his technique of working, in overcoat and gloves and blankets taken from his bed. He found no disappointment over this, but he did become despondent when he found himself thrown back, for his reading, on his own resources, and disappointed that Mr. Wigan had not continued his promised role of mentor. He became frustrated, too, as he realized that all the church work he was expected to do was eating too heavily into his own reading time; it irritated him to have to admit that he was really just a full-time curate, and the knowledge that he was not even paid for it irked him. So he had very largely to revert to his own habit of selecting for himself his own post-school reading, at the same time secretly continuing with the writing of his, by now maturing, poetry.

He was certainly overworking during those two years at Dunsden, and sitting in his cold bedroom did not help to check the chest colds he was so constantly plagued with. What was really depressing him now was the growing certainty that there was no longer any avenue left open to him through which he could go up to a university. His chance for his coveted degree had disappeared for ever through his renunciation of the Church. To remain any longer in Oxfordshire he knew would be futile.

In his anxiety and frustration, he had developed an extremely low physical resistance point; he became drawn and white faced. A stray influenza germ did the rest and brought him home a shivering wreck. My mother's nursing staved off immediate danger, but could not prevent a serious congestion of the lungs. With his illness came depression, but very gradually this was thrown off and with the throwing off came a return of his old fire, and a renewal of his habit of collecting scathing remarks with which to scald us all from time to time. A great relief welled up in us all over this, for we had not liked to see him lying in bed so motionless and quiet, with his bedclothes wrapped so tightly over his head and face, leaving only his eyes to glow out darkly towards us, burning with a strange unnatural fire of gentleness and docility that we could not understand at all.

10. *Disappointment and Uncertainty*

It was the winter of 1912–13. I was happily working away at my painting under Mr. Weaver, and I had already passed several of my technical examinations.

I was about half-way through these, and final qualification seemed not only possible but extremely probable before I was sixteen or seventeen years old, when the wretched bombshell burst, shattering my small hopes and schemes with its violence. An official edict emanating from some Government Department stated that in future students would not be allowed to qualify, as they had been until now, as soon as they were competent to do so, irrespective of age. The substantiation of a diploma would be withheld until the minimum age of twenty-one had been reached, which meant of course that employment as junior art masters, except as pupil-teachers, would be debarred until this necessary age was attained. Everything had depended upon my qualifying very early, and obtaining the junior mastership which Mr. Weaver had promised me in time to prevent my being caught up in some lesser wage-earning occupation at sixteen or earlier.

Consultations between my father and Mr. Weaver followed. Defeatism swept the family so far as this career for me was concerned. It could not sweep me, for I was already defeated by the question which was now put to me as to how I thought I could exist until I was twenty-one without a money earning job. To this of course I had no ready answer, but I caught up with one in a few weeks' time, for in my disappointment I made vehement application to Mr. Weaver. In his energetic way, he saw the right people and presented to me a cast-iron offer of a pupil teachership which would last until I should be old enough to take a permanent mastership; the value of this was fifteen pounds a year, which, when I worked it out, I found would be about six shillings a week. Such sums now seem ridiculously small, but to me at my age in pre-1914 it seemed adequate to justify my continued living at home and so going on with my painting. Triumphantly, I shot my great news at my family, rather innocently congratulating myself upon having ironed out all the difficulties. However, my news only seemed to create consternation, and after the preliminary hesitancies I could see that the tide was setting against me very strongly indeed. Swiftly my father told me that I must give up all thought of any career in the Arts and set about finding myself a job. Equally swiftly I pleaded my marvellous offer of fifteen pounds a year as a pupil-teacher, but this he told me he could not consider. Uncontrollably rebellious now, I heatedly retorted that except for his keep it was more than Wilfred was earning—who was so much older than I was. My father flinched at this, but although softening his brusqueness he continued to undermine my revolt. Diffidently, but with harsh affection, he darkly hinted at his precarious financial position and the dreadful outlook for the rest of us should he suddenly die or in any other way lose his salary. He probably had been more realistic than he intended; his habit of using words too stark for his meaning was not suitable for immature minds, and by doing so he—unconsciously perhaps—over-painted his real intention. I felt miserable and awed by the prospect of disaster that seemed to me to be lurking all ready to pounce. I was wholly oppressed by the weight of seeming responsibility which was being placed on me for my own future. My father offered help, but only in a negative, slightly sentimental, manner and did not put forward any concrete suggestion or recognizable plan. Quite suddenly he terminated the discussion, leaving me with a feeling of dreary desolation and a suspicion that he was wishful of casting off all responsibility for me, and that from now onwards I should only be able to look to myself for help in my struggle for establishment in life and for ordinary security. With a panicky feeling that this was going to be extraordinarily difficult to attain, and with an unendurable upsurging of aloneness, I heard him tell me that he would give me a few weeks in which to think things out for myself, by which time he would expect me to have something arranged. Failure on my part would mean the immediate acceptance of the first paid job that he could procure for me, no matter how lowly or unpromising.

That night I hung back until the others had gone to bed, meaning to go to my mother's room to have a talk with her before my father came up. Our talk did not get going well. At first we only discussed rather aimlessly and with some futility what it would be best for me to do. I was rather disappointed at my mother's complacent acceptance that I should give up any thought of the Arts as a career, and her insistence that this was my right course, and surprised that she should consider my drawing so relatively unimportant. For I was still vaguely hoping that although my father was so adamant she might somehow arrange things for me, as she had done for Wilfred. Instead, she begged me to do all I could to find a job for myself, and anyhow to accept without demur any post—no matter what it was —that Father might be able to find for me. Otherwise, he would certainly insist against all her supplications in sending me to sea at once. This last was told to me almost as a secret, and certainly with the sure feeling that it would be a spur to me to be compliant and accept anything that came along. I was astonished by this revelation. The idea came with complete freshness to me for, in spite of so much sea talk and my father's so often expressed regrets at not being at sea himself, I had never associated any connection with myself in it at all.

My mother of course meant this as a warning to me but, after my first startled surprise, far from being alarmed I began to feel the idea was attractive. I immediately became flooded with romantic visions of myself in all sorts of heroic roles at sea, so that instead of appearing smitten by the thought I accepted it calmly and almost blithely. But the next day I awoke with a sense of dread at the prospect of suddenly being plunged into an alien sea world. And I had unpleasant mental pictures of iron-fisted mates, hard driving captains and drunken bo'suns—for my reading had included some of the more lurid sea stories which, salted by my father's over-enthusiastic exaggeration of the immense capacity for hardship and brutality which first-class seamen were required to cultivate, made me shrink from the idea; and the small, tall sailing ships and huge cargo steamers which had seemed so romantic in the early Birkenhead days now seemed to loom about me with a grim menace of the unknown which I found it unwise to dwell on. There was, too, about this thought of going to sea a horribly terminating sensation—as though by embarking upon it I should be wilfully severing my life—so that I longed passionately to retain for myself the known structure of my own family and surroundings.

While my father held forth so much about the need for me to seek independence, yet the suggestion of sending me to sea had not again been brought up. Perhaps he was being pulled two ways and found it difficult to be decisive. On the one hand, he had his life-long desire to see a son of his commanding a ship; on the other hand my rather surprising bent and enthusiasm for a painting career had awakened in him an intellectual hunger and a desire to see expressed through his blood the innate but so long suppressed urge—so strong in himself—for creation and the fostering of fine thought.

However, with this general unsettlement about Wilfred—for this was when Wilfred was obviously becoming dissatisfied with his life at Dunsden—and my own recent realization that my father was losing interest in what I ought to do, it was not surprising perhaps that I at last became convinced of the impossibility of my being able to continue in my School of Art career. I found myself accepting this knowledge, if not happily, at least without resentment. Instead, I found myself with a growing realization that the economics of the family did demand my early independence.

Curiously enough, it was my interest in paintings which in the end gave me such a vision of life at sea; wholly erroneous, but sufficiently strong to cut across my indecision, and bolster up my quailing resolve. For interspersed between my over-romantic longings and golden visions of foreign lands, terrifying waves of clear-sighted realism would sweep over me so that I was frightened by what I saw. I would dread the pangs of thought which projected me so vividly into lonely and perhaps helpless desolation in distant seaports of the world. I hated the thought of leaving the known safety and the warm familiarity of my home and family, yet the alternative seemed some dreary somnolence in a musty office. In the end, as I shall tell, it was the intense experience of a picture which finally swept away my doubts, and with easing quickness made me decide to go to sea and that as swiftly as possible.

11. *Sea-going Decision*

It was not many days after I had come to this decision to get myself to sea, that my father returning late one evening from his office told me he had an appointment with a doctor who lived on the other side of the town. It was January and this particular night was one of bitter cold with a blizzard of fine snow that was tearing horizontally across the streets blotting out the friendly glow from the lamp-posts. This of course did not deter my father, but just the same I am certain he was feeling very much in need of a companion; anyway, he told me rather brusquely to put on my coat and he would take me with him. It was a shy but at the same time very peremptory order. I had been hoping so much he would tell me that what he really wanted

was my companionship, for I dearly loved an invitation to share anything with my father. I always liked any nocturnal excursion through
the town, and the worse the weather was the more I enjoyed it, for
the streets would be deserted, our four boots would make delightfully invincible thuds on the gleaming pavements, and, although
surreptitiously blowing on our frozen fingers and suppressing violent
shivering shudders, we would square our shoulders and feel fine and
tough. My father would every now and again blow through his
long moustaches to make disparaging remarks about weaklings
who sat in front of fires, instead of battling through storms and dirty
weather as we were doing, and these remarks would make me try
to break my short-legged trot—for my father was a fast mover
—into a more impressive and resounding tread, so that I could pound
along as he did; then indeed I would feel heroic and very superior to
Wilfred who preferred to stop at home and read.

We set off; and perhaps to offset his earlier brusqueness and to
entertain us both, my father launched into disjointed sea anecdotes,
well laced with salty nautical clichés—which he was more familiar
with and often more accurate in using than most practising seamen.
We ranged from 'cracking on with every stitch of canvas set in the
Roaring Forties' to 'clawing off a lee shore' or 'lying becalmed in the
doldrums in a blazing inferno of heat and thirst'—for we had to be
short of water—with the caulking boiling out of the deck seams and
taking the skin off our bare feet.

By the time we reached the doctor's house, we had literally had a
fair sample of bad weather and both of us were wet through and
numb with cold. It was for this reason that the doctor insisted upon
my coming into the consulting-room with my father, instead of
staying in the dismal and chilly waiting-room. In the doctor's surgery
there was a fire, throwing out great shafts of heat and supplying most
of the light as well, for there was only a single concentrated pool of
light on the desk. The sudden heat, and warm flickering firelight
melted me into a lovely soothing lassitude—it was probably near
sleep—in that enchanted border-land where the body is able to take
the ease of sleep and the brain remain driftingly alert; when a
separation of the mind from the body becomes possible and fantastic
flights out of reality seem not only more completely natural, but
more real than actuality.

Floating about in my trance like this I was unencumbered with my
body; my drifting consciousness was caught and held by the painting
of a ship in full sail and beam-on to me, which seemed to be sailing

through the night with a luminous, gossamer beauty that enthralled me. The creamy green of the stretching sails seemed to be wrapped around with the velvety blue-blackness of a hot tropical night, and so real did this become that I floated out of the room and in imagination found myself aboard her, idly spinning a gigantic wheel in control of this vast network of cordage, wood, and canvas. Power and exhilaration possessed me; so much so that I could feel the slanting tremble of the vessel under me, as I careered her to my will, and hear the sibilant hiss of the black, warm water sliding down her gleaming side as I heeled her over. . . .

In my imaginings I was deeply in love with my ship that slid so perfectly through the ghostly air and the swelling oily seas. . . .

It was the doctor's quiet, pleasant voice which brought me back to reality: 'Young man, you show such intense interest in my painting, tell me what you see in it?' But he had brought me back from my voyaging to fifteen-year-old diffidence, and I could do no more than mutter polite inconsequences about liking all pictures.

After we left the doctor's house that night and plunged once again into the bitter, ice-laden wind, I tried to think up ways of telling my father that I had made up my mind to go to sea. I always found the greatest difficulty in making any statement about myself to anyone, and more especially to my father, and it was not until we were in our own road again that at last I managed—although my heart was choking me with sledge-hammer blows—to stutter out through chattering teeth that—that—yes, that was what I meant to do.

It must have taken him completely by surprise, for he stopped dead and, peering down at me, told me to speak up more clearly. Having broken through the barrier, I was more able to do this. He seemed surprised and shaken, and seeing our own gate looming up close in the darkness, slowed up his walk and, taking my arm, turned me about and with a warmly conspiring air told me we must not go in yet, for he did not know what my mother would say to this and we had better think and talk a bit first. He must have done a lot of thinking, for he certainly did very little talking but paced slowly along seeming distrait and anxious. Then he said abruptly he must discuss this with my mother and, turning about once more, set off for home, this time sharply.

Nothing more was said that evening, but I suspect my father and mother talked it over when we children were in bed, and I think not only without arriving at any agreement but with worried, fluctuating discussion, which led neither of them to any decisive opinion. This left me high and dry, not knowing very much what they thought about my decision, for the question was not brought up specifically with me but instead with wavering indecisiveness worked its way into the general family conversation, so that the initiative seemed to be taken away from me; discussion now seemed to centre on whether, after all, it wasn't the only thing to do with me. I was quite willing to go to sea, but I did not like the idea of being sent.

This took a good lot of gilt off my gingerbread and left me feeling flat and disappointed, for I had really expected my announcement to create a little more drama among the family, having felt that my adventurous decision deserved it. My father did not talk to me about my idea of going to sea, as I had hoped so much he would do, but contented himself with short and irritable references to such a possibility, if it could be brought about. Even going to sea, he kept reminding me, was not so easy as it sounded. His cold reserve damped my spirits and displaced the pleasing glow which had warmed the idea for me so comfortably up till now; in its place came a creeping foreboding until the whole idea began to appear a threat instead of a promise.

The heroic role I had hoped I would play seemed in some extraordinary way to have vanished, and left me only with a feeling of being under some disagreeable sentence. My father's strange disinclination to talk to me about going to sea came to an end at last, as usual rather abruptly. One evening when he arrived home from his office, instead of repairing to the sitting-room which was his undeviating habit, he came straight up to the bedroom Colin and I shared. I knew the unusualness of this proceeding portended seriousness, much as it had done the last time, for apart from the stealthy dawn calls to get me up or the ordinary seven o'clock burstings in to pull us out of bed, he never intruded on our juvenile pursuits if we happened to be in our bedroom, preferring to call out for us to go to him. I was half-heartedly and ineffectually finishing off a book cover design when he came into the room.

After stamping about uncomfortably in the congested space and making several false starts, he quite grumpily got out that if I still thought about going to sea these papers might help me to get myself there. One was a draft letter of application for a position as a sea-going deck officer apprentice/cadet (some of the more important shipping lines nominated their apprentices as cadets, but these crack lines mostly selected their boys from *Conway* or *Worcester*). The other paper was a long list of the shipping companies all over the

British Isles. He told me to start writing to them at once, and to be careful to write well and not use my usual careless scrawl, and to watch my spelling and punctuation, for if even the lesser companies suspected my indifferent education I would not stand a chance—all this in a voice very cross and clearly admonitory.

Glaring fiercely at me and humming and hawing, he seemed to be trying to get something else out, but after a little more snorting he abruptly gave it up and changing his mood to one of boyish jollity announced that, having settled that, we would celebrate by all of us going to the moving pictures. This expelled all other thought from my mind and with excited cries I rushed in search of my co-devotee, little Colin, to share with him as quickly as possible the exciting news.

For, indeed, it was the greatest treat that could be bestowed upon us, beside which the concerts—often good ones—to which my father got complimentary tickets, faded into staid affairs, and the Literary Society's lectures to which he took us on Monday evenings paled into dreary boredom. The cinema was, of course, in its infancy and a real permanent cinema had only recently been opened in the town. A year or two before this time my father had taken us all to some local hall, specially hired for the occasion, to see the first of the travelling moving pictures—a blurred and rainy version of the Kelly Gang, a magnificent drama of train robbery, with splendid bandits holding up trains and shooting people down like ninepins. Colin and I were enthralled and infatuated, Wilfred the tiniest bit superior about it, and Mary very much unmoved. My mother was certainly sceptical about the morality of the whole business, although the fact that the actors and actresses were not seen actually in the flesh seemed in some remote way to commend itself to her. My father, too, was dubious, and both of them sincerely indignant when, in later years, what had been a religious building—a chapel of one of the various denominations—was bought and turned into a picture-house.

My mother maintained her prejudice and would never enter the place, but my father's curiosity and nodding acquaintance with the manager overcame his scruples and on very rare occasions he would suggest taking his family to see the new invention. The family always dwindled down to himself and Colin and me, Wilfred being aloof about it all and considering it poor entertainment and a gross waste of time. My father soon found the heated atmosphere too exhausting after a day's work, but Colin and I retained our ardent passion for the place and were eventually allowed to visit the evening shows by our-selves. It was seen to that this was not allowed to become habitual or even regular, which was perhaps why it held its savour. In those early days, the highest bliss for both of us was to be given our threepence each for our seats and sent off to enjoy ourselves. The whole ritual had a perfection of its own; the longish dark walk to the town and then through the lighted streets titillated with mounting joy our speculation as to what lay ahead for us in the next two hours. Our excited exhilaration would bubble so high that oblivious of the traffic we would make wild rushes across the roads, dodging the fast van-horses with some agility and much greater luck, and then worm our way into the milling throng, praying for our favourite seats; once safely in possession of these everything took on a lurid beauty for us. The hall—it was little more—was extremely primitive and until the show started pandemonium reigned with cat-calls and stampings and a discordant banging on a single upright piano, which for us, in some magnificent way, had a most exciting effect. The hall itself was practically dark, and to begin with the atmosphere was thick and dankly stale, but the temperature would rapidly rise with a steamy heat that brought us out in prickles of perspiration. We loved it all and, clutching ourselves, waited for the appearance of the proprietor.

He would arrive resplendent in boiled shirt and tails, and after making us a speech of thanks for attending his show, would whet our appetites with a synopsis of what was to come. He would appear on the low stage to announce each separate picture. In the intervals, he came on again to give imaginative descriptions of the treats in store for the next week.

The films themselves once started gripped us to the very end. The pianist would work himself and his instrument into a frenzy of speed and noise to keep pace with the shootings and wildly galloping horses. These horses performed incredible feats and seemed always to be ridden down sheer mountainsides, sliding for yards on their haunches and sending up clouds of dust and showers of rocks and pebbles. The whole picture was accompanied by very loud and realistic noises off-stage—that the manipulator was often visible to the audience did not seem to detract from the realism! The thunder would roll, the cascading water-falls would roar, and the pistols crack in astounding synchronization with the blurred and flickering incidents that raced sideways across the screen. The dramatic situations would often raise the audience to its feet and deeds of the hero or heroine would bring storms of furious applause from adults and children.

Looking back on these early films, it seems to me how morally sound they were—even innocent, so that after nerve-stretching tension truth always ascended over deception, and good always triumphed over evil. The tortuous rounding up of gangs of rustlers or blood-thirsty bandits, and their wholesale shooting down so that they toppled off their horses and rolled splendidly in the thick white dust had no connection with death or slaughter, but seemed only an exciting, wholly right, and convenient way of preserving the safety of the true law-abiders. The slight love themes which ran through them were concerned only with the honourable winning of the heroine from the designs of the villain, leading always to a finale of orthodox and proper marriage. The entertainment always concluded with an address of thanks from the proprietor to the audience for their patronage.

Our blood boiling now, our faces moist and scarlet, and breathing quickly from the blue, suffocating air, we would struggle our way through the over-heated crowd, and reaching the street gasp in the fresh air. On the way home—which always seemed too short—Colin and I would enthusiastically gild the lily or lay on pitch to the black, with a sublime agreement of thought, our only variance being competition as to which of us could agree the most heartily with the other.

At home a very special supper would have been prepared by my mother. Afterwards we would all sit round the fire—if the family mood was just right—my father smoking his evening pipes or his single cigar, my mother busy with needlework. It was rare, indeed, ever to see her sitting without work for her hands, either plain family mending, fine crochet, knitting, or exquisitely fine needlework. Mary sat with a book or more likely her set-piece of embroidery in coloured silks. Sometimes Wilfred would glide silently down from his attic and quietly taking a place in the room would listen while my father drew us out about the films we had seen. Wilfred enjoyed this second-hand entertainment, which belied his customary parting shot to us when we were leaving about wasting our own time and the family money on frivolous mechanical entertainment.

I had laboriously written out and posted my letters of application to the shipping companies, and the answers were beginning to trickle in; but they were all alarmingly negative and Wilfred was not slow to inform me that if my ambition could fly no higher than getting myself to sea—the last resort of the unintelligent—I must expect, owing to my deficient education, to be elbowed out. Thinking of my offer of fifteen pounds a year as a junior art master, I was furiously angry with him and immediately wrote off another batch of letters. One of these produced an offer of an apprenticeship in a coal tramp where a vacancy had occurred through the loss overboard of one of her apprentices. The ship was not likely to touch in England for years to come, so that if I accepted it would be with the proviso that I should have to get myself to Algiers and remain there to await her arrival; when this would occur was uncertain.

It is strange, and indicative of my father's over-anxiety to have me settled and independent, that he could contemplate allowing me, an inexperienced boy, to set off for Algiers, of all places, under such vague conditions and without preliminary arrangements for my well-being. He knew, too, that if he sent me off it would have to be without sufficient money for a return ticket, as a safeguard against the likelihood of the ship being diverted from the port, or at best seriously delayed. He was all for my going, as it now seemed that most of the shipping lines had no vacancies.

He had actually opened negotiations about my passage with the Company, and I was prepared to be ready to go. The idea of going to Algiers attracted me, but what I was dreading so much—and it made me completely miserable—was the thought of not coming home or seeing my family for four years—the length of seafaring indentures. That this might happen had never occurred to me, as my father had always told me that the average voyage for a steamer was six months and a sailing ship eighteen months, but four years seemed to me at that age a period which would take me almost to the end of my life, so that I had the truly miserable and mournful sensation that I was about to say good-bye for ever to all and everything I had known. I could hardly bear the thought. All the same, I could not now bring myself to ask not to have to go.

Last-minute doubts must have assailed my father. In any case he wrote—just before it was too late—to his brother-in-law, Uncle Edward Quayle, the tin-plate broker in Liverpool, for information concerning the Company. The reply was immediate and unfavourable in every particular, for the small firm I was dealing with had an unenviable reputation, and my uncle pleaded with him not to allow me to get vaguely stranded in Algiers or any other foreign port. As it seemed, however, that I really was determined to go to sea, he ended by suggesting that if I had any other letters which were not absolute refusals from the other Lines to whom I had applied, I should be sent to Liverpool to visit him and he might be able to make things easier for me, as he was well known to most of the shipping houses.

This was unexpectedly good news to my father and he promptly, but not without difficulty, extricated me from the Algiers proposal.

I was happy again, and after the awful thought of going away for four or five years, found myself contemplating with easy complacency all sorts of risks and hardships—provided my absence from home was measured in months and not years.

After several more refusals from the shipping people, two replies arrived with offers which seemed hopeful. Armed with these, a free railway pass from my father, and one and fourpence in my pocket for lunch and expenses, I set off very early one morning to call upon my uncle in his offices in Liverpool.

I was feeling very diffident about the visit to my uncle. The magnificence of the Liver Building with its resplendent janitors and porters did nothing to dispel this uneasiness. The rushing about of hundreds of apparently immensely important men, all jostling one another and seemingly intent upon business affairs of the utmost urgency and apparently world importance, I found more than a little breath-taking. The deference shown to me when I made myself known to the reception clerks restored my morale, and I was able to enter my uncle's large and airy office with reasonable confidence. He received me with extreme kindness and introduced me to his partner and senior clerks with some ceremony. He was, I think, a little nonplussed by my juvenile appearance, for I had still not yet advanced to the maturity of long trousers.

When we were alone again in his inner sanctum, he shot a lot of questions at me in his quick-firing, big-business manner, and finally exploded with a query as to 'why the devil my father had not bought me a long-trousered suit'. Unthinkingly, I replied that my father had promised to do so as soon as ever he could afford it. Looking at me intently, he muttered something about, '. . . as bad as that, is it?' and eased the point off by offering me a cigarette—which I had the sense to take. Saying my chances with the ship people might have been easier if I had looked a trifle older, he rang for his confidential clerk, and proceeded to give instructions about appointments and generally to manœuvre things for me to my advantage. Having arranged this, he seized his partner by one arm and me by the other and rushed us out of the Liver Building exclaiming, as we sped along, that he could not allow me to leave without letting me see the really big men of Liverpool, the men who carried all the huge business of the port on their shoulders, shipowners, cotton brokers, and big merchants of all descriptions.

In something of a daze, I found myself seated at a table upon which immediately appeared as if by magic fragrant pots of coffee and cigarettes in glass boxes. The room seemed to me immensely large. It was low-ceilinged and pleasantly but dimly lit, which gave it a cave-like mystery, so that it appeared to stretch away without walls. This effect was increased by the many pillars which interspersed themselves between the tables, for the place was underground. I was impressed with the lazy activity, which hummed throughout—the comings and goings and interchange of places at the coffee tables. My uncle told me that big business was being done all the time. I was pleased and proud to be with my uncle, for he was hailed from all sides with quiet joviality or deferential greeting. I suspect he did quite a lot of good business himself, for there were hurried conversations in strange jargon, but mostly in nods and head-shakes or gay banter, alternating with stiff curtness.

I remember thinking to myself that if this was business, how different it was from what I had expected and feeling attracted to the air of suppressed excitement that tingled through the place. It seemed to charge the manipulation of money and merchandise with such infectious gambling glamour—until I remembered the white-faced subservient clerks; old and young, in my uncle's outer offices; and knowing that my lot—if I had renounced the sea—could hardly even be equal to theirs, my resolution for the sea stiffened again. This was just as well, for the hours ahead were to be busy with interviews in shipping offices and with marine superintendents—until finally my uncle told me that I should get a berth in a steamer belonging to one of the firms from which I had heard—not a sailing ship, that was impossible. Swallowing my disappointment, for I had set my heart on sail, I said my thank-you's, which were brushed aside, whereupon he told me that we had had just got time to go and buy my kit. He knew the exact store to which we must go and where I could get everything I should need: not very much as my berth would be in a tramp steamer. But here I remonstrated, saying I could not pay for this kit, and I would not commit my father for any sum whatsoever—never mind a frighteningly unknown one. At once—because I had crossed him—my uncle became snappily angry and demanded to know how the devil I thought I could go to sea, even in a god-damned tramp steamer, without kit, and did I seriously propose to join a ship in my child's knickerbockers? But the thought of my father's worried face over a bill of eighteen and threepence, and well knowing that his expenditure of even one pound had to be thought over and schemed about, gave me courage to oppose my uncle, and I stubbornly refused to spend any money which I did not even know if my father possessed. My uncle, like so many successful business men, was affable, generous, and kindly so long as he was controlling every move, but once he encountered opposition he would completely change. This had happened now, for he had wished, in order to please and satisfy himself, to round off the whole thing by ordering the necessary equipment.

By this time we had reached his office again, and he barked at me that I might get orders in a day or two to join a ship, so I had better agree to his suggestion and he would write to my father and put everything right. But I still didn't like it, and bluntly and stiffly told him that my father had always looked after me and would manage somehow to do so now. With electric swiftness, his mood changed, and roaring with laughter he called in his partner to tell him that he had been bested on his own stamping ground by his own nephew.

Returning to kindly seriousness, he told me: 'All right, we will leave Tom, your father, out of this and we will see if you are business-like enough to take a chance entirely on your own. I here and now, as one professional man to another, offer to purchase for you immediately the necessary sea-going gear. I will hand to you the receipted bill, and you will undertake to produce this receipt and repay me from your own earnings when it is reasonably possible—not before—for you to do so. I only want one word for an answer; it must be "yes" or "no".'

'Yes.' And something in this fantastic atmosphere of money warned me not to add 'thank you'.

Out shot his hand, with the true Lancashire spirit of sealing a bargain, and, telling me I had negotiated my first financial commitment and 'a damned good one, too', he wished me good luck and good business, adding, 'But of course the sea is no place to make real money. It's right here, in Liverpool, you should be, and if I had not got two sons of my own, by God, it's here I would have you.'

Without more ado, we found ourselves inside a huge seafaring stores. He at once demanded the manager's personal attention and, rushing the wretched man from department to department at incredible speed, chose and bought without hesitation, striking out each item on the list he had procured from the shipping people as the various things were obtained, the final purchase being a sea-chest. I still have it intact and use it in my studio, as a memento of those early sea-going days. He paid in cash, and handing the receipt to me asked me to produce it when I honoured my bond.

The sum involved was exactly seventeen pounds, ten shillings. When paying, he had insisted upon reduction to exact figures with no odd shillings or pence, and paid in gold.

My uncle now prepared to make his way home to his house on the outskirts of Liverpool, and I myself to make my way back to Shrewsbury. In putting my hand in my pocket, I was surprised to discover that I had not spent a penny since leaving home. Crossing the Mersey to get to Birkenhead, a sense of inevitability gave me unhappy qualms about what I was letting myself in for, and I knew then for certain that quite soon I would be boxed up in one of the gaunt ships I remembered from my early dockland days—and without possibility of escape—steaming down the grey tideway of the sullen Mersey out towards the hungry looking sea. I timidly hoped the ship would not be riding light and showing the horrid upward-towering expanse of red lead and streaky rust.

In my quailing heart I knew she would.

My arrival home aroused flattering interest and my dramatic announcement that everything was fixed and that I might be called upon to join a ship any day now sprang me at once into a personality in the family, as nothing else had ever been able to do before. My mother bustled away to prepare choice food for me. It was, I think, her remedy for all troubles. It was as if, unable to alter our destinies, at least she could ease the difficulties for us by feeding our bodies. In these years, how beautifully she attempted to do this, and docketed in her mind what for each of us was a special delicacy to be magically produced in honour of our several special occasions. It was her remedy for all our ills.

Colin reacted unexpectedly with joyful exuberance that with me away at sea the old bicycle would become his undivided property.

Mary was quietly sombre and, saying nothing, suffered from her thoughts and sensed the coming violation of the intactness of her beloved family.

My father, after solemnly reminding me that I had incurred upon myself a serious debt, told me that he had already arranged with a local outfitter to get very extended credit to cover my needs for uniform and sea-going clothes. But with this explanation he closed the matter, though not until he had again impressed upon me the seriousness of my financial position, and that although it was a straightforward enough transaction that I had concluded with my uncle—he was quite happy about it and I myself need not be over worried—I must never forget my uncle's generosity and, at the same time and above all, must commence at once to set aside small sums until I had sufficient to repay the whole amount. Having thus delivered himself, he forced himself into good humour.

12. *Leaving Home*

One morning an important-looking letter arrived addressed to me, and the gaily coloured house-flag stamped on the back told me at once what it was. Sure enough, it was the offer of a ship sailing from Liverpool in ten days' time. She was destined for the Far East, Calcutta, Karachi, and Ceylon, putting into unknown Mediterranean ports outward and homeward bound, returning to Antwerp and possibly London. The arrival of this letter, with its implication of definite commitment, brought with it a sense of finality and agreeable relief after the vacillating family conversations which had floated around and about me for so long.

If, at moments, I was assailed with regrets for my School of Art and all its associations which I was so soon to leave, this was greatly offset by the heady air of importance which seemed now to surround me. I was genuinely and most pleasantly surprised, too, by the effect my carefully nonchalant announcement had on people, especially my few contemporaries, and the—to me—quite splendid envy it aroused, especially as I could name my ship, and to a chosen one or two show my unworn uniform in all its glory of lapel gold lace and brass buttons and the peaked cap with its gay badge of brightly coloured silks and silver anchor, surrounded so skilfully and plumply with golden leaves.

Perhaps most exciting of all were the white tropical drill patrol suits, with their neatly pleated pockets and snugly fitting, upstanding collars—these, indeed, smacked of the tropics and when coupled with the magic names of Naples, Malta, Suez, Aden, Rangoon, and Calcutta made strong meat, conjuring up for me visions of magnificent adventure and untold romance. . . .

Another beflagged envelope arrived, addressed to me, with a letter inside ordering me to report on board a ship lying in the docks in Liverpool prepared to sail at once. After the first shock of elated speculation and the pleasant self-satisfying glow of achievement which came with it, an extremely unhappy timidity began to assail me and sneaking whispers of doubt fingered about in my mind, so that I was ridden with a feeling of impending loss and began to wonder most unhappily what I should feel like when I left behind me all that was known and familiar to me and, for that reason, precious beyond measure. The prospect in front of me took on a cold and hungry look that shrivelled me and made me feel small and deflated.

Although I had my black qualms about how I was going to manage everything when I got to sea, I was secretly pleased about the inevitability of my move which, once the plunge was made, would open up excitements and adventures and show me something of the world I was to live in. It seemed to me worth the effort, and if I was diffident I was most certainly not sorry for myself. I made my small round of farewell visits, getting the worst boring ones over first and reserving the one I valued most—the School of Art—for the very last one.

My good-bye to the School of Art surprised me with its warmth of good wishes from students and staff. Even the old janitor—old as I thought of him—for the first time unbent to become almost amiable.

He had always resented my getting past him for an interview with Mr. Weaver, when I had first of all demanded entry into the building on my way home from the board school on that summer afternoon that now seemed such a long time ago. My unorthodox full-time attendance had always met with his suspicious disapproval, so that he was invariably ready to compare me unfavourably with Wilfred (the Technical School was in the same building), whose air of preoccupied quiet studiousness and gentle withdrawal from any high spirits had established him with the janitor as a permanently favourite student.

The pleasantness of my good-byes keyed up my emotional sensitiveness and almost undid me, so bitterly did I regret leaving the safety and charmed certainty of the warm, oily mustiness of the painting rooms; and in those few stabbing moments I longed to put time back and was sorry I had so impetuously thrown down a challenge by demanding for my drawing and painting all or nothing and, failing to get all, and repudiating any compromise, had thrust out instead for something seemingly so opposed to it.

Mr. Weaver, who led me into his sanctum for a final few words, was warm in his expression of regard and assurances that this must be looked upon as an interruption and not a severance, and sternly bade me paint everything I could on what he called my travels in foreign parts. This made me feel better and more hopeful and less guilty about my water-colour box and sketching block that I had secreted in my sea-chest amongst the long thick woollen drawers and vests which my mother considered an essential part of a seaman's outfit.

At the forlorn moment when I was saying good-bye to my family, Wilfred was suffering from one of his heavy chest colds and was laid up in bed. I remember so well the sparsely furnished, dreary little bedroom, made more grey and cold by the driven slush that spattered across the windows, violently flung there by the March gale. As was his wont, he was curled up in the bed with only his head and his book showing, the blankets dragged tightly round his neck. Wearily, for he seemed to be possessed with a sad tiredness, he gazed at me quietly, then turning away his face on the pillow whispered in his almost inaudible way, 'If I can't please Father and I never seem to be able to—at least I should think you must be doing so now.' Then his mind began to work enviously and he irritably told me how much more profitable it would be for him to be going instead of me, and with some rhetoric said, 'Give me only Italy—and you may have the rest.' I wished very much just then that he was going to sea and not me. I quickly smiled—rather crookedly—my good-bye, for downstairs my father was champing in the little hall. He smiled back very sweetly and waving his fingers at me—we did not shake hands—bade me go to my sea and leave him to his books. I went down the stairs to join my father and Colin, who was to come with us to see the ship. It was thought that this would take the edge off the separation, for now that the time had come neither of us was feeling too cheerful about my going, and even the magic thought of undisputed ownership of the old bicycle had somehow lost its charm for Colin.

I do not recall much of the journey to Liverpool until we arrived in the dark sulphur-smelling murk of Birkenhead Station, with its resounding echoes of imprisoned steam demoniacally thrashing its way to screaming escape and the clang of riveting from the nearby shipbuilding yards. My father quickly took us into a pierhead café and ordered coffee and cakes. The hot coffee and the unlimited buns and cakes—for my father was in a reckless mood—worked wonders.

When my father told us it was time to cross the river and find my ship, I stepped out quite happily and was even able to negotiate the long covered gangways, where the water surged and sucked so

hungrily underneath me. Once over on the other side and in Liverpool I felt altogether better; I liked the look and sound of the
rumbling drays, piled high with merchandise of all kinds, mostly
with huge brown bales of raw cotton, drawn by teams of massive
horses that struck fire from the bumpy cobble-set roads. The
great iron-banded wheels thundered along, the wheels themselves
reverberating so that the very pavements trembled and pulsed with
life.

By the time we reached the docks snow-clouds had piled up in the
north-east and long slivers of frozen rain were lancing down on the
bitter wind. We had a long way to walk to find the vessel, which was
in a far basin. As we made our tortuous way through the maze of
warehouses, stepping over wire springs, hawsers, and lines that
stretched across the quay sides, I thought of the days—in reality not
so very long ago—when my father had taken me round with him
on his visits to the ships, as though even then I had somehow sensed
the threat of my ultimate connection with the immense—and
intensely male—activity of the seething ships and hordes of dockers,
who looked so enormously large and strong. Then it had been vague
and comfortably far off, with only the merest possibility of ultimate
actuality. Now it was real enough, and I knew that in less than an
hour I should be a part of this world of derricks and giddily whirling
slings, a part which would leave me unaccompanied and dependent
wholly upon myself for existence in it.

I was surprised by a tingle of pleased satisfaction with myself; a
gratified feeling that I was competent to grapple with what lay ahead
raised my spirits. This did much to offset the uncertainty I had felt, to
soften my regrets about leaving the peaceful quietude of the School of
Art, and to dim the memories of the deep water-meadows where I
had so often painted the slanting sunlight. These thoughts had been
assailing me all the way from home. Already it all seemed so far
away and impossibly unrealistic. Ships and seamen were taking hold
of me, and the entwining and utterly demanding bewitchment of the
sea was closing about me.

We had difficulty in finding the ship. My new and shiny buttons
brought forth one or two cheerful calls wishing me 'good luck' from
stevedores and dockers, who had quickly sized me up for what I was
—a new apprentice looking for his first ship. In the genuine and
simple way of the sea, they were cheering me on and showing their
comradely acceptance of a boy whose uniform proclaimed him now
as one of themselves. I was grateful to them for their heartening

robust friendliness. Occasionally there was other good-natured chaff about little boys being sent off to sea, but this was bandied about amongst themselves and not called out directly as the 'good luck' shouts had been to me. My father's stern and dignified bearing, despite his small stature, precluded anything like that.

We found the ship at last. I knew before my father spoke that here she was. There was no mistaking the high red sides of her, streaked, as I had known she would be, with vivid rust. We came up to her under her counter, the space under which echoed cavernously with the slap of the oily, turgid water: her gaunt sides loomed up to merge with her white-painted but blackened top hamper. She was riding light and her decks we could not see. A long plume of grey-brown smoke was streaming away from her funnel and showering us with gritty cinders that crunched under our feet.

My father, remarking with too much stress, I thought, on what a fine ship she was and what a lucky boy I was to be sailing in her, led the way up the steeply-rising gang-plank. Going up it I thought I was in for a return of the childish vertigo that used to attack me when my father had insisted upon my walking on the very edge of the graving-dock parapets, but I was able to suppress it satisfactorily. Clambering over the brow, we stepped on to the coal-dust-covered deck. There was a deserted atmosphere about the ship and the cold waning light of the winter afternoon lent her an air of desolation. The Lascar crew must have been below decks. However, I was warmed a little to see that my sea-chest had been hoisted on board and although it looked forlorn and disowned slung so carelessly on its side, just as the grappling hooks had left it, it was nice to see it and a relief to know of its safe arrival.

Presently, after we had been peering about uncertainly, an old day-watchman looking very like an ancient brown rat shuffled out of some hidden hole and in a quavering voice inquired our business. Then, turning about, he beckoned us to follow him and with shambling gait led us through dark and tortuous alleyways. They were over-crowded with brown-skinned, black-haired men in various states of nakedness, all of them shivering with cold. I noticed they were all either shaving or washing out of funny little pannikins of water on which ice was already forming. Wicked draughts of freezing air whistled through the narrow alleyways, but apart from their violent shiverings the men seemed unperturbed, keeping up all the time a high-pitched staccato jabber in Hindustani. They did not look up as we threaded our way in and out of their chattering groups, but continued their frenzied washing and hair oiling—the smell of them was rancid.

After climbing up and down companion ladders, our guide, stopping outside a cabin door, mumbled 'Chief Officer in there' and left us. The withered-up rat-like old man was wrong though, for after knocking sharply on the door, my father turned the handle to find the door locked. He seemed a little put out about this. I have no doubt he would have liked to have had a word or two with some responsible person in the ship. We made our way to the Upper Deck and righted my sea chest and then the three of us sat on it shaking with cold, my father pulling nervously at his watch all the time and muttering about 'time he was getting back'. Then he suddenly jumped up and told Colin to stop where he was until we came back, said he and I were going to have a look at the ship from the quay side, and walked me down the gang-plank with him. This must have been only a pretext for, giving only the most cursory glance backwards, he hurried along peering all around. Eventually we came out on a quay on the blind side of a great warehouse and, looking around anxiously to make sure we could not be overlooked, he put his hand out in farewell but, thinking better of this, quickly withdrew it and drawing me to him, kissed me on both cheeks instead, muttering something about 'wanting to do that and a last chance, when I came back I should be too old for that sort of thing'.

To cover his embarrassment, he assumed again his fierce expression, throwing out one or two admonitory comments about my future behaviour for good measure, and stepping out briskly now we returned to the ship.

On board again, my father, after hesitating for a few seconds as if about to say something, changed his mind, clearing his throat rather noisily instead; jumping up very suddenly from the sea-chest where we had all seated ourselves again he whisked up Colin and very quickly strode over the gang-plank. It was almost dark now; swiftly I moved over to the bulwarks to keep them in my sight as long as possible. At first I could see them threading their way through mazes of piled cargo or stepping over heavy mooring lines that led from bollards to ships . . . ships . . . ships everywhere. . . .

After this their way led through patches of black darkness; in these I lost them altogether, but I knew that as they crossed through the pools of light made by the glaring arc-lights I should be able to see them, getting smaller and more indistinct as they got farther and farther away from me. It was when they walked into the last circle

of light—faint now—before they would have to turn behind the
dockyard wall that they stopped and turned, as I knew they would,
to look towards me and wave. I waved back to them although I knew
that standing among the black superstructure, as I was, they could
not see me. . . . I knew, too, that my father's eyes would not be fierce
or hard now, and that Colin would be miserable. . . . I watched the
short sturdy figure of my father and the slight smallness of Colin,
both dwarfed with distance but still recognizable, until I saw my
father, holding Colin by the hand, walk out of the light towards the
dock gates. Colin I thought still had his head turned looking towards
me as they merged into the far darkness and then almost with a click
disappeared completely. A painful stab drove through me as I
wondered if I should ever see them again.

Turning about I looked around me, but except for the towering
masts and smoking funnel which stood out sharply against the
luminous darkness of the sky, everything else about the ship was
melted into inky gloom, and as I stumbled across the deck I felt all
around me the immensity of the darkening docks. The iron of loneliness bit deep into me.

13. *Joining Ship*

I was wondering where I could go to get warm and wishing that
someone would come who would show me my cabin, when a man
came aboard and, after introducing himself as the Second Officer,
told me to go along with him and we made a tour of inspection. He
said I could doss down in his cabin as mine was not yet free and as he
himself proposed going ashore to spend a few more hours with his
wife. He also told me that there was a night watchman on board and
he handed me the keys of his room and also of the chart room, for
he was the navigator. He said that I should be required to attend him
aft when casting off next morning on the early tide, and making a
final suggestion that it would be a good idea to persuade the senior
white quartermaster, who would be aboard any time now, to show
me round the bridge, wheel-house, and chart-room, of which I
already had the keys, he went ashore and left me to myself.

As mostly happened with me, I was quite happy alone, and after
carefully locking the cabin found my way up to the deck. There
seemed to be more lights about now; in any case the strangeness of
walking on iron was beginning to wear off and a picture of the ship

was already forming in my mind. The snow-laden rain had ceased, but it was colder than ever. I was just thinking of finding my way back to the steam pipes that I had noticed hissing and clanking in one of the passages, so that I could warm my hands, when a man in a blue jersey, carrying an immense white canvas sea-bag across his shoulders, strode over the gangway. Sliding the bag down his back, so that it fell with a thud on the iron-plated deck, he asked me if I was the new apprentice. When I told him I was, he told me that he was the senior quartermaster and suggested that we should dig out the night-watchman and see if there was any tea going. I thought this was a fine idea and immediately said so, whereupon we threaded our way through the winches, cargo slings, and other pre-sailing debris that cluttered up the decks, until we came to the watertight iron doors of the galley. Opening these by their queer lever fastenings, we were hardly inside before we were bidden angrily to 'shut the bloody door'. The room—really, it was more like an iron box than a room—was eerily lighted by a weak electric bulb lost in the fog of steam and sulphury smoke that eddied thickly from shoulder-level upwards, and I immediately thought of a description Wilfred had once beguiled us with of Dante's inferno. The surly watchman was real enough though and so was the billy-can of black tea bubbling thickly on the top of the closed-in fire. Pouring out three cups of the treacly black fluid, the watchman spurted condensed milk from a tin on to each of them. He did this by first removing two filthy screws of paper from two punctures in the lid and then applying his mouth —horribly fringed with a glutinous moustache—to one and blowing sharply. The result was a curving arc, and a yellow blob which plopped very neatly into the cups. This delicate operation over, the watchman sank back on to his locker, and pursing his lips shot out a stream of black tobacco juice, accurately aimed between the mugs, to land with a smacking hiss and crackle on the hot iron of the fire-plate. He seemed absorbed with this accurate squirting and glared resentfully when the quartermaster, thinking perhaps that this precise exactitude might not last for ever, hastily seized a cup for himself and handed one to me. Unabashed by the quartermaster's withdrawal of the already loathsome cups to a safer place, the filthy old ancient continued with his vile squirting, encircling his own cup with the brown blobs, only pausing to work away with his jaws to produce fresh supplies of ammunition. The only variations to the cup-ringing came when a rat, made bold by hunger, eased its twitching nose around a flour-bin, and the old man, with barely perceptible movement, diverted the attack towards the creature, whereupon it leapt off its feet with a squeal of pain as the blinding stream of nicotine hit it full in the eyes; or now and again the poisonous jet would be sped towards the low deck-head itself, where a cockroach, its antennae waving with slow, obscene inquisitiveness, crawled about upside down. Not until the insect was in position over the fire-top was the shot discharged. Its impact momentarily pinned the cockroach to the ceiling, and a second later the horrible kicking clot of insect and juice slowly dislodged itself and fell to the hot iron to be boiled and roasted.

I was becoming uncomfortably aware of the vast multitudes of verminous livestock which seemed to be sharing the very atmosphere with us, and my wandering eyes noticed the large heaps of sweepings pushed in broom-patterned piles against any convenient bulkhead. They seemed to be grey flour or biscuit sweepings, but far the greater proportion, I saw, was made up of rat ordure. Now and again they would pulse disgustingly, as the cockroaches burrowed and fed under the filthy mounds.

With the cups in our hands, I looked towards the quartermaster, hoping he would not drink his tea, but I saw that he was quite unperturbed and presently began to drink with great relishing gulps, swirling the mixture around and around to stir up the sugar. I began to realize a bit that there was much more in this sea-going business than the violent gales and tropic seas and the pure cleanliness of the salt elements that my father had spoken about with such yearning nostalgia; I wondered if he had forgotten the rats and cockroaches and the blind, legless weevils; I supposed that he must have done.

Thinking that as I was now in for the sea-life I had better—for my own sake—embrace it and its customs as soon as possible, I made a brave attempt to drink my brew. But it was no good, for after the first determined sip the picture of the night-watchman's gluten-encrusted moustache, as it had flared and oozed over the tin of milk, kept imposing itself between me and my cup. For one awful second I thought I would have to be sick, but the thought which immediately followed, that if I was, it would be mistaken for pre-sailing sea-sickness, steadied me; and putting the cup down as casually as I could I felt fine again. The quartermaster, with a mumbled 'If it's all the same to you', immediately seized my cup, drank it up and with a nod of thanks to the dirty old man in the corner made for the door.

It was nice to get outside into the bitter cold wind and nicer still to climb up the steep companion ladders with their slippery hand rails and mounting to the bridge lean over the furled canvas dodgers to look at all the ships lying so quietly in their dark settlements all around us; I liked the sound of the fussing yelps of the tugs and the deep-throated answering bays from the liners and big ships moving in the river.

The transition from the rat-infested galley, with its foul air, to the clean, clear blackness of night cleared my head. I enjoyed the darkness; the cloaking density of it hid all the dirt and general rubbish of the docks, disguising even the oily scum pollution of the dock water so that its surface where it caught some vivid light possessed a gem-like brilliance. As a setting for these immediate dock water reflections which attracted me so much, there was the backcloth of the lit-up pulsing glow from Liverpool and more distant the hard glitter from Birkenhead. Still, it was too cold to stop on the unprotected bridge for long, so we soon unlocked the wheel-house and chart-room and went inside to get out of the wind.

I remember I was deeply impressed with the clutter of navigational instruments, the compass and chronometers, and when the quartermaster brought out some charts I began to get an awed feeling that I was desperately ill-equipped to set about mastering all the mass of navigational mathematics which seemed essential to final qualification. When he commenced talking airily about Euclid and trigonometry being the key to all the mystery—for I had only the vaguest ideas about Euclid and none whatsoever about trigonometry and logarithms—my heart sank down and for a burning second or two I was filled with violent resentment that I should be expected with so little preparation to compete with these mysteries. Deep down in my heart I had a feeling that my affairs had been very mismanaged and wished Wilfred had been a little more encouraging and amiable over his periods of spasmodic tuition. The quartermaster, busying himself with tidying up the charts, kept up a running commentary about how easy it was for young 'gents' such as myself, who had had a good education to master all this navigational stuff: it would, he said, be child's play for me. It was poor bloody bastards like himself, with no education, that never had a dog's chance, and could never better themselves, but instead had to remain before the mast all their lives. His whining self-pity somehow irritated me, and thinking of my own beastly board schools, a hot childish denial nearly sprang out of me but something—my brass-bound reefer jacket I think—made me bite the words back in time. I kept my silence; and in so doing I took one of my first real steps out of boyhood.

A little resentfully now, the embittered man exclaimed loudly, 'I knew it, easy as falling off a log for you young gents, but—don't forget—all the bloody book-learning in the world won't make a seaman of you. That is something you have bloody well got to go through.' Thinking of the astronomy and the wretched trigonometry, I thought to myself that the practical seamanship was going to be the easiest part of it, but maintained my silence. Saying that he would see too much of the bridge once we were at sea, and bidding me to be careful to lock up properly, he took himself off.

Left alone, I felt a wave of encouragement that anyhow if my ignorance was colossal it did not seem to appear to be alarmingly apparent to others. I was pleased, too, that I had caught myself in time, and not responded to the quartermaster's confidences. I was able to remind myself that four years had got to pass before I could even sit for an examination, and that seemed a comfortably immense length of time. Feeling rather good now, I had another look at the charts, and then switching off the main light studied the compass by the soft glow of the binnacle lamp. The diffused radiance melted the wheel-house and the bridge into splendid mystery, the topmost spokes of the wheel throwing off a living gleam from the natural polish which countless seamen's horn-palmed hands had wrought upon them—she was an oldish ship. Standing there I did not look much into the compass, but instead, felt my blood run tinglingly; it seemed to me the ship quickened and I had again the absurd wish I had in the doctor's consulting room, that I would like to take her out alone and sail her to unknown seas in solitude. Drifting across my mind, I could see again the painting of the ship as it had hung on the wall of the fire-lit surgery; I felt now, as I had then, the dreamlike quality of the sea and all to do with it, only this time it was real. Almost caressingly, I put my hand out and stroked the hard smoothness of the wheel. The sea had entered into me and claimed me for her own. . . .

For ever afterwards a binnacle-lighted wheel-house in any type of vessel, whether a drifter or a battleship, had the power to move me strangely.

I walked outside and looked down on the black fore-deck of my ship, the long shape of her just densified against her surrounding atmosphere. Right forward, a thin pencil of yellow light stood up like a rod. It was light escaping between the nearly closed doors of the deckhead leading down to the Lascars' fo'c'sle, and every now and then my ears caught the sharp excited chatter of muted Hindustani; the Indian crew was settling in. From the docks, I could hear a maudlin English song, broken every now and then by blasphemous ribaldry as some drunken sailor reeled about trying to find his ship. Turning again, I looked once more at the pale amber squares of the wheel-house window and after locking up began the descent to the lower decks and the officer's cabin. The ship seemed quite deserted now and I could neither see nor hear any sign of life.

I found my way to the Second Officer's cabin and lay down on the settee, but felt unnatural doing this in my clothes. I tried sitting up and looking through a magazine that had been carelessly thrown on a chair, but I was restless and unable to concentrate on the pages. Leaving the cabin again, I wandered about the ship until I came to a lighted lower deck. This seemed rather pleasanter than the cabin and I thought I would stay here for a bit. I walked up and down to keep myself warm, whistling for all I was worth to keep my spirits up— I felt them to be slipping down a bit. I was a cheerful if ill-tuned whistler in those days and went through my whole repertoire, even managing a fair representation of one of Wilfred's favourite pieces, a Chopin nocturne. When I had completed my extraordinary version of this, I was a little startled and sad to realize that my rendering could not now irritate Wilfred as it had done so frequently in the days at home.

Having finished my untuneful noises, it was about now that I thought to myself I would be justified in looking again at my lovely golden sovereign. This had come to me as a farewell tip from my Uncle Edward Quayle. I had never before owned anything approaching this sum of money and its possession was giving me a most pleasant 'capitalistic' feeling and fine sense of independence. After all, with a whole splendid sovereign behind you, nothing at all seemed in any way quite impossible. I had taken it out of my leather purse —a much prized present from Mary—and was turning it over in my hands, enjoying the feel of its solid weightiness, when suddenly it was out of my hands and bowling merrily across the hatch boards of one of the holds. I was after it like a flash, but I was too late, for striking an interstice, it gave a twist and disappeared—to drop soundlessly to its final resting-place somewhere amongst thousands of tons of cargo. I took it, I remember, quite philosophically—thinking all the same what a pity it was that the whole of my wealth should be stripped from me with such unexpected suddenness—although I realized with something of a jolt that I was penniless again. However,

I should not need any money at sea and by the time we reached a port where I could go ashore I would be able to draw a 'sub' against my minute pay.

I was tantalized most by the thought that I might as well have bought the really magnificent professional artist's water-colour box, which I had known for a long time could be got for eighteen and sixpence; from Winsor and Newtons, too.

This was soon crowded out of my mind though, for something else seemed to be tugging and pulling, and somehow invading my being. I could not find out what it was, but it was nothing to do with the sovereign, the mates, or the ship, or yet anything at all that had happened immediately or even in my own lifetime. It was a call, almost perhaps a song, that was drifting and clinging around me and was reaching out to me—clear, with taut-strung, vibrating shrillness. I knew that it was coming down through the centuries, primeval in its powerful urge upon my mind. I did not know how to define it, but my whole being leapt to accept the powerful influence of its potency. I had a fine, clear sense of immaterialism, the immediate moment was unimportant, my touchable surroundings became insignificant so that everything—my own small venture of going to sea, my own future comforts, hazards, or dislikes—seemed to melt away to utter unimportance in a way which for me in those short hours became absolute. Out of the dark and unknown swirl of the past, there uprose in me a conviction of an innate propensity; a connection with existence that had never ceased to live in the æons before I was born. I knew it to be something enduring and everlasting welling up out of the timelessness of the centuries. . . .

Presently escaping a little from these deep undertows or, more truly, ceasing to wonder and question, my thoughts wandered floatingly over my family: now, for the first time, I was able to look at them from the outside and in doing this all the small tyrannies and irritations and short-tempered intolerances seemed not so much to fall away as never to have happened. Only warmth and love and loyalty seemed to form my pictures of all of them.

A lot of this sort of homesick thinking was running through my head at great speed with kaleidoscopic flashings but with little sequence so that I jumped back and forth from one incident to another; but it was always the five other individuals of the family who persisted in my thoughts. I myself felt curiously remote from it all; pictures of myself came to me very little. It was as if a great blotting out had taken place, so that my School of Art, all my hopes of painting, and all that had been individual to myself, no longer mattered or counted; and the transition to seafaring seemed already, in these few hours, to be for me of lengthy establishment.

The rain had cleared now, and I found myself climbing up to the bridge again. As I gained it and leant my arms over the broad teak rail, I noticed arc lights flooding in a nearby dock; half a steamer was lit up, the other half of her was cut off by the sooty blackness of a cargo warehouse. It added sharpness to the glare of the cargo lights that chequered the black and white of her midships and forepart. I remember she had a black funnel with wide stripes around it, one blue and one white. The blue and white merged together and seemed to flare brilliantly amongst the florescent yellowish-white light and the hard blackness. Donkey engines were groaning and whining to life, and huge derricks erected themselves from the decks and moved around in slow tentative gropings, blindly seeking for weight to steady and tense their strength. Presently great activity worked up, and with it the hum of straining wire and whine of descending cargo slings; the clank and rattle as the great iron grappling hooks hit the quayside proclaimed her as loading last-minute freight. Beyond wondering where she would be bound for, and if she would sail before we did, my attention refused to be held by her or my actual surroundings; my thoughts kept flying back to the dingy little house in the insignificant little road that I had left that morning, as it seemed to me for ever.

The fo'c'sle-head doors had been closed and even the monkey-chatter from the Lascars had now died away. All of the lights about the ship had been put out, even the one in the main alleyway. I had the strong impression that the ship and I were alone and sharing a silent deserted solitude. No light showed and no sound came from the galley. I supposed if the dirty old watchman was on board at all, he would be sprawled in disgusting slumber in some noisome hole. I had no intention of finding out if I could possibly avoid it. In my walks around the ship I met nobody, but the ship herself felt friendly, although she was not without aloofness, so that I could not get away from the drag and pull from the little house in Shrewsbury with its people, who had been my people and were still my people. That morning I had been one of them and always with them; now I was not any longer one of them; forlornly, I thought that now I never should be really one of them again. The knowledge made me feel a great gulf opening between me and them; all my feelings flowed mercurially with runs of liquid movement that saturated me with swelling tenderness. I could remember only the lovely things about my people, and harshness seemed never to have been.

I was possessed by a great and lonely longing to be back again in the security and warmth of everything I had known all my life.

I was shivering now and painful with cold. Looking around me I was suddenly aware of the rift I had made for myself, with the future looking incalculable and, to my chilled body, desolate and altogether forbidding. I became once more realistically aware of my actual surroundings. As I looked I could see nothing but icy water or cold forbidding ironwork. I saw, too, that the water dripping down the iron walls of the ship was freezing into hard blue ice. My breath was vaporizing and rasping my throat. Realizing my plight and need for warmth I stumbled along to the cabin. I tried my whistling trick to revive my fallen spirits but my teeth were chattering too violently and I could make no sound come. All I did was to open up a crack in my split lip, the sting of this and the freezing air bringing smarting water to my eyes and the salt taste of blood into my mouth. I wished there was someone on board just to speak to.

Stumbling around the ship, I somehow found the Second Mate's cabin; I slumped on to the settee, and fell into an exhausted sleep.

14. *At Sea*

It seemed only seconds later when I was awakened by a rough shake and a rougher voice bidding me stir myself and get aft and report to the officer in charge, for we were about to cast off and I was wanted on the poop at once.

After shaking off the confusion of my sudden awakening, I felt a fine exhilaration, and by the seeping light coming with daybreak soon found my way aft. Through my infant tours with my father, I was familiar with the general lay-out of ships and well versed in nautical terms. As I climbed the ladder up to the poop deck, I recognized the Second Officer, and going towards him not knowing quite what else to do I politely raised my cap to him. This nonplussed him for a moment but, recovering himself, he returned the courtesy by gravely shaking hands with me, remarking at the same time that if I could stick the life and take the knocks which would be coming to me he, for his part, would make a sailor of me; but I must remember it would be tough going at times. In the meantime I was to follow him around and do what he told me.

Suddenly breaking off, he yelled 'And for Christ's sake, if you don't
want both legs amputated, stand clear of that straining wire spring.'
As another warning shout went up, he picked me up bodily and threw
me to one side. Jumping up, I was in time to see the wire draw itself
into a steel bar, part itself, and whip round with a vicious whistle. As
it cut through the air, both ends spreading into bunches of razor-
edged strands, a terrible scream rang out and a Lascar seaman fell
writhing to the deck. One of the lethal ends, travelling faster than
sound, had brushed against his legs. He was gathered up and rushed
for'ard, and our bows being still alongside, a gang-plank was run out
and he was hurriedly carried ashore moaning horribly.

As the tugs edged us out into the Mersey, I could hear the frantic
ringing of the ambulance bells. Although I had dogged the Second
Officer up to the bridge, I could still see in my mind the thin brown
figure, in its faded blue cotton, squirming and spinning so terribly in
its pool of red blood. The Second Mate's comment to me was, 'You
see what happens if you don't obey orders. I told the silly son of a
pig to stand clear. Now we shall be shorthanded until we get to
Calcutta.'

I thought to myself rather dizzily that I did see only too well; but
I was able to shake off my nausea, deluded a little by the speed and
incredibly calm efficiency with which the accident had been handled
and the complete nonchalance of all concerned, as if really it was no
concern whatsoever of theirs. A little leathery-faced man, whom I
took to be the First Officer, summed it up and dismissed the whole
episode by saying, 'Thank the bloody Christ it didn't happen at sea, I
don't fancy my surgical skill too well.' We were well out into the
river now and under way with our own steam, and the incredible
truth broke upon me that, come what might, nothing now could
stop me from at least having got myself to sea. From today onwards
I would be able to lay claim to having been a sailor. Thinking
of my father drinking his early morning tea, I hoped that he was
pleased.

My first voyage had begun and, looking round me as we steamed
down the Mersey in the grey cold of that bitter wintry morning, I
could see the murk of Birkenhead lying in its blanket of yellow
smoke-vapour, and thought of the miserable house in the dark and
filthy street and was reminded of my mother's bitter struggle to keep
the house, herself and us children in decent cleanliness, and of the
war that was so unceasingly waged to keep the permeating squalor of
our surroundings from creeping in upon us and so destroying the

seclusion of our damp and mildewed home. If with the memory my mind flashed back as well to remembrances of my mother's exasperated, short temper and how often I was the wretched scape-goat—often well merited, but not always so—I found I could think of these trivialities not only without resentment but with an awaking awareness of dim understanding. With my going to sea, I was growing up.

The receding gloomy pall of Birkenhead made me conscious perhaps for the first time in a thinking way of the progression of ourselves as a family since we had moved away and left behind us the truly acrid poverty of the early days in that dark district of mean streets that lay somewhere in the seaport that was now being swal-lowed up in a lovely pearly-coloured river haze. Shrewsbury in comparison seemed warm and fresh and cleanly. Thinking like this of our advancement, I was filled with cheer and hope for the future and, if at the back of my mind my painting career nagged at me, I had a comfortable feeling that I should be able somehow to manipu-late things all right. The thought of my paint-box and Whatman block tucked away in my sea-chest and the fine new fat red-sable brush that lay with them made me scheme and wonder how soon I should find some chance to use them. I swore to myself it should not be long. At this moment a change of course must have swung us full into the wind, and the next instant my lovely new cap with its splen-did gold badge was whipped off my head—to sail away. For one heartening instant it settled on the foredeck far below me, and recovery seemed possible, only the next second to be fluted into the air again to plane down gracefully into the grey waters where it winked a last glint at me before sinking out of sight. This struck me badly as a major disaster, for it was the only one I had and I felt denuded and all wrong without it. Even before the sucking grasp of the greedy river quite drew it down, I found myself composing a letter to my father demanding instant replacement and despatch of another with utmost speed.

The voyage did not seem to be beginning very well, and I hated the old Mersey more than ever. The Captain cursed me roundly—the first notice he had taken of me—for my unseamanlike carelessness. He was a large, purple-faced man, somewhat gross in build, with a funny accent. He was, I think, Danish—certainly not wholly English. I did not think he liked the look of me much and was glad when he told me to get to hell out of it down below and find myself another cap. Later, the Third Mate came to my aid with the loan of one but it only had a working badge and the leaves were in black mohair instead of gold thread, which did not seem the same thing to me. I could not be philosophical about the loss; my regret was bitter, and lasted until I got another cap and gold badge.

First, my sovereign, which I did not mind nearly so much; then the flayed and bloody Lascar; and now my cap. As I stumbled down from the bridge I thought to myself that things were happening very quickly and that I did not seem to be making much of a start. I was more than ever certain that gold and I were not made for sticking together at all well.

Below decks it was warmer but the air was thick with the smell of hot oil and fresh paint, and another indescribable sourness of air, a combination—I always think—peculiar to cargo ships. After a few days in it, consciousness of it wears off, but always when I met it again after a spell ashore it hit me with unfailing force so that I was reminded vividly of my first ship and those strange and not very happy weeks that began my sea career.

However, caps and sovereigns and all other trivialities were soon put out of my head in the general shake-down of joining a ship for the first time; of being thrown into immediate and too intimate contact with the other apprentice who was my senior in years and in voyages, a mean-faced youth to whom I took an instant dislike; of getting to know the officers and their idiosyncrasies and of trying above all to grasp my duties and the variously assorted jobs allotted to apprentices. Still, I had run the gauntlet of tough schools and tougher gangs of little Birkenhead bandits and Shrewsbury slum-boys, so that although mentally I was innocent and physically immature, I knew many of the ropes and was prepared, and in a pugnaciously hard way able, if not always to take care of myself, at least to hold my own to good advantage.

I can see now that I had acquired, owing to my back-street experiences and the consequent craft it had imbued me with, a cunning ability to read the portents and therefore be able to forestall many of the indignities that at that time it was thought fitting to apply to a young boy first going to sea.

I possessed as well—as I see now—a naïve trait of digging my toes in and saying 'No'. I would then become completely uninterested and —more valuable still—was able to communicate this lack of interest to my opponent or oppressor. This, combined with a stubborn refusal to move—come what might—in any direction whatsoever, caused them to be highly suspicious of my unorthodox tactics. This course I found nearly always succeeded in nonplussing my temporary enemies in a most satisfactory manner. The hardened little urchins of the streets had not taught me self-defence but something more valuable still, tactics, and these last I found always bewildered and nearly always without violence defeated those who wished to dominate me or demand submission. Some of this useful experience stood me in good stead and did much to offset my small stature and deceiving gentleness of manner, which apparently was inviting and provocative to would-be assailants. Altogether, I shook down without too much difficulty and certainly without undue physical combat.

The first few days were helped a lot by the extreme violence of the weather, for soon out of Liverpool we ran into some of the heaviest weather I was ever to encounter in my years at sea. I rarely met its equal again, and only twice experienced worse and more dangerous seas; once off Cape Pillar, north-west of Cape Horn, in a tramp steamer, and once during a passage from Kirkwall through the Pentland Firth to Thurso in a naval drifter.

So, in the first days no one had any time for attention to anything except keeping the ship head-on and ourselves from being swept overboard. We were rolling bulwarks under and shipping immense seas; lifelines were ordered to be rigged everywhere—an unusual proceeding in a large steamer. I was detailed to join the party of white men, officers, and quartermasters, with only the Indian serang, or bo'sun, and two other picked Lascars. I could have been of little use and was indeed most concerned with remaining on board at all, let alone upright on my two legs. We were completing the rigging of the final line on the most exposed stretch of deck when a sea came over that picked us up bodily as a party and burying us swept us seemingly over the side; but the bulwarks brought us up short and, fortunately for me, I was jammed underneath the experienced seamen. Actually one of the quartermasters had me in a bear's grip. Bruised and with torn skins, we came into the air again, spitting and choking with sea-water. I was terribly encumbered with my great heavy sea-boots and the stiff newness of my unaccustomed oilskins; my hands and body were frozen to uselessness. The Captain signalled violently to abandon any further attempt to continue the rigging. Lines were thrown to us, one of which was immediately secured around my middle by the little brown-faced First Officer, and all of us—scrabbling with bleeding fingernails for any hold on the slippery precipice of the deck—slid and rolled to safety. Off the dangerous open deck, the Mate turned to me and chucking me under the chin, said: 'Well, youngster what do you think of going to sea now? More in it than a pretty uniform, eh?'

Still spitting sea-water and with the breath still not back in me, I nodded my head and managed to croak that 'I liked it very much, thank you, sir.' Whereupon he swung me round and hit me a great whack between the shoulder blades, roaring out, 'That's to knock the sea-water out of you and a bit of bloody sense into you, and just remember this: if any apprentice goes overboard we never bother to put a boat out for him. If you go overboard you are a poor seaman, and we don't waste time rescuing that sort. Get up to the bridge and finish your watch on deck.'

When I ventured to suggest that he himself had been more nearly overboard than I had, he gave me a friendly good-humoured grin, and remarked: 'Good for you, boy. Now, get to hell out of it.' It seems I was always being told to get to hell out of it.

The bad weather continued until we had weathered around the coast of Spain and Portugal and were well into the Mediterranean, where we ran out of it and into brilliant warm weather.

The exceptionally rough passage was invaluable to me, for I had not been seasick and had not even felt like it, and to this day I have been immune from what observation has so often shown me must be a ghastly experience. The damages and bruises which I had sustained had taught me more in seventy-two hours than the same number of days of moderate weather would have done. I was finding my sea-legs very rapidly, and throughout I had felt a fine exhilaration and delight in the maniacal fury of the great mounds of water which so perpetually hurled themselves at us and over us, and I had found myself unconsciously challenging their determination to overwhelm us. The constant, never-ceasing scream of the wind as it tore away at the wave-tops in a frenzy to hollow out the sea to its very bed, did something to me which I liked. I found myself egging the ship on to pitch still more steeply and roll even more drunkenly. There was a savage cheerfulness, too, in the constant smashing that was going on all the time from stoved-in boats to landslides of crockery. This destruction—wanton in its fury—was exciting to me and made the niggling care with which we had been trained at home to handle our meagre possessions seem insignificant and altogether futile.

Running into the good weather, I was able for the first time to see the ship properly and to take some stock of those around me. Owing to the rough weather, up to now the ship's company had been

employed entirely with battening down and generally keeping the
ship in seaworthy condition; as far as I myself was concerned I soon
discovered that I had no time to think of anything at all except how
to keep upright on my two legs in my efforts to escape injury or even
drowning. I had been sent along with the working parties, improvis-
ing repairs and securing with extra lashings everything on deck that
was not swept away, including a nightmarish descent into dark holds
to capture and secure shifting cargo. I was not, of course, any use
whatsoever, but I did my best to do what I was told.

From the point of view of seamanship and ship matters in general,
as distinct from incident, this voyage to India was not my most
interesting. This was largely due to the invariable practice of manning
ships on the India trade with Lascar crews. This meant that we
apprentices were not allowed to work with the Indian sailors, which
debarred us from real sailoring and confined us, when at sea, to the
bridge or at best to working parties made up of the few white quartermasters, so that we got little of the real working of the ship; what little
contact we had with the Indian seamen themselves was entirely
supervisory. We were given plenty of hard work to do but always
alone, painting, scraping, and chipping ironwork. I would have
preferred going along with the main body of the crew. When, later
on, I changed to ships carrying nondescript crews mostly of European
extraction but with sprinklings of Negroes, Chinese, and Malays, I
got my wish brimming over with a vengeance; and if at times working with a ship's crew was heartbreaking, hard, and rough, it taught
me seamanship and most valuable of all the ability to work alongside
all sorts and kinds of human beings.

However, I was not getting on very well with the other apprentice,
but so far there had been no open breach and so no violence; but I
sensed that this might not be long delayed so strongly were we
opposed to one another. Otherwise, everything seemed pleasant
enough. I was getting to know, and to like very much, the three deck
officers and generally was settling down happily enough. Homesickness had not yet had time to make its real onslaught upon me. This
was to come with added strength later. I had really been too intrigued
and interested in everything around me to have much time to think.
In later voyages, when I was seasoned and there was not so much to
enthral me, I was to suffer some ghastly bouts of this, especially
on some of the long, dreary 'legs' I was to sail down into the South
Atlantic.

Malta, our first port of call, enchanted me. The pinks and whites and yellows, surrounded by the brilliant blues of the sea and sky, impressed me very much. I remember my surprise when I noticed that in spite of the burning dazzle of the harbour the island as a whole retained a cool and fresh look. The fussiness of the minarets and narrow height of the buildings seemed to lose their niggly quality in a splendour of massed glitter.

We went right into the harbour: I was captivated with the noisy bustle as the bum-boats came tearing out to meet us, crowding each other about and skimming the water like intoxicated water-beetles, their owners, when not quarrelling amongst themselves, screaming their heads off in their excitement and lively anxiety to sell their wares. The ripe Eastern smells nearly intoxicated me, so satisfying did I think them, warmed as they were by the hot sunlight.

We were not given shore leave, but I was delegated to the Captain's boat to take him ashore on his official visit to the Company's Agents. While he was engaged in this, I had an hour or two of freedom and spent them wandering about the harbour streets of Valetta. I remember being astonished at the number of goats that seemed to be meandering about, feeding on garbage and street rubbish. They had an unpossessed appearance and were prone to gaze at me with a yellow look so malevolent and prescient that I found them uncomfortable to watch; but I enjoyed the human throngs and the babble and wharf noises going on around me. The heat of the sun made me feel fine. I would have liked to have explored even farther up the steep and narrow streets of the sunflaked houses, the hot discoloration of which made me want to paint them.

Before we left Malta, I and the other apprentice were sent out for boat practice and we rowed close around the great ships of war that were lying in the harbour. When we had passed them as we steamed into the roads, I had been fascinated by their motionless solidity and the threat of immense power that their grey forms seemed to throw off. Close up to them I was charmed with the immaculate austerity of their decks, companionways, booms, pinnaces, and boats, and above all by their perfectly set awnings, so brilliantly white on top, so coolly pleasant and green looking underneath.

The sight of the midshipmen—magic word—in their attractive uniforms filled my small soul with bitter envy. I discovered that poisonous jabs of discontent were stabbing into me so that I began angrily questioning myself why it was that if I had got to give up my School of Art, desert my painting, and go to sea, why could not I be a midshipman in a cruiser instead of an apprentice in a cargo steamer. I found no satisfactory answer to my silent argumentation.

On that sunlit afternoon in Malta Harbour, so great was my passionate childish desire to be a midshipman in the Navy instead of an apprentice in the Merchant Service, that had some genie suddenly sprung the chance upon me and, as a bargain, demanded my soul and the certainty of eternal damnation, I know that I would with unperturbed blitheness of spirit have closed with the offer. Something of my enthusiasm must have spilled outside of me, for the other apprentice—I will call him Atkins—was disparagingly anti-Navy, and detecting my admiration became aggressive. We quarrelled violently and altogether most unpleasantly all the way back to the ship. In the ship again I tried to avoid Atkins but the quarters were too confined. I had started by disliking my fellow apprentice but now I found myself detesting him, especially as he was one of those persistent nuisances who refused to understand that others might prefer to be alone now and again.

His way of following me around whenever I tried to get away from him and his stupid determination to continue our argumentative quarrel irked me; and his provincial outlook and lauding of his native town, with all the inveterate inverted snobbishness that went with it, infuriated me. I hated the sound of his blasted Newcastle-on-Tyne or West Hartlepool, or wherever it was he came from. I told him so, and we became openly hostile to one another.

The smothering heat of coaling operations at Suez—I was put to tallying the baskets of coal which the sweating coolies, trotting up and down the narrow planks from ship to shore in an endless human chain, tipped off their heads into the bunkers—and our subsequent slow run through the Red Sea and the Gulf of Aden, with the burning torture of a light following wind, only added to our panting dislike of one another. It was not until we found comparative coolness in the Indian Ocean that we resumed a guarded friendliness.

Our bad feeling had one good effect for me, for it emboldened me to bring out my paint-box. I had been diffident and shy about this, and had I wished to hold the regard of my fellow apprentice I would have deferred doing so until I was more established.

My father had been sceptical about my taking my painting things at all, and had seriously warned me not to attempt any sketching aboard ship, but if I must do it at all to do it only when I was ashore and then secretly. He feared, I know, that my drawing would be looked upon as effeminate by the Captain and ship's officers and thereby I might be deemed unsuitable for the hard life of a ship's officer.

Anyway, I brought my watercolours out of hiding; as I expected, it brought forth jibes and sneers from Atkins and with glee he immediately set about noising it abroad that the new apprentice was 'a softie', who daubed pictures like a schoolgirl. But his triumph was stillborn, for his only success was to evoke interest in the dreary monotony of shipboard life. This was news, and quite soon the curious began to trickle down to our cabin to see what I was doing. I had an instant success—to the complete chagrin and real amazement of Atkins. One of the passengers offered me ten shillings there and then for the sketch of Malta, but I was still in love with it myself and would not sell. Still, before we reached Calcutta, I had sold three that I did not like so well for five shillings each which, when exchanged into rupees, would ensure many evenings ashore and some local travelling from the docks to the city. My 'fame' even reached the Captain, who sent a message to the Chief Officer ordering me to report in his cabin with the 'pictures'. The Captain peered at them rather blearily, and then barked at me: 'Boy, what the hell are you doing at sea? Stop ashore and make a fortune.'

15. Calcutta

We had laboured along at our nine or ten knots through the Indian Ocean into the Bay of Bengal, until one evening we knew ourselves to be standing close off the mouth of the Hooghli River, that great and shifting-bedded stream that runs in ochre-coloured muddiness from Hooghli down past Calcutta to the sea. It was midnight when we made the mouth itself, and put out our signals for the pilot.

I had the morning watch, so that I should have been below sleeping from twelve to four, but I had heard so much during our few weeks at sea about the wonders of the Hooghli River Pilot Service that I made up my mind to stay on deck and watch the embarkation. In any case it was too suffocatingly hot down below. The iron cabin where my bunk was had been pulsing out heat all day long. There was a stir of air on deck and the Indian night was lovely and very beautiful in its wealth of blue and silver, and black and gold.

Folding my arms, I leaned over the rail in an angle of the fore-deck, and presently out of the indigo darkness I espied the pilot yacht, gliding like some monstrous and lovely seabird straight towards us.

She slid over the gently heaving ink of the sea, throwing off cascades of liquid gold and jewelled fire from her creaming breast. The phosphorescence was brilliantly active tonight. As she closed with us in a sweep, she showed her gleaming ivory side that was full of grace. Gangway lights shone down, and immediately a small white cutter detached itself from her, looking, I thought, for all the world like an adventurous sea infant escaping from its parent. As the cutter came alongside, I saw that she was manned by lithe young Indians, superbly uniformed in white linens and scarlet sashes and puggarees. The pilot and his assistant climbed up our rusted, salt-encrusted side and, with engine-room telegraphs ringing, we swung to a course and commenced our journey up the long river.

For reasons of my own, I had taken great note of the pilot's assistant as he came aboard; I was surprised to see how old he was, at least twenty-five. Secretly I was enamoured of this Hooghli Pilot Service, for I had been much impressed with the stories of its reputation as the finest pilot service in the world and the cream of all Merchant Service posts, unattainable except to a few minutely selected candidates. The pilots, I had been told, earned incredible sums of money, upwards of one thousand pounds a year, and possessed superb quarters in the pilot yachts, which they commanded and practically owned; ashore they possessed bungalows and enjoyed numerous clubs.

The romantic approach of the white craft, stealing so silently out of the Indian night, added fire to my imaginative idea that I might one day become a Hooghli pilot. I thought it would be lovely to lie in wait, riding the oily swell like some sleeping seagull, waiting to swoop out so skilfully upon the great liners and ungainly steamers and, seizing upon them, transform their fumbling clumsiness into assured manœuvring.

We made our moorings in Kiddapore Reach late in the afternoon of a burning Indian day just before sunset, the evening atmosphere aflame with light, alive, it seemed, with myriads of glowing particles that danced and floated in a red transparent mist like living red-hot brick dust that parched my nostrils and burned my chest as I breathed. We moored in the stream, as there was no hold for anchors; bare cable-ends were run through the hawse-pipes and dropped in the mud of the river-bed. Naked river-men dived down after them and, in the darkness and swirling murk of the churned-up bottom, shackled our cable-ends to permanent ring-bolts secured in the river-bed. They seemed to take astonishing risks with running cables, and remained submerged for an incredible number of minutes, so that I wondered if they would ever come up again. Then I glanced at the cosy-looking, half-hooded river-boats, rubbing with friendly gentleness alongside each other in their countless rows, and when the tiny charcoal braziers twinkling out so merrily in the suddenly fallen darkness, with here and there a woman kneeling over one in an attitude of prayer and blowing the twinkle to a sparkling glitter of welcome. I thought how nice it would be to paint this river scene, and as soon as we were finished tying up and I was free from work, I went below to try out some sketches. But it was no good. The tiny iron room was palpitating with vicious throbs of heat, and I was forced up on deck—where it was not much better, but at least I was not enclosed.

I was not allowed ashore that evening, but expected shore-leave most evenings afterwards. I was impatient to land and explore beyond the riverside and wharves into Calcutta itself.

As I wandered from one part of the ship to another seeking for some stirring of movement in the intolerably heated air, I had no presentiment of the disaster which was to strike me down so unexpectedly in less than a week's time. I was always glad afterwards that I had made the best use of the first few evenings I had ashore.

My daytime hours were, with the exception of one Sunday morning, entirely occupied in the monotonous work of supervising the discharge of cargo, either on the iron decks directly in the rays of the livid and dangerous Indian sun, or in the suffocating furnace-like heat of the reeking holds many decks below.

I was, as I was to learn afterwards—and too late—inclined to take my daily orders much too seriously and too literally; but I was over-conscientious and anxious to prove my worthiness for trust and responsibility and, as well, to prove my physical strength and endurance under rigour, and establish my general suitability for the harsh roughness of life in cargo ships. All of this and especially the extraordinary carelessness of the master and mates in not keeping a better eye on so young a boy out East for the first time—and in Indian midsummer, too—combined together to spell out the catastrophe which was so nearly to finish my sea career for ever.

Still, before this happened, small incidents crowded around me and impressions imprinted themselves upon my mind.

The evening of the day after our arrival in the river Atkins, with surprising affability, invited me to go ashore with him, explaining that he knew the ropes very well and would put me right about transport and so on. I thought this a good idea and readily agreed. I did, however, stipulate that our first objective should be the swimming baths for, after the heat and dryness of the ship, I longed to feel water around me. However, he would not accompany me into the baths. I was not sorry about this, for I knew I should do better alone. In any case, he wanted to look up some friends, so we arranged to meet in an hour's time in a restaurant where we had a rendezvous with our own junior engineers and some apprentices from other ships.

I enjoyed my splashing and sliding about in the water, for it was a magnificent bath and fitted with ingenious chutes, trapezes, and so on, which provided pleasure without much effort of movement. The water, although cooler than the air, was still too warm for actual swimming to be enjoyable. I felt very much better after this sporting about in the water. It was in a freshened state that I made my way to the restaurant, looking forward to the coffee I was going to have with the other young men. They had chosen a large and garish place, but the coffee was good and I thought it all tremendous entertainment.

When Atkins and I left our ship, he had suggested that if I paid all our expenses to the city, he would pay them on the return journey; not having very much in my pocket I would have preferred that each of us should have paid as we went, so that I could budget more easily; however, I agreed readily enough. My two rupees to the Swimming Club though had by now depleted me badly. All the same, being the newcomer and 'green-hand', as it were, I was anxious to pay the bill for our coffee, but before doing this I was prudent enough to demand assurance from Atkins that he would have sufficient funds to get us both back to the ship. I did notice that these questions of mine evoked sly looks and undue hilarity but put it down to experienced amusement over what, perhaps, appeared to them as my over-cautious newness.

After we left the restaurant we wandered about the city, which I began to feel was very perplexing to find the way about in, for the party seemed bent on twisting and turning in and out of the maze of streets through dark alleys on the fringes of the native quarter.

It was in the New Market that one of them suggested that I should buy some fruit; indeed I was longing to do so, for the green, golden, and red heaps of it so cunningly mounded up were most tempting. But I refused, saying that I had only a few annas left, and thinking to myself that it was quite time somebody else started to do some of the paying. It was at this point that the party started thinning out, first one peeling off—without any leave-taking—and then another, until only Atkins and myself were left. I was beginning to think this very odd and, turning around to question him about it, found that he too had disappeared. Looking round, I moved about to see where he had got to and caught sight of his grinning face peering at me from behind a square pillar. I knew instantly that I was the victim of some sort of practical joke, and it did not take me long to realize what this was—to leave me thoroughly lost and with no money in the maze of Calcutta, miles and miles from the ship. My first instinct was to rush after Atkins, which was what may have been expected of me. If I had done this, he would no doubt have led me on a sort of paper chase, finally losing me; the others, likewise, being at vantage points to watch the fun. But the sight of his stupidly grinning face so infuriated me that, after looking towards him with what I hoped was an appearance of icy disdain, I assumed tremendous nonchalance and wandered off in the opposite direction.

I knew myself to be hopelessly lost and had no idea in which direction the main part of the city lay; but I was not at all depressed and with the glorious assurance of extreme youth had no doubt of my ability not only to find my way but to undertake the long walk back to the docks and river. The real difficulty that I foresaw was how I was going to get from the shore to the ship. The tariff for this was two rupees; I had exactly four annas.

In my optimistic frame of mind, the whole night walking about ashore would not have daunted me. My main anxiety was that if I did not report on board I should be considered failing in responsibility and duty; but again with the divine arrogance of youth I decided that I would manage to get aboard somehow.

In the meantime I thought I might as well wander about and enjoy myself; enchantment drew me on, so that I had little thought about where it might lead me; it was not until I had been walking for some time that looking around me I suddenly realized that I was by now deep into the labyrinths of the native quarter. I was fascinated by the innumerable little native shops, the wares often only spread on the ground around the owners who, squatting on their skinny haunches, ceaselessly extolled their miserable merchandise of rotting fruit and sticky sweetmeats, around which swarms of fat, nasty-looking flies eddied and hummed, with here and there remnants of lovely pure-coloured cotton pieces, which caught the light from the naphtha flares. But best of all I liked the lurid mystery of the shadows thrown by the flaming torches, with here and there a silversmith trader whose silver and brass twinkled and flashed out of the depths of the massed black shadows, and I was astonished to see set in between the brass and silver work, empty English ginger-beer bottles —even these spittle-polished prosaics had caught something from the surroundings and threw out rays of rosy light. They were evidently much prized, for I noticed a brisk and extensive trade in them.

I had put aside my predicament of being more or less lost and without money in a strange foreign place; instead I was enjoying it all immensely and drinking in the atmosphere in great gulps of satisfaction. The hot purple night, the yellow glow from the flares, the excited chattering of the brown people, with here and there a tethered buffalo covered in terrible living sores, the tired exhaling of whose breath blew out little hollow scoops in the thick parched dust beneath their pendant heads—woven into all this was the low intermittent drone of the muted native music pulsing from tiny drums, threaded with the sweetish, rather sickly cadence of the reeds and pipes. All of this helped to lull me into a sense of reality, so that I was contentedly absorbed and knew that to feel like this was to be really living, and that life—as I had known it—in Birkenhead and Shrewsbury had not really been reality.

I was brought back rather sharply to my immediate surroundings by a furtive plucking at my sleeve and, looking round, found myself face to face with a grinning leer—so full of evil that I recoiled, but although I shook off actual contact, I had difficulty in evading the filthy diseased-looking individual, for he kept up a running patter half in Hindustani and half in broken English. He again attempted to clutch my sleeve. This was too much for me and with some violence I pushed him in the chest with the flat of my hand. This was a mistake, the more so as for some reason or another he fell over on his back. A clamour of excitement instantaneously broke around us, the stall-holders and vendors running towards us from every quarter like dark brown rabbits. I was encircled by a shouting and gesticulating mob; hysteria was rising and I had no doubts about the hostility of the ring around me, and thought it quite time I got away. I managed this more easily than I had hoped, for I found that by just walking straight ahead the ranks opened on either side and I was able to march through unmolested.

Having walked some distance, I was still completely without any idea of direction. I had been looking around for some European so that I might ask my way, but I had not seen one for a long time now, and I noticed that the natives were eyeing me with speculative curiosity, which I did not much like; so I decided to try and get some information from one of the bazaar keepers. This was a second mistake, for my attempts at inquiry were mistaken for a wish to purchase, and competition from all sides immediately became acute. The importuning was good-natured enough but was gaining me nothing—except an embarrassing following of would-be sellers. I was beginning to wonder how I could shake them off, for my negative signs seemed only to exhort them to fresh waves of silly mania to sell me something. Despairingly I turned off into one of the hundreds of side-alleys. I noticed as I did so that two things happened very quickly: one was an abrupt diminishing of my unwanted entourage, and the other that the native shops here were of a higher class than the squalid squattings I had just turned away from. For these were low buildings, with glassless windows, seemingly built of mud or soft yellow stones. Not far away I could see one of these native shops that especially drew me, for it was beautiful. The soft crumbly-looking peach-coloured stone caught and softened the harsh light from the torches by throwing into relief the platform raised some three feet from the ground, which served as the display table—all of which was recessed back by the overhung balustrade which projected into the passage-way forming a glowing frame to the small dark interior, mysterious in its indigo blueness and warm, deep brownness, the wares themselves glinting colourfully in the hot, shaded darkness. It was perhaps the deep overhang, reaching out over the interior, that gave to the small opening such a look of obscurity and mystery.

Approaching closely, I saw sitting cross-legged the still figure of a black-bearded Indian, radiating great dignity; so that I averted my eyes from rude staring and pretended interest in the wares. What I was really doing was unconsciously recording a mental impression of this mystical setting for a future painting. The quiet stillness of the Indian did not alter, nor had he spoken, but I felt his eyes were scrutinizing me. It was as I was about to move away that, still quite motionless, he spoke: 'English boy, this place not good for you. Night too late. You go—you go, not stop.' Encouraged by these few English words, I asked in English how to find my way back to the city and docks. He considered this, but shook his head without real comprehension. But with signs and head shakings, I did make him understand my need, and he gave me an emphatic direction with an outstretched arm, as if he wished to hurry me on my way with great speed. I had taken a few steps in this general direction, when his low voice arrested me again: 'Come back, I help.' Looking at me very intently, he exclaimed, 'Lost, not find? Lost?' I nodded vigorously. Relief may have shown in my face, for he smiled with great pleasantness for the first time, and turning his head, sent a low call into the deep interior behind him.

Almost at once a sweeter call answered back and I saw coming towards us a small figure. At first, I took this to be a very small child, but as it came into the flickering light I saw that it was a tiny adult human being—a woman of incredibly small stature not reaching three feet in height, but most perfectly made, with a head of startling beauty set in a perfection of miniature proportion, with lovely little white teeth and brilliant eyes. Pierced through the centre cartilage of the perfect little nose was a gold ring, and from her ears—no bigger than my finger-nail—fire was dripping from pendant stones. She was probably twenty-five years of age. I was enchanted. And when she proffered her hand in the English fashion, I bent low— actuated more from a desire to pay homage to this beautiful and perfect little being than from the necessity to bridge the physical distance. Straightening myself again, I looked towards the bearded Indian, and saw in his eyes a gratified smile. He arose now, and the two of them spoke together, looking from time to time towards me. Presently the small person turned to me and, with more English words than the man possessed, attempted to give me directions; but I could make little of it. I was about to take my leave of them, just hoping that I would be able to find my own way, when the tiny person turned with vehement speech to the gaunt Sikh, and it seemed to me that she was pleading for a permission of some sort. Momentary doubt crossed the man's face, but quite quickly he seemed to make up his mind, and waving towards the girl, said to me: 'Follow, follow.'

Immediately the small person, smiling sweetly at me, reached up and lightly touching my sleeve, bade me with her eyes to go with her. I knew then that I was to be guided out of the native quarter.

We must have made a strange pair, as we threaded our way in and out of the tortuous ramifications of the lanes and passages. I must have penetrated even farther than I had supposed. For the most part we travelled in silence, only from time to time would we attempt some broken speech; every now and again she would raise her tiny arm and placing her tinier hand on my fingers would exert a delicate tug to show me the way she wished me to follow. Walking with her

gave me an enormous sense of safe-conduct; I noticed, too, that a
hush went before us through the bazaar and that never once was an
exhortation or importunity addressed to either of us. Behind us, a
low murmuring rippled away—to end in a strange silence. I was
bewitched with delight in the experience, and had a most extraordinary feeling of high privilege and could not avoid the sensation
that I was in the company of a superior being: it was as if I were
escorting spiritual royalty.

She took me almost to the edge of the bazaars, so that I could hear
the rumble of European traffic. Stopping, she extended both her
small arms, palms upturned, in emphatic direction. Smiling up at
me, she turned away and slowly walked into the fugitively lit lanes.
Spellbound, I watched her diminutive figure melt into the background
until she was gone. Then shaking myself, I made my way to the neatly
tree-planted pavements and the clanging trams.

It was now very late indeed and I was beginning to tire, for I had
had a long hot day in the ship, and the heat, although not burning
now, was still suffocating, so that I longed only to drink some water
and lie down; but I was still far from the ship and the streets seemed
long and directionless. I had already crossed the Maidan, pausing
midway to listen to the shrill metallic ringing of the cicadas and, as I
had thought, progressed some distance towards the docks, only to
find myself back on the edge of another part of the same open space.
Every street and place seemed strangely deserted. I was conscious
every now and again of a queer silence which fell around me; the
local noises went on, but behind the trivial sounds the unbearable
quietness of tropical heat lay in brooding menace. I did not recognize
the actuality of this as I wandered about Calcutta seeking my way.
It was only after I had been in many other countries that I was
able to put this subconscious awareness into formalized recognition.
I had got my bearings now but my trivial adventures were not over
yet, for although I reached the riverside more or less at the right place
for embarkation, I had still to get across the river with only four
annas in my pocket. It must have been about two o'clock in the
morning now; all was still and quiet among the huddled river craft.
It felt very lonely; I had hoped to fall in with some English sailors
returning to their ships, but I could see no sign of a white man anywhere. It was dark with the purple darkness of the East, and again I
had the eerie sensation of an unearthly silence. The air was hot and
thickly turgid by the water's edge, and hanging in the water mist was

the acrid permeation of smouldering buffalo dung; nearer to hand, arising from the medley of small craft, came the sour spicy smell from the cooled brass cooking-pots and curry-stick grinders, and drifting with it the fermenting sweat-smell of thousands of sleeping coolies.

I had stopped short of the point where I would be espied and pounced upon by the boatmen as a prospective fare. The vastness of the violet night and the excitement of my evening's happenings had tired me so that a lassitude fell upon me, and knowing that I had now only the river journey to negotiate, I was content to sit for a while on a derelict crate.

My solitary contemplation and slight feeling of loneliness must have turned my thoughts towards home and I found myself speculating that if—just supposing—some incredible magic could plump one of my family down beside me for the next hour or two, which one of them I would choose. My mother I was able to dismiss at once. The family legend of her extreme physical delicacy was so powerful that it was not possible, even in imagination, to bring about such an incredible transplantation.

Mary, I thought, would be great fun and would provide me with a splendid chance to indulge in some show of the worldly-wise and strong and competent brother.

Colin, I thought to myself, would be grand indeed to have, and his cheerful companionship was just what I wanted. I felt as well that he would be a great help in getting us on board the ship. But I thought rather differently about my father and Wilfred.

I took Wilfred first, and decided quite quickly that it would not do at all. I was somehow sure he would be a great responsibility and would not be capable of co-operation; also I was quite certain he would be very cross with me and in some way make my evening's behaviour seem rather silly and stupid, and so spoil much of what I had enjoyed and, indeed, was still enjoying. No, I thought, he would be quite out of place, and I could not see him dealing with the Lascars, crews, and rivermen, as I was learning to do. I was sure, too, he would himself get caught up in some predicament from which our united efforts would fail to extricate us. So, I put Wilfred back in his attic— poring over his books and from time to time furiously writing notes or memorizing great pages of prose or poetry.

My father came last, but rushed in with a bang. His short, thick-set little figure, with its red-brown face, seemed at first to fit in perfectly, and promised ability to deal with hordes of foreigners and strange seaports, until it was spoilt for me by the ludicrous idea that he might suggest that we should swim out to the ship. He was quite capable of such madness and of being angry, disappointed, and vexed with me if I refused to do so, perhaps chiding me for lack of courage. This image of him spoilt my illusion.

Here of all places, an Indian waterfront at three o'clock in the morning, was where he should have been. Out of them all at home it should have been my father more than any of the others who ought to have been with me, but the picture of him weighing up the chances of our swimming out to the ship came between us. In the hot Indian night so charged with mystery and romance I felt I could not bear a trivial misunderstanding with him, and perhaps because of this his image vanished, and unbidden he slipped away from me and back to his hated Shrewsbury. Anyhow, I was tiring of these illusionary visions of my family. Chancing to look up into the immensity of the brilliantly star-lighted sky I felt curiously unrelated. The solitary prospect of this made me feel a little bleak; in spite of the humid heat, a shiver ran up and down my back, so sliding my legs down off the crate and unconsciously squaring my shoulders, I set off to bargain with a dinghy crew and get myself on board. I had little doubt that I should manage it somehow.

My hail for a boat let loose pandemonium. I was at once besieged by crews anxious to earn a rupee or two, and I have no doubt that to their experienced eyes I appeared an easy victim to fleece. Excited bargaining soon turned to angry gesticulations and frenzied screams of refusal when I offered four annas. It did not occur to me to cheat them by promising to pay the recognized two rupees, which of course I had not got, but just the same I was quite determined to force a boat to take me out for the few pence I did have. Even native persistence began to flag in face of my stubborn disregard of their justified pleas for a fair price and with unpleasant mutterings they began to peel off and return to their moorings. I had, however, noticed one crew who seemed to be wavering and discussing it amongst themselves. Fearing I was going to be left on the beach without more ado I stepped into their boat, putting on a detestable air of command and English arrogance. Actually I did not find this very difficult to do, for I was losing temper myself and was sick of their clipped screaming noises. My upbraiding in English, interspersed with the few foul Hindustani insults I had picked up, helped me to overbear them and my action in finally pushing off the boat myself turned the trick. They laid on the oars and we were under way.

They had a funny little lantern on board and, by its flickering rays, I could see that I had picked an ugly-looking crew. There were four of them, and they were discussing me amongst themselves in a way which I did not like. Apart from this and the treacherous and nasty looks thrown at me, we made fair progress until we were about half-way to my ship; it was in this broad and deserted piece of water, out of hailing distance of any anchored vessels, that the headman—taking a careful look all around—gave some order to the others and they all stopped rowing and held water. The infernal bickering demands started all over again, but now I thought there was real menace. As far as I could make out they were demanding five rupees, all the time pointing their skinny fingers into the deep black water. This, I supposed, was the alternative to my not coughing up some money. I certainly wished that I did have some, for quite apart from the slightly dangerous situation, I had not at all liked the idea of this high-handed forcing. I felt uncomfortably that there was an unfair colour advantage somewhere. They were, I am certain, convinced that I had money on me. I stormed and abused them in an effort to get them going again but the answer I got was a snakelike forward movement by the headman, who was rowing stroke, in an effort either to overcome me or to wrench my pockets open.

I was genuinely livid with rage at the insulting effrontery of this and in a very passion of anger, and forgetting all good seamanship, I sprang up and striking down his reaching arms thrust him back with great violence on to his fellows. These were overbalanced in turn, and the boat slewed broadside on to the current most alarmingly, so that we were in immediate danger of capsizing. Loud conciliatory cries of 'Nay, Nay, Nay,' now came up from the jumble of arms and legs in the boat.

Actually, although against all good seamanship, it was quite the most fortunate action I could have taken, for although they were in the mood to strip me and then slide me quietly into the river, they had no wish to join me. The diversion in righting the craft and gaining control gave me the advantage I needed, and wrenching up a bottom board, still standing, I brandished it with what I hoped was a show of belligerent confidence. Their half-hearted effort at domination having failed they were cowed and frightened now. Displaying fatal indecision they lost all determination, became conciliatory and abject, and began rowing like mad for the ship. I refused to sit again, and remained standing, driving them unmercifully, rocking the boat perilously, which brought forth despairing cries of fear, if I saw the slightest sign of slackening; but I was myself too frightened to relax. I was also flooded with a buoyant sense of power and hurled my few Hindustani insults at them with enormous gusto and delight. It was my first dangerous intoxication, engendered by my instinctive know-ledge of easy power.

We went alongside the ship's gangway in creaming style and, stepping out, I resisted the temptation to throw my wretched four annas into the ringleader's face; instead, I gravely handed them to him. There was much abject head-touching and sickening salaaming over this, and, feeling rather like a 'little Clive of India', I climbed on board.

No sooner was I aboard, than my nose began to pour with blood; except for the bother of mopping and trying to stop the bleeding, I was not greatly concerned about this, as I was much given to this nuisance. While I was lying in my bunk waiting for it to stop, I reviewed my first evening ashore and realized that I had enjoyed it very much and that, on the whole, I was going to like this sea-going business, particularly the going ashore part of it. I especially thought I should like it as I knew now that I would be able to go on doing my bits of painting. It was while I was composing—as I thought—a lovely water-colour of the deeply recessed little Indian shop, which had attracted me so much in the native part, that I fell asleep. When I awoke in the morning I had an unusual headache, and I thought it was hotter than ever—so that the day's work ahead of me seemed particularly uninviting and threatening, as indeed it was; but I sponged myself down as best I could in the suffocating air of the cabin, and reported for duty cheerfully enough at a quarter to six.

Each day I started work at six in the morning when the cargo coolies came aboard, and continued on duty throughout the day until after six o'clock in the evening, when the cargo working ceased. We were only relieved at meal times—for as long as it took to swallow some food, about fifteen minutes or so. I was put in charge of a hold in the foredeck, and the Second Mate had impressed upon me the responsibility invested in me and the extreme importance of never relaxing vigilance or snatching any spell of rest.

I had to make a check of, and notes about, any broken cases or damage to any of the mixed cargo we were unloading.

The coolie labour was under its own gangers and stevedores, but I in turn had to supervise these and above all prevent pilfering. I was made to understand that I was responsible for the general smooth and efficient working of my hold. If extra large or heavy stuff required unloading—we were carrying a considerable amount of plant and machinery—I had to put in hand the rigging of extra tackle and gear; this again was carried out under the experienced direction of our own serang.

Under temperate climatic conditions the work itself, although it amounted to more than a thirteen-hour working day, would not have been unduly hard, but under the fierce Indian sun it was much more than arduous; and the long hours stretching ahead under these conditions often appeared unbearable. I was taking my duties very seriously: more seriously, I knew afterwards, than it was ever intended or thought possible I would do by my superior officers.

My upbringing precluded—as of course it did with the rest of my family—even the thought entering my head that I should in any way make things easier for myself, never mind discard actual responsibility; so that if my duty called for me to be in the sun, in the sun I knew I must remain. The temptation to take a spell off or seek alleviation in any way (for as each day grew hotter, instinctive self-preservation did bring temptation along) could not be succumbed to.

Another reason for my 'unreasonable application to duty' (as it was afterwards called when being argued out in Liverpool) was my real and serious wish to make a success—now that I had set my hand to it—of my sea career. Anyhow, the fact remains that on each of those four or five burning days, I set about and stuck to my work, at first with real zest and later, when conditions became even more intolerable and my body began to rebel, with a forced and conscious application.

In spite of my slight physical rebellion against the long hours and stunning heat of the holds and iron decks, I was far too young and inexperienced to recognize this in any way as a warning; instead I accepted it as something which was part and parcel of my chosen career in a merchant ship, my only real concern being that I should prove myself able enough to keep on top of it.

Although this work during my thirteen hours of duty was so insufferably arduous and difficult to sustain, just as soon as I was free I would change into a fresh duck suit and get myself ashore. For one thing I noticed that it was cooler there, and although Calcutta itself still throbbed with stored-up heat from the parching scorch of the day's onslaught from the sun, in the open spaces there did seem to be whispers of faint land breezes and tiny stirrings of the air, which were absent in the ship. Here the radiating heat forced itself out of the burning ironwork, consuming any currents of mounting air and leaving only a molten stillness which was alive in its vibrating ferocity. I looked forward to my evening swim, for if it did not refresh me very much at least it made me feel nice and clean after the dust of the ship's holds.

I had completely ignored Atkins' silly efforts towards humour on our first evening ashore, and as I had refused to satisfy his intense curiosity as to how I had spent the evening or got back on board, an unpleasant—to him anyhow—silence had fallen between us and we were only on perfunctory speaking terms. This suited me very well and left me quite free to go ashore by myself. I must have traversed quite a lot of the city during my few evenings of freedom for I loved just walking about and finding something new at every turn.

I made more excursions into the native quarter, but I did not penetrate so deeply and I was careful not to get lost in them again.

I was quite intrigued by the number of Indian children, who darted in and out of the crowds like minnows. All seemed to be little boys, and most of them were smoking voraciously and incessantly. None of them looked to be more than eight or nine years old and some of them were much younger—five or six—but they were drawing into their lungs the strong Indian cigarette tobacco or were dragging away at the stronger-leafed cheroot stubs. Their greediness in drawing the smoke into their bodies was made more obvious by the peculiar way in which they all smoked: instead of holding the cigarette in their lips, they held it in the fingers on the far side of both their cupped hands, and placing their mouths to the orifice formed by their crossed thumbs, drew in deep dragging breaths so that the smoke was drawn from the distant cigarette through the vacuum in their hands and so right down to the deepest parts of their emaciated little bodies. I was quite horrified by their tearing coughs and the craving greed that showed in their too-brilliant, glittering eyes. They were indeed drinking in smoke with both hands.

The great New Market attracted me for short spells. It was, I remember, divided into numerous aisles on the sides of some of which were banked great mounds of fruit and vegetables; on others, cages with live birds, beasts, and reptiles of a hundred species. In other stalls were brass and silverware, basketwork, sweetmeats, and cakes. The conglomeration was fascinating and I enjoyed the crowding throngs of natives in their plain white or brightly coloured garments. The noise, too, mingling in the hot air gave an impression of excited liveliness: the shrieks of the demented parrots and the clicking mutterings of the depressed monkeys were almost indistinguishable from the frantic vendors and the haggling purchasers. It was always, though, the more mysterious labyrinths of the native bazaars that really drew me, so that I wandered and lingered—enjoying the hot, rancid smells that intermingled so alluringly with the intermittent drumming music, the dark squalidness impregnating it with —to me—an indefinable and strange beauty.

I was very tempted to spend my money—there seemed to be so many things I would like to buy—but I had budgeted out very carefully the small amount which I would have available for the Calcutta stay and knew that if I was to have, as I meant to, my nightly evening coffee, I must not spend much on anything else except an anna now and again for an orange or two bananas. The fares from the ship to the city and back drained most of my small money away. However we were due to move out of the stream and berth alongside the wharves quite soon. I was looking forward to this mostly on account of the rupees I should save on river fares from ship to shore which would leave me more to spend in the bazaars.

Before we moved alongside, I was to have a long trip up the Hooghli. It was a Sunday morning so we were not working ship, and I was wondering if I could get permission to go ashore when the Captain sent for me and, giving me a letter, told me to deliver it to the Captain of a ship moored some distance away. It was, I think, the old *Ganges* but I am not quite certain. I was commiserated with by some of the others for having caught this Sunday job, but I was excited about it.

The heat was certainly increasing each day, and this Sunday morning was promising to surpass everything. The trip in the open native boat up the unshaded river did seem a little formidable, but all the same I was very pleased and did not bother myself much about the heat, thinking it could not be any hotter than on the sizzling ship. The trip promised me views of the river banks and Indian countryside, and I felt certain I should get some good ideas for sketches. I had a light four-oared craft, which necessitated my steering, and I was determined to hug the bank so that I could see all that there was to see; by doing this I brought forth discontented expostulations from the Indian rowers but I had the trick of dealing with these boatmen now and soon put a stop to their mutterings.

I was wrong about it not being hotter on the river; the blazing sun overhead struck the water to rebound upwards with penetrating

violence, so that heat was all around me: it was driving so fiercely
into me that I could feel my bones getting hot. I found the glassy
shimmer of the water painful to look at as well, but mostly I was
able to look at the banks. I liked the brickish-red colour of the flat
land, changing as it did here and there to patches of hot and dusty
ochre. The straggling villages enthralled me; I thought they were
quite lovely in their parched aridity, the thatched huts with their
long, sloping roofs nearly reaching to the ground; and there was, I
thought, a natural sense of design about these clustering little homes.
In and out amongst them were the tall, straight palms, intermixed
with the unruffled columns of wood and dung smoke; and always
banked behind the grouped huts were dense masses of trees, whose
rich dark-green foliage threw the brick-dust reds, the paler greens of
the thatches, and the ochres of the foreground into brilliant relief.

The inhabitants, squatting motionless and silent in the black pools
of shade, were statuesque in their quietness. Only near the water's
edge was there life and movement, for it was here that the countless
children moved and rolled about. They were collected together in
small groups, interestedly chattering or gambolling about in lethargic play. They had great variety of colour, from a pale stain of brown
to an almost rusty-black. All of them were entirely unclothed, which
interested me very much, for it was my first impact with unconscious
nakedness. They were all ages—from little round squabs to children
of twelve or more. I liked the little girls but thought the small boys
rather ugly.

I was especially taken with a child I noticed standing perfectly still
on a small promontory which ran out into the river. I had pulled
towards the bank so that I might pass her closely, for there was
something about her very immobility which drew me strangely.
She was probably nine or ten years old. The lack of movement
emphasized the upright straightness of her pose; her arms were
hanging straight down, with her extended fingers lying closely against
the outer sides of her thighs; her knees were close together, accentu-
ating the sweet outline of the young body; the beautiful inner lines
of the light brown body itself were unbroken and unmarred by any
hair. She was completely naked. As I closed nearer to her, I saw that
her eyes were following mine in the boat, but seemed to be cast a
fraction above my own gaze. Her only movement was this following
swing of the eyes, locked just above my own. Her small head never
moved, and as soon as I had swung away and passed her, our inter-
locking stare was broken.

My boatmen set up a lewd cackle and illustrated their conclusions
with pantomimic gestures. I quelled them with my fiercest insults. I
had found the little figure extraordinarily lovely, standing so
straightly upright in the simplicity of her nakedness that I had, I
knew, unconsciously smiled towards her, but from the dark eyes
there came no answering gleam—only the slow swivel as they
followed the sound of the boat. It was not until I was past her and
turning my head to look back that I realized with a stabbing jolt
that the statued, slender little creature was blind.

The heat around my boat was increasing now, and the glare from
the water was sending little darts of pain in through my eyes and out
through the nape of my neck. I was beginning to wonder when we
should come up with the ship; we had been on the river for an hour
and I was longing very much for the respite of shade of any sort. The
increase in the temperature coming up from the molten-looking
water was liquefying my interest in everything except for a consuming
desire for the relief of cover from this terrible burning. Villages,
peculiar river craft, and the naked children all slid past me without
any more arousing my interest or notice. I was a bit bothered too, by
the curious way that every now and then a curtain of blood-red mist
came down between me and the brightness of the river and its green-
backed banks, so that I was seeing them as a monochrome of fiery
red; but I put it down to the flaring light, and as it only lasted for
seconds at a time, I took no notice of it.

The return trip to my own ship was I thought hotter than ever and
I had a boiled feeling inside me, although my skin was perfectly dry;
but I was not bothered with the red mistiness any more and arrived
on board in quite good order. After the sun had gone down, I went
ashore, thinking perhaps to find it cooler than the ship and shake off
a lassitude which I could not ignore but did not want to admit to; but
my eagerness had gone so that I wandered around Calcutta rather
disconsolately until my nose began to bleed again. I was near the
Maidan and, looking for a dark patch, I found a seat so that I could
deal with this gushing nuisance out of sight.

It was only a short bout, which surprised and pleased me; I felt
relieved and less oppressed after it stopped, which was unusual, but I
still could not regain my enthusiasm and decided to go back to the
ship, turn in, and try to sleep. On board again, I had the feeling that
my nose was trying to bleed and couldn't. I wished very much that
it would, and even gave it a few tentative taps to see if I could start
it off, but beyond a horrible seepage which trickled down the back

of my throat, it would not flow. Lying on my bunk, I discovered I was panting a little, which made me think rather wretchedly how much I should like to be at home and I wondered if it was a lovely cool evening there. Supine under the roasting iron bulkhead, I found I was panting much harder and began to think with some dread of the twelve-hour spell in the sun and in the holds that lay in store for me tomorrow. I hardly dared to think that this would be only one of the eighteen or twenty days which had to be got through before we completed our unloading and loading up again and could get to sea out of this terrible heat. What bothered me most was the feeling that I might not be able to stand up to it and so be proved lacking for a sailor's life. I made great determination that no matter how intolerable the working conditions became, I would never give in. And having consoled myself with this heartening thought, I must have slept, for I awakened with a renewed feeling of zest and with some shame for my doleful spirits of the evening before.

In spite of my good beginning, this day was to prove more exacting than any which had gone before. The pitiless rays of the sun smote our ship until every piece of ironwork was outlined with a nimbus of trembling gaseous heat. It was in fact necessary to wrap rags around our hands before descending the iron ladders to the holds, for where the sun had licked them they were too hot to grip. The coolie cargo workers had quickly sensed the threatening menace that lay in the day ahead and with savage looks had at first refused to continue working and had to be driven back to the holds with blackguardly threats. They were in an altogether ugly mood, which was probably why there was such an unusual number of broken cases in the hold and careless or deliberate mishandling on deck. This it was that kept me running up and down the perpendicular ladders from the naked heat of the sun on deck to the intolerable furnace of the ship's entrails. So frequent were the broken cases that until the gangs had settled down I had little respite from these up-and-down climbings.

It was around about noon when I began to realize that all was not well with me; the red mists were again assailing me, but what was much worse I was getting attacks of losing my sense of balance, so that it required a conscious effort to prevent myself from reeling. When I was relieved for lunch, I did not go near the saloon, as I knew I could not possibly eat anything; instead, I made my way to where the bucket of tepid—nearly hot—drinking water was kept, to try to ease the unnatural thirst that was raging in me, but the water only increased the thirst. I noticed my skin was dry with a crackling dryness. I wished very much that the day's work was over so that I could lie down somewhere—anywhere, and wondered, in a troubled way, if I could get through the afternoon without falling, and dreaded the possibility that I might not.

It was mid-afternoon when I was hit by a severe attack of staggering instability. I was in the lowermost deck of all and had just finished checking a damaged barrel when a feeling of dazed and blind uncertainty made me rock and reel. Cries of concern went up from the native workers and when the blindness disappeared and I was steady in my body again, they made signs to me to go up on deck and lie down, bending their heads on the flat of their hands to indicate sleep or rest; others pointing fingers at the sun overhead and then at their own heads, and nodding these violently, yelled, 'Nay, nay, nay—no good', trying to convey to me the immediate and deadly danger I was in. They were in fact far ahead of the white officers in diagnosing what was going wrong with me. I was due on deck anyhow; so while I was still free of the awful feeling, I thought I would go up. For the first time I was seriously alarmed, for my weakness became obvious to me when I had the greatest difficulty in climbing the last ten rungs of the ladder. When I did somehow scramble over the hatch-combing, I felt bemused and terribly ill. I had made up my mind to find an officer or any white man and say so. It was now that the Second Mate chose this moment to come along. Taking one look at me, he shouted: 'Christ, boy, what's wrong with you? You're half asleep. Can't you see there's another crate broken open in the lower hold? Dammit, pull yourself together and get to hell down that bloody hold. You are supposed to be looking out for me. Blast it, I thought I could really trust you.' I was too stupefied from the rocking attacks of blinding awfulness to feel resentment at this outburst, but it did jerk me back to more or less ordinary consciousness and I recall thinking that perhaps, after all, I had been just about to make a fuss and complain of illness when there was really nothing wrong with me at all; so to put things right with myself I immediately climbed back over the combing and made the giddy descent to the bottom of the hold. My reappearance was greeted with consternation and angry mutterings from the sweating coolies. Before I had finished checking the staved-in cargo I was struck again by the terrible loss of co-ordination. This time I was aware as well of searing darts of pain which burst like rockets in my head and a suffocating, choking breathlessness. My mind was at once illuminated with an urgent awareness of real and frightful danger, and in a clear moment I knew that if I did not gain the deck immediately, final and everlasting obliteration would take place in me.

Groping my way to the ladder I commenced the nightmare ascent. Once started I was in a tiny enclosed world of my own: I was deaf and nearly blind in a blood-red sea; my will had only one object—somehow to gain the deck.

Half-way up, another attack of rocking horror smote me, and for a second my will relaxed and I was tempted to let go. There was of course no desire for death in this. It was only a fractional realization of temptation. There was to me in those terrible seconds no alternative that could possibly be worse, and with searing clarity I knew that my present consciousness was far more intolerable to bear than final oblivion. Existence in that split-second of time had become too dreadful to wish for.

But I survived both the reeling, head-bursting terror and the demand being made upon me to release control of my will, and continued my slow weaving—as I swayed my weakening body with horrible uncertainty—upwards, upwards—I must fight only to get upwards from rung to rung. The last ten or fifteen rungs would I think have defeated me except that in my distress I had forgotten my protective hand rags and the pain of the impact of my bare palms on the heated iron, where the vertical rays of the sun were striking, forced my consciousness to clear with bitter resolve—so that I finished the last flight in a desperate effort of speed, in a concentration of determination to succeed in spite of the pain in my blistering hands. This localized pain had pitted itself against my general exhaustion and it was the ensuing concentration which won for me the safety of the deck.

It was the little Chief Officer who was at the top of the ladder to confront me with furious mien: 'Good God, young Owen, what the hell is happening here? The whole of your gang have stopped work and are screaming their silly heads off that you are dead or dying. Even if you were, we can't have the brown bastards stopping work like this. Anyway, what's the matter with you? You look drunk to me, by Christ. I believe you are, young man. Are you?' This was too much for me, and there must have been some urgency in my denial which reached him, for looking at me closely, he said, 'No, no, Owen, I'm sorry, it's not that. But what the hell is the matter with you? D'you feel ill?'

The relief of reaching the deck had temporarily restored my strength, but the nervous reaction was wearing off and I heard a voice—which I thought must be mine—saying 'Yes, I am afraid I do—really.' It seemed a long way off. Muttering to himself and saying that he did not know what the hell to make of me, the Chief Officer led me off to be inspected by the Captain.

In a very vague way, I managed to follow along, for waves of instability were sweeping me again. The Captain questioned me with scant sympathy and concluded there was nothing much wrong, telling me to go to the saloon, get a cup of tea and sit down for half-an-hour; after which I was to go back to work, and with this he dismissed me.

By paying the greatest attention to every move of my feet and hands, I managed to reach the saloon, but could not try to drink the tea. Something else was bothering me now, for try as I would I found I could not hold my water for more than two or three minutes at a time; but my half-hour was up and desperately praying that I should not become incontinent, I weaved my way up the companion-ladders and through the alleyways to get back to my work in the hold.

It was while I was passing the open door of the Second Officer's cabin that the cascading, exploding rockets burst inside my head and a red-hot flaming abyss opened up under me and as I plummeted down swallowed me into its fiery maw. I still fought for consciousness and before this slid from me, only to be replaced by unconscious nightmare, I remembered being lifted on to the Second Officer's settee where I had been carried and someone saying angrily: 'You damned fool, don't try to take his clothes off. Cut them off.' I could hear the tearing hisses as the knife slit open the neck and sleeves of my tunic. I struggled furiously against this wanton destruction of my suit even as I heard the frantic cries—an immense distance off—of, 'Ice. Ice. For Christ's sake, find some ice.' . . . I lost consciousness of all that was happening, and entered a disassociated world of tormented nightmare, of struggle and suffocation.

True to the tradition of the Merchant Service, so long as a man or boy could stand on his feet, he was considered a fit man.

Even in these years, a legacy from the old sailing-ship days, the days of shanghai-ing drunken sailors, the days of man-driving by bony-fisted mates, and the days when all that mattered to the officers was working their ships at the greatest possible speed and at the cheapest possible cost, crews were looked upon as a crowd of bodies, to be driven to breaking-point. Captains and officers from the beginning had never been trained to consider the welfare of their men, much less to give a thought to their happiness. This would have been looked upon as softness indeed, and bad all round for saving on the running costs and the speed in sailing their ships.

All this did have a reverse side to it, and this was always manifested brilliantly in a crisis or emergency. The very mates who had bulldozed, hated, and hammered the men, or perhaps gone as far as 'keel-hauling' them, could be humane, and would be the first, if a man went overboard in impossible weather, to volunteer to put a boat out to try to pick him up.

It must have been something derived from this heritage which brought about the situation whereby it was possible for an illiterate Indian coolie gang, dazed with betel-nut chewing, to notice, recognize, and resent the peril I was in when the sun was doing its deadly work with me, and for the white officers—even when my condition was forced upon their notice—to treat it with unconcern and, in the Captain's case, to dismiss the symptoms with complete nonchalance and with only an accusation that I was attempting to evade work. It does, I think, throw the attitude into a higher light, when—as I learned afterwards—in dismissing me the Captain had turned to the Chief Officer: 'There's nothing wrong with the bloody little fool, and if there is it will be cholera—so there's damned little to be done anyway. And, Mr. Mate, see that the boy is back down his hold in less than half-an-hour. I'll have no scrimshanking in this ship.' When, however, my brain exploded with skull-cracking pain so that I fell to the deck outside the Second Officer's cabin, the reverse side showed itself and immediate and efficient action sprang into instant life.

The Second Mate cut off all my constricting clothes, sent for some ice from a nearby German Hansa liner, and ordering two of the other officers to hold me down for, although unconscious, I was struggling wildly, tore off to find a conveyance of some sort. There were no telephones and apparently no ambulance could be got. In the end, he commandeered an already occupied gharry, with what—as he told me afterwards—was a likely-looking nag between the shafts which looked as if it still had a turn of speed left in it. Spilling the indignant occupants on to the pavement, he mounted the box beside the driver and, threatening him with painful death if he did not get his horse

going, galloped to the ship. He was a great powerful man and under-
took to get me safely to the hospital himself.

Word had gone forth as to what was happening and as the Second
Officer urging on the gharry raced along with me, sailors—Indian
and white—lined the route all armed with ice of some sort. Running
alongside the vehicle they pitched the quickly melting stuff into the
gharry. But I had not yet reached my crescendo of tormented
strength, and before we left the dock area the Second had to call in
another young ship's officer from the ice-bearers to help control
my unconscious violence. Before we reached the hospital I had
damaged them both considerably and in my possessed strength
had snapped the Second's old-fashioned thick gold watch-chain in
two places. But through all my maniacal struggling—they told me
I was 'fighting mad'—no outside hurt had come to me. It was not
until we arrived at the hospital and I was being negotiated up some
narrow iron stairs that I sustained some superficial injuries.

Once inside, the doctors and nurses took charge. It took four
doctors to control me. And I was first of all stuffed well and truly
inside with finely crushed ice, after which I was placed in a bath and
completely buried in more ice, only the small space around my lips
and nostrils being left uncovered.

My temperature was rising furiously, and they told me afterwards
that they had no hope for my life: but as my young body refused to
succumb they fought on.

My temperature which had gone on boiling up with fantastic
determination reached 108·9 before it could be checked; after considerable hesitation it at last started to fall. I was unconscious for
nearly five days.

Whilst I was in this state, although oblivious to my surroundings,
a dreadful inner awareness was still with me: it seemed to me that I
was back at home in the familiar swimming baths in Shrewsbury, but
instead of being filled with water they were tightly packed with blood-
red cotton wool; I was in the deep end lying on the bottom, I could
neither breathe nor make a sound of any sort, and I knew as well that
I was blind. Although I knew it was cotton wool which was smothering me, it was so immensely heavy and was exerting such paralysing
pressure from all sides that I felt entombed in blood and wool.
Although I felt clamped into helplessness some part of me still went
on fighting to try and reach surface to find again sight and air. Sub-
consciously, but to me in dreadful consciousness, I knew that to
survive I must fight my way first to an upright position, for the

weight was holding me down flat on my back, and then that I must claw my way upwards and out of this suffocating mass. This most probably accounts for the extraordinary and unnatural violence with which I tore and struck at all around me.

I suppose some sort of climax must have come about and as it reached me I plunged immediately out of the circle of known and familiar things—I was no longer in the swimming baths at home. Now my delirium sped me on journeyings into the abyss, and led me towards far distant celestial worlds, into fantastic chaos.

Out of this welter of the known and unknown, waves of unearthly clarity broke over me, excruciating in their spirituality, twisting and twining themselves amongst the incoherent journeys through delirium; I was aware of a terrible struggle for separation going on between what I recognized as my spiritual entity and something else which I now realized was only my body. In an ecstasy of terror, I could feel in me something insistent that this violent struggle for division should not be allowed to come about but must be denied and prevented at whatever cost: I knew with devastating knowledge that these two must never be allowed to lose union. It was to prevent this that I found myself fighting.

I was aware of prolonged separation between myself and my body. I realized now that a distinction existed between these two entities. This was clear beyond all uncertainty; I accepted this with complete absoluteness. In some remote and dreadful way, I could watch what I knew to be my real self being drawn away out from my body; it was just as if that part of me was attached to the rest of me with an elastic string. I could feel and see myself being drawn away into infinite space, with only this thin—and ever-thinning—elastic connection holding my two separated selves in frail tenuity. I seemed at times to be flying out and away from my body with astonishing speed. This seemed to project me in a long straight and lonely flight away from my body until the elastic stretched to humming frightening vibration; at this point I would become possessed with the utter need to impel out of my dormant body some exudation of vital force to sustain strength in the thin straining cord that was holding me. I fought with despairing urgency to imbue this fragile bond with a holding power that would preserve this stretching gossamer. If I could not prevent it from breaking I knew with profound certainty that the one part of me would shoot off into eternal space and never stop travelling. If once this tenuous cord snapped I would not, I knew, be able to draw this other part of me back again and life would go out of my body.

I desperately did not want this to happen and in an agony of concentration pitted my fevered determination to implant in this ever-tautening thread the strength to hold and draw the one escaping part of me back to the other. Always just as the point of breaking was reached, I struggled and fought with frenzied anxiety to reinforce the link with possessive strength.

Each time, it seemed, I just won, and in its defeat the tensioned bond relaxed, and recoiling shot my spirit back into my body again. I was dimly conscious of a clicking reunion as the two slotted together again; until with tearing pain they sprang apart once more and with refound strength the one part of me tore yet again out on its frantic journey to gain separation and escape into void. Then the frightful struggle would start all over again. . . .

In adult life, when in the presence of still living but so-called 'unconscious' persons, I am always obsessed with the conviction that their consciousness, instead of leaving them, has only been plunged into a more horrible sphere of realization, and the most kindly and expert medical refutations that this is physically impossible always fails to ease my distress about them.

16. *Hospital*

It was on the morning of the sixth day that I came suddenly and easily back to consciousness. I say 'easily' for the great long, wide ward with the double rows of countless beds strangely enough gave me no shock. Gone were my terrible pain and oppression; I felt as light as swansdown and as if I might just as easily be wafted blissfully about. For some seconds, I had a feeling of most profound and pure happiness. I realized without any apprehension that I was too weak to make any movement except with my eyes and this exalted the floating sensation of relaxed and exquisite languor. I was vaguely aware that I had come through some unknown but great combat and I was also deliciously aware that I had conclusively won—of that I had no doubt whatsoever. With this feathery feeling of exaltation there came to me the strangest feeling that I had returned from some age-long existence which could not be measured: my few years of life which up until this moment had seemed of enormous length to me—now seemed minutely unimportant and wholly dwarfed by the timelessness of my voyage away from and out of myself.

So real was this sensation that I could feel no surprise; I did not wonder at all why I was in an unknown hospital ward instead of on board my ship. In some curious way my immediate and present existence coming back to me like this after my profound experience did not seem to matter.

Presently I felt gentle fingers laid on my wrist and looking up I saw that a nurse was looking intently at me.

I was quiescent for many days; my weakness was so pronounced that I was unable to move any part of me except my eyes. Nevertheless, recovery commenced from the moment I became conscious. My resilience astonished the hospital staff. I became an 'interesting medical case-history'. Doctors from outside the hospital were allowed to study the phenomenal survival. I was much helped by my extreme youth, and although strength was slow in returning, progress never faltered, so that each day I gained momentum. The speeding-up process was, I think, helped along a lot by my absolute determination to rejoin my ship before she sailed. I felt so much that if only I could do this, and take up my duties again, it would go far to wipe out what I looked upon as a stigma upon me through my failure to stand up to sea conditions. I was quite determined the ship should not sail without me, and when it became almost a certainty that this would happen I laid plans to escape if I was not discharged. In the end, it was a little of both which got me back on board an hour before my ship cast off.

My stay in the hospital ran the usual course of such things. I hated being washed and attended to, but to make up for this I liked the waking up in the morning with the early sun streaming through the verandahs and lying in golden squares on the floor; and the pleasant swishing noise as the sweepers plied their ten-foot reed besoms so skilfully in and out amongst the beds, and the cheerful clatter of cups heralding tea, and the knowledge that breakfast was not far behind. Each morning I envied the other men being lathered and shaved so luxuriantly by the visiting native barbers, and would stroke my smooth cheeks regretfully—but not very hopefully.

Although I was unable to walk, in about ten days I was allowed to career about in a self-propelling wheel-chair, and much enjoyed the manipulative navigation involved.

Another thing which was full of brightness and did much to mitigate the slight misery and real loneliness was the ministering friendship—I use the words with care—of one of the nurses. She was very young and I liked her dark eyes that glowed so well with warmth. She had, in fact, been called to deal with the emergency of my arrival and been detailed to my case during my unconsciousness and remained with me until I came to, when she was switched away; but she continued to visit and cheer me whenever possible and generally showed me great affection. There was some comment among the more senior staff, but she had a quality of imperviousness and was quite indifferent. She needed to be, because—as she told me herself—she was Eurasian and therefore outcast.

The relationship was quite delightful and completely devoid of coquetry, or the usual boring flippancy. She would steal into the ward during her off-duty time and if she found I was not sleeping would sit talking to me quietly and pleasantly, bringing me cool drinks and oranges and other forbidden luxuries. There was no hint of flirtatiousness in our relationship. It was, perhaps that most delightful of all relationships—the mutual liking for one another of two very young people, both of whom were feeling thrown out into the world; she because of her mixed blood, I because I was friendless in a strange hospital separated by thousands of miles of sea from everything that was familiar to me.

The doctors, while agreeing that I had made a splendid and surprising recovery, were unanimous in their declaration that never again must I come East or visit tropical climates. They were categorical about this, and told me that to do so was not only a positive risk to my life but a suicidal invitation to death; except in temperate waters, it was impossible for me to go to sea again; they strongly advised me not to do even this but find a comfortable job ashore.

On the face of it, my sea career did seem to me quickly and ingloriously finished off. At the bottom of my heart I knew perfectly well that this was not so, and that sooner or later I should be back at sea, though not of course with the Line of ships I was now in, for the hospital authorities had informed the Captain and the Company's agents to the same effect. Further employment by them I knew to be out of the question. It was the interim period, between leaving this ship when we got back to England and scheming up something else for myself, that worried me. I detested the sense of failure which I could not help feeling would tinge with defeat my deflated homecoming.

I had two or three days to think over this before I got myself out of hospital; but it was rather despondent thinking. I was being pulled in two directions and it looked to me as if, after all, I was going to be left somewhere in the middle as an office boy or the equivalent. The study of art would, I knew, still be denied me and it seemed also that the sea was now closed. The devastating crack I was just recovering from was too recent, and the memory of my boiling blood too painful, for me to feel much like courting any repetition of that just yet, anyhow. My physical weakness and weariness from thinking over this new complication must have left me a little disarmed, for I remember an unusual lowness of spirits damping down my ordinarily confident outlook, so that bitter and envious thoughts gripped hold of me. I felt a wave of loneliness wash over me—and I was a little afraid. I found myself longing with unnatural intensity that I could be a boy again and have a few more years of instruction and guidance, so that I could feel my way with more certainty. I experienced the depressing feeling that I was being committed to courses of action long before I was ready, so that I felt a blindness of direction. It was natural, perhaps, thinking as I was, that my mind should stray to Wilfred and wonder how he was getting on in his Oxfordshire vicarage.

Out of my own depression, my first real understanding of Wilfred came to me. Gone for ever was my childish blatancy and intolerance of his application to books and learning. I found myself admiring his secular attitude and the sacrifices he was making and, above all, his determination to pursue his course by laying his own foundations even at the cost of alienating my father's esteem. It was, perhaps, a sign of growing maturity in myself that I apprehended in Wilfred the sensitivity which made this last another and distressing obstacle in his path, and it came to me with a—still very undeveloped—prescience that, at whatever cost to tranquillity of mind, he was and would be impelled to surmount this and all the other setbacks that came his way. It was borne in on me that he, like myself, was still groping not so much for his positive direction as for the means by which he might get there. I felt a new kinship with him over this, but it was tinged with admiring envy, for I realized that he had already laid his foundation, was certain of his goal—writing—and that his need now was only to build on to his foundations and the rest would come to him. I felt very sure for him about this as I lay thinking. For myself I could only feel underneath me and my half-visualized aspirations a shifting looseness that refused me support. I wondered rather vaguely and not at all happily how I could build some foundation for myself. As I lay in the crowded hospital ward it all seemed very difficult—I wished I had somebody to talk to.

I had for some days now been allowed to walk about the ward. As soon as this had happened I pestered the doctors about rejoining my ship, for I had heard that she was due to sail any time now, but they were unhelpful and completely non-committal. To rejoin her had become something of an obsession with me, but apart from this I was sick and tired of the hospital and only longed to be out of it. To this end I had taken the little Eurasian into my confidence; I found in her an intelligent and eager accomplice. She not only discovered some channel through which she could keep us posted upon the likely day that my ship would sail—we had decided that I must join her only just before she sailed or I might be sent back—but had made all arrangements to hide my money and few belongings in a place where I could pick them up in the most casual manner.

On this afternoon she had come to tell me my ship was sailing next day and while I surreptitiously tucked into the fruit and sweets, we discussed—with alluring conspiracy—last-minute plans. We decided the best thing for me to do would be to collect my things, wander out into the grounds in a casual way, meander about aimlessly looking at the flower-beds, but all the time increasing my distance from the hospital building, until I reached the main gates when I would just walk out. By now we had finished our tea and eaten all our sweets and fruit. So, leaning towards me, in a whisper she told me where—if I decided to go—I should be able to find my belongings, and gave me some final instructions about how to time my escape.

With quick darting movements she sped out of the ward and was gone. I never saw her again.

My little Eurasian's advice and timing must have been very good and the next day everything went to plan; I was able to take myself out of the hospital with the greatest of ease.

Once I was out of sight of the hospital buildings I had walked through the adjoining gardens gaily enough and with a fine free feeling, but when I had left the precincts of these and found myself in the city streets I soon became disconcerted to find how shaky I was on my legs and to discover that walking along the fiery pavements was altogether different from wandering about in the comparative coolness of the hospital wards. The pitiless sun, I could not help thinking, was singling me out again. I could feel it scorching through my thin cotton suit and burning my skin; the pavements were biting savagely at my feet as well. For a few moments, nausea and giddiness attacked me; I felt alone and friendless, and so I was. I had no notion of my whereabouts, or in which direction the docks and ship lay.

For a few awful moments my purpose wavered and weakened and I wished to myself that I had not been in such haste to take myself out of hospital and wondered for a little if I ought to go back. It seemed there was no shade anywhere. I did not seem able to avoid the fierce yellow blaze of heat; the dust and glare hurt my eyes and a parching dryness rasped my throat and tongue. But I rallied my wilting determination and doing so felt better.

I kept on walking until I reached the other side of the city, and decided that from here on I would have enough money to pay the gharry fare for the remaining distance to the ship. I made up my mind that anyhow I must chance this: do something quickly and stop walking about in the sun; for the doctor's unambiguous warnings about what would happen if I exposed myself too much to intense heat were ringing with realistic and actual threat in my ears.

It was nice sitting back in the gharry, and I did not mind the terrific smell that came out of it—a heady mixture of sun-cracked leather, flea-ridden fillings, and stale horse manure, with a strong dash of dried-out urine. I remember thinking to myself what a pleasantly living, animal smell it was and enjoying the richness of it very much, after the deadening carbolic sterility of the hospital; but I wished that I had drunk some more water before I had come away. As I drove along through the streets, I thought once again how gimcrack the place appeared, and was puzzled, for the general impression of flimsiness was difficult to define and unsatisfactory to account for. I took good looks around for I thought it most likely that I should never see Calcutta again. I wished I could have another long evening ashore and penetrate just once more far into the native quarter, for I knew that if I could do so, I would search and seek, and seek with care, until I found again the tall bearded Indian and my diminutive guide, the sweet little midget woman who had threaded her way with so much dignity to steer me out of the dark, mysterious labyrinths and so cleverly set me on my way. I found myself with a great longing to see her once more before I left India. But we were sailing in a few hours' time, so I knew this was impossible.

My arrival on board occasioned considerable surprise, as the Captain had been informed that I would not be fit enough to rejoin before the sailing date. However, these sort of things that happened to apprentices were never really anybody's business, so nobody got excited—much less took any action. The whole ship was in the throes of port clearance and preparation for sea. My unexpected reappearance was a *fait accompli*, and as such was accepted; explanations—if anyone showed sufficient curiosity to demand them—could be dealt with when the ship was at sea. I was actually rushed before the Captain, but he only stared at me in a befuddled sort of way, rather as if some long-forgotten small ghost had suddenly been re-presented to him. Still glaring bemusedly towards me, with liverish bad temper he ordered the Chief Officer to get me to hell out of his cabin and to set me to work at once. Giving me a pleasant and knowing wink, the little Chief hurriedly bundled himself and me out of the Captain's cabin. Outside he ordered me to the poop to assist the Second Officer in the business of casting-off ship. I skipped aft gladly enough, for I was delighted to have got myself back on board —glad in the general sense to be free of the clutching discipline of the hospital and relieved in the immediate sense that the open sea with its respite from the burning ache of the merciless sunlight was coming near and, best of all, that soon we should be steaming away from these intolerable docks with their burden of heat and smell. The thought of a cool wind in my face was hard to wait for.

On the poop the Second Mate with worried but well-meant hectoring cursed me for my eagerness to rejoin the ship, telling me I ought to have stopped in hospital where I was well off. I found out later he was worried in case of any compensation claims being made, as it had been he who had been responsible for detailing me to the arduous cargo working. However, he absolved me with lurid certainty from immediate duties, demanding only that I should remain inactive under his eye until we should be free of the infernal heat of the river.

I was glad of respite, for I was very tired from my weak-legged journey to the ship. Although my body was languid, my mind seemed unduly alive and receptive. The smells of the ship herself, heavy with the oily pungency of sun-heated painted iron, and the musty taint of the heaving bodies of the sweating Lascars permeated the air with acrid bitter odour. The biting smells all round me reminded me vividly of the evening only a few weeks ago—which now seemed to me a lifetime away—when we had steamed up to Calcutta and I had had my first sight of the waterfront. I found myself, as we moved slowly down to the sea, looking again towards the rows and rows of small craft which lay floating with murmurous rubbings on the sludgy waters that gurgled past the river bank; I remembered my first evening in the river and the magic of the myriad tiny breaking lights sparkling like shivering diamonds on hot black velvet, the tiny braziers that glowed and quivered like living liquid gold; I knew

with absolute certainty that although I was again looking towards
the same scene that had enchanted me so much that first evening
after we had sailed up-river and let go our mooring chains, I was
looking at it differently.

This late afternoon was of an incredible Indian loveliness; the
atmosphere seemed to be made up of a glow of slanting light suffused
with the colour of pale Venetian Red. The night, when it fell, was
gorgeous with intermittent soundless lightning. As the diffused
brilliance lit up the sky it showed for fractional seconds the huddled
villages lining the river banks. Enchanted by the beauty of it all I
could not bring myself to leave the deck to face the stuffy airlessness
between decks and worse still have to deal with Atkins as he spewed
out his questions about all that had taken place in the hospital. Some
rumours of the friendship which the Eurasian girl had so unselfishly
given to me had inevitably found their way to the ship, but beyond
some light-hearted and entirely pleasant banter from the two officers
who had visited me nothing untoward had come from it. With
Atkins I knew it would be very different. If he spoke of it at all I
would have to hit him and hope to hurt him. In my weakened state
I was not very hopeful about this last; but—like a good little general
—I hoped I would be able to delay combat until I had my forces
marshalled. At the best if I tried to sleep in the cabin, I should in any
case have to endure the sound of his heavy open-mouthed breathing
and the odour of his sweat-soaked body.

So, against ship's regulations, I found myself a corner on deck, and
curling up with a blanket watched the play of lightning until sleep
overcame me.

It was another late afternoon when, after throbbing steadily down
the Hooghli on our tortuous course to the sea, we came to the mouths
of the Ganges and prepared to drop our pilots and nose our bows into
the merging waters of the Bay of Bengal. Once again the atmosphere
seemed charged with a molecular quality that flamed with a strange
red glow of illumination. Coming down the river we had twice run
into violent storm squalls, the hard driving wind from them sweeping
through the ship, clearing her and ourselves of the dust and musty
odours we had collected in Calcutta. The relief of the wind was
exquisite and the glory of the continuous lightning as it spent itself
in brilliant discharges all about us seemed boundless. I was stationed
amidships—supposedly to assist in the disembarkation of the pilots;
as I stood there looking round me, I remember a surge of unaccount-

able elation and happiness welled up inside me. The land was still around us, and as I gazed, I saw banked before me the rich green darkness of the trees silhouetted against the falling sun, swathed in an aura of fiery copper; mingled with this luminosity the grey-blue smoke of the cooking fires drifted in wind-strewn wraiths, wreathed into blue and gold loveliness as it faded away to nothingness. The solid edges of the trees as they lay against the sky were a glittering line of emerald sparks, where the level rays of the sun struck green fire from the rain-wetted topmost fronds. As I looked and drank it all in, I heard our bridge telegraphs ringing down to the engine room for full speed ahead; the emerald jewels snapped out, the banked trees melted into the indigo sky. Now, it was only over the open sea that there was a faint phosphorescent glow; this too, died, and then the sun, without warning, plummeted through the horizon and purple blackness fell like a cloak over the widening delta of the Ganges. . . .

When I had rejoined the ship, there was considerable comment upon my changed appearance and loss of weight. Until my attention was drawn to it like this I had not noticed it, but now examining myself I saw how spindly I had become. My boyish roundness had certainly disappeared, as it turned out for ever; my round chubby face was quite gone; in its place I saw had come a gaunt thinness, with much bone showing. On the whole, I was really pleased about this for peering in the glass I thought I looked more hard-bitten, which I so much desired to do, and very pleasantly older-looking; with some pride and satisfaction I concluded I looked quite old, at least eighteen, and if I frowned I might even pass for nineteen or twenty. The extreme pallor of my face I thought did not quite fit in with the hard-bitten aspect, but I hoped a little sunburn would put that right pretty soon.

For the first few days out at sea there was quite a lot of fuss and to-do about keeping me out of the sun and heat. I had not expected this, but apparently the doctors from the hospital had been severely critical to the Captain about the whole episode; and, although it did not occur to me at the time, there was great anxiety amongst the ship's officers lest, upon my return home, my father might bring a claim for compensation and generally make things awkward all round for everyone concerned. Still, even this consideration did not last very long, and when it seemed obvious that I was not going to succumb any further, I was soon put back into the ordinary routine of the ship. By the time we were in the Red Sea, I was chipping and scraping the ship's masts from a bosun's chair in the blazing sun again: but we had a head-wind so that the heat was not intolerable and I came to no harm.

My great anxiety on the voyage home was as to whether, by cracking up like this and being medically forbidden to undertake further voyages, I should be involving my father in some financial difficulties, for I well remembered the frighteningly legal-looking document which I had had to sign when completing the indentures which bound me to the shipping company for four years, and the dire-sounding penalties which would fall on my father if I broke the agreement. I seemed to recall that when the deed was being muttered over to me before I signed it terrifying forfeitures, vast sums of money like fifty and one hundred pounds, were mentioned as possible penalties. This bothered me a lot, and I cursed the interfering parson who had visited me in hospital and who had taken upon himself to write to my father informing him of my illness in an unnecessary and wholly alarming manner. It if had not been for this give-away, I fondly imagined I might have gone on saying nothing, for I had been careful not to disclose anything of my sudden illness when writing home from the hospital and had only written on ship's note-paper, giving the impression that I was doing ordinary work aboard in the normal way. The interfering clergyman had complicated things frightfully for them at home and caused my family no end of mystified and alarmed anxiety which I had myself been at such pains to avoid. However, I had discovered the parson's action, and had at once written off reassuringly—this time giving full details and explanations.

On the whole, I thought to myself, I had made a pretty good mess of everything and altogether did not think much of myself for it; I wondered unhappily if I was about to bring financial ruin upon the whole family, or at best, perhaps, through this unsettlement of mine, jeopardize Wilfred's chances of continuing his own studies and independent career. But it did not amount to depression. I was young and eager and in my own way able to put aside gloomy thinking and turn instead to a forward-looking optimism. I was up against a setback but I had a youthful confidence that I could make things work out somehow; anyway so long as this setback did not entail some awful unfindable sum of money. I had my own debt of seventeen pounds ten shillings, the loan from my uncle, to think about; but this was my own concern. I was already beginning to realize that responsibilities confined to my own actions were easier to contemplate than any which involved other people.

Soon after leaving Calcutta I learned from the Chief Officer that we were bound for home—a rather usual run: perhaps Bombay, Colombo, Aden, Suez, Malta, the Italian ports, Antwerp, and Rotterdam, and then London. For the most part, the voyage was uneventful.

Atkins and I were still disagreeable to each other. My rejoining of the ship had increased the hostility between us. We had not been many days out from Calcutta before the tension between us came to breaking point as I had known so well it would on that first night of rejoining, just as, in the same way, I had known that if he insisted on mouthing his foul innuendoes I should hit him. I did—thinking to settle the unpleasantness there and then, expecting him to retaliate and let the silly business take its natural course. Atkins refused to strike back and instead with low cunning inveigled me into a position from which I found it impossible to extricate myself by challenging me to an arranged fight, which was something I did not want at all. A rough and tumble there and then was one thing, but a serious fight was quite another; my generalship had collapsed disastrously. I detested the idea in itself, and as well I was far from free from serious alarm, for I knew I was in no state to fight. However, it seemed unavoidable. On the voyage out Atkins in spite of my obvious hostility towards him had skilfully avoided getting involved with me in anything more than exchanges of insults; but now, my state of weakened muscles was too much of a temptation to his mean disposition and he saw in it a grand opportunity to establish once and for all physical superiority over me. The fight was to take place in secret on the fo'c'sle-head after dark; it was to be bare-knuckled, no seconds, and all in. All day, the thought of this beastly business nauseated me. I had never, as yet, engaged in a prearranged post-dated fight. So great was my dislike of Atkins that I would have welcomed a spontaneous flare-up and a sudden exchange of blows, but the idea of a calculated trial of strength with him made me feel sick. I disliked Atkins so intensely that the very idea of the actual physical contact and the close grappling which such a contest meant, filled me with loathing; the thought of his horrid sweaty skin coming even against my knuckles disgusted me. I did not think the outlook too bright for me, for I had a strong suspicion that I would not last any time in my condition, and also Atkins had some reputation as a clever boxer. I had never boxed and could only be dangerous in hot blood.

In the end, it was his overweening vanity which was my salvation and his undoing. He just could not bear the thought that the easy victory he was so certain about should go unwitnessed. Unknown to me, he had invited two of the quartermasters from the white crew to take up hidden vantage points and watch the slaughter.

No sooner had we squared up to one another than furious anger over the whole beastly business flooded me, so that I went into the attack with flailing speed. For a short time I did have him on the run, and for a few splendid seconds in the light of the moon, I saw doubt and apprehension come into his ferret-eyes and blood run out of his nose. But I had no reserve of strength to keep it up; I was exhausted, and a few good blows from him around my heart had me reeling. I saw the lust of triumph, as he came in for a kill, but before he could really get in, roars of rage came from behind the capstan and the two hidden onlookers sprang around and Atkins found himself securely held between the two seamen. With no ceremony they shook Atkins until he rattled, and with rich eloquence denounced him for a coward for fighting with me when I was only just out of hospital and still weak. Pinioning his arms behind him, they begged me to take free blows at the unprotected wretch. When I refused, they chorused, 'Right, little toff—if you won't, we bloody well will.' They let him go and then without any brutality set about giving him an open-handed slamming and buffeting. I left them to it and went below.

It was a frightened and trembling boy who joined me there ten minutes later. We should I suppose have become friends after this, but we never did. It completely cured him as far as I was concerned of his unpleasant aggressiveness; we were able to live together for the rest of the voyage with mutual hostility but no violence. I found myself in a position of such moral ascendancy that I was able to control the goings-on in the cabin we shared. This meant I was able to do my water-colour sketching without interference from him although I still had to put up with his contemptuous sneering; but this did not bother me very much. In any case we were in separate watches now so that quite often I was alone in the cabin.

I was very elated about this. I had so many would-be pictures and sketches running about in my mind that I was restless to get them drawn and safely recorded on paper. I did not know then that I would possess a mind which could, and did, hold the minutest details of these early imaginings for paintings, so much so that even the ones I never drew I could recall at will forty years later.

The first one I did was my little Indian shop. It went with great surety and turned out one of my very best. The next thing I tried to do was an attempt to seal in paint the exhilarating moment I had experienced when steaming out of the Hooghli into the sunset over the Indian Ocean. I tried with all my limited skill to capture the lovely greens and fiery ochres and the cooler, translucent overhanging purples that had wrapped so much joy around me as I stood on the deck in the Indian stillness and watched the flowerless land melt away into the indigo curtain of the night. I was disconcerted with the result, and I felt it had the unhappy and unbelievable air of a bad picture postcard, so that I tore it up—not only in shame, but also because I felt it was damaging to what I really had felt yet could not portray. Being out of the mood for painting, I wrote to my mother instead and found myself colouring the memory of the evening with words. I remember feeling well satisfied after I had done this. Curiously, I no longer had any desire to paint it. This troubled me a bit at the time. It was perhaps the first onslaught of querulous doubtings about the validity of my chosen medium for my own expression; I became unsettled by a nagging distrust and a feeling of disloyalty to my painting as I realized that my imagining had flowed more easily in written words than it had in the studied use of paint.

In any case my next drawing was to trap me into false security again. It was prosaic enough—a cluster of native river-craft. The perspective was excellent and the drawing good; for what it was, it was quite satisfying. I was pleased, for I could not yet distinguish between the skill of the fingers and the imaginative qualities and capacities of the mind.

While we were sailing through the Red Sea I was sent aloft most of my working time, scaling and painting the foremast and greasing down the ratlines and rigging. It was very hot again, and I had one or two moments when the doctors' warnings drifted uneasily across my mind, especially when I was exposed to the sun and could feel it savagely probing my spine. But when I had endured a few days' exposure to the Red Sea heat without feeling any real ill-effects from the sun, I felt not only pleased but inordinately proud of myself. The fact that I was doing ordinary ship's work again in some relieving way offset what I still looked upon as my defection in Calcutta.

It was while we were steaming through these blazing land-bound waters that very early one morning I was detailed to scrape and paint around the truck at the mast-head. I had thought, from my inexperienced reading of the chart whilst standing my watch on the bridge during the night, that we were likely to pass close to some of the sea's many barren islands.

As I was being hauled up to the mast-top, I thought—more in order to keep my mind off the horrid feeling of suspended insecurity than anything else—what a good view I should get when day broke; but even so, I was not prepared for the strange unfolding that was about to take place before me. As I swayed dizzily about in my bo'sun's chair at the mast-top, I looked around me and there, slowly at first, as the rim of the sun lifted behind its turreted rocks, and then swiftly as the ball of fire shot upwards, out from the breaking light of the bursting day, swam an enchanted island. Indeed, it was not swimming so much as floating, caught as it was between the smoking sea-vapour and the brilliance of the rising sun. For seconds it remained suspended, aloof and unconnected with sea or sky, ethereal and magically mysterious. I saw that all about it hung a most extraordinary air of austerity. I was astonished by a sensation of familiarity which came over me, looking towards this citadel rising out of the sea, and I had the strangest sensation that I had in some way been at some time closely connected with it; I could not dispel a pronounced conviction that none of this was new to me, it seemed in a remote way to recall a journey . . . a journey upon which a separate part of me had been floated out to travel a great distance away from my real self . . . I knew in me a persistent tugging connected I thought with my recent delirium when I had been two entities —one of me migrating out, always far out on the end of my string— but this time I was enjoying the tenuous separation, here before me in actuality. Glittering in front of me lay something which I knew all about; here it was—the reality of silver light that I thought did not exist outside my own secret journeyings, the delicate fortress set like a jewel in its sea of solid silver.

As the sun swept upwards it burned away some of the smoky films of drapery and the island slowly emerged to lie motionless on the polished sea, but still separated by a girdle of silvery mist. With the heat of the sun slowly disrobing the island, my feeling of transmigration increased, as rocky minarets and boulder formations crept into translucent detail. I saw that there was no vegetation, not even a dead shrub or a piece of driftwood; it was devoid of any vestige of life whatsoever; its utter aridity held a perfection of barrenness, the rocky natural towers guarded by the serrated pinnacles mounted like a thousand lances piercing upwards in perpendicular slenderness, coloured multitudinously in a lovely delicate monochrome of light red, too true in colour to have any suggestion of pink. Here and there in the deeper clefts the shaded monochrome was glazed with an overlay of violet, or stained with a film of pale purple-browns.

Perhaps my own suspensive lodgement between sea and sky lent an air of unreality to the whole thing or perhaps after all I had left the hospital too soon; whatever it was, I could not throw off the feeling that I was looking at a spired citadel—a citadel wrapped about with terrible severity and separated from my own world in bleak remoteness—an island of the dead. The silvers, pale reds, violets, and brown-purples were pearl-strung with morning sea-mist, but none of this could belie the stark austerity, the purity of its naked simplicity, nor yet the powerful aloofness that disdained the minutest softening by vegetation. I found it hard to believe that beneath its fluted loveliness there lay a mass of unyielding rock.

I was brought back to reality by the little Chief Officer roaring up at me and bellowing through cupped hands to know why the hell my paint-brush wasn't working. I was vexed with myself for being caught out day-dreaming like this, and at once set to and slapped away with my brush with great vigour to make up for lost time. I remember thinking as my gaze travelled astern to the receding island —but keeping my paint-brush working now—how much I wished Wilfred were with me, not only so that he could see it too, but because I felt if he were with me I could have put into words to him something of what I was feeling. I was aware that if we could have been together at this moment a communication would have been established which might have put an end for ever to my petulant rejection of his proclaimed asceticism and his too-frequent gibes at me for my lack of regard for everything except the commonplace. I had a queer idea that the sense of impregnability and utter stillness that had radiated from what I had just seen and felt would have bonded us with more understanding had we been with each other.

I have always linked this island in my mind with the name of Lecotral. It probably isn't. The name most likely stuck from my constant scanning of charts; it is more than possible that I may, during my many voyages, have become confused and although I am certain that somewhere in the world there is an Island of Lecotral, it may not be in the Red Sea at all. But I do not mind about this, for I like the name for it—it fits so perfectly—so that, for me, it shall always be Lecotral.

Before we finished our voyage I managed to do a number of sketches, none of them very satisfactory; however, to make up, I did a considerable amount of 'fancy painting' for the ship. I emblazoned house-flags and the ship's name on life-boats, belts, and buoys and anywhere else the touchy little Chief Officer could think of as fitting or even remotely suitable for my heraldic efforts. This endeared me to him very much and he would rub his hands with glee, as he surveyed some brilliantly coloured effort of mine, over the thought of how much he would score over zealous and jealous mates of other ships when we got to a home port. I enjoyed this work quite inordinately and revelled in the fine, rich sea smell of the lamp-room and paint lockers where I was allowed to mix my vivid hues. I took great pains and almost more pride in the design and colouring and thought it most tremendously worth while doing. Before we got home, the Chief Officer and I had formed quite a conspiratorial alliance in seeking out likely places to embellish. When we did eventually arrive in London, and my first—and as it looked—my last voyage was nearly over, there was a pleasant and unexpected surprise waiting for me.

Soon after we had tied up in Tilbury Docks, the Captain sent for me and told me the Company had suggested to him that I should be allowed to go home from London, instead of going around with the ship to Liverpool, as I was supposed to do. Advancing me a sovereign for expenses, he told me I could get away any time the next morning. My father was behind this. The Calcutta episode had given him a very bad fright, and he had got into touch with the Liverpool offices to arrange that I should be allowed to do this.

My father was waiting on the platform at Shrewsbury when my train drew in, and my heart gave a great leap when I espied his short, thick-set, smoothly clothed figure as I was carried past him. I grinned to myself as I thought how cross he would be when he found he had taken his stance at the wrong end of the platform. But still he had got the time of my arrival right, which was something. If any one of our family made a mistake about private railway times, it was certain to be him, which was curious, for in his official railway work he was extremely accurate. When we found each other, sure enough he was looking red-faced and furious, and immediately upbraided me for travelling in such a silly part of the train. I did not realize at the time, of course, that this was all in order to cover up his embarrassed shyness about meeting me; but as he gave me a quick look his eyes crinkled up into his warm smile, to revert immediately to petty annoyance as he fussed and fretted over my sea-chest and ticket— which I had forgotten all about. Having denounced and panicked several porters and inspectors in a grossly unjust manner, he cooled down, and making the excuse that he must sign some letters before we could go home, led me off at a great pace towards the station offices. Actually what he was dying to do was to show me off as his son home from a voyage—and that before I had a chance to get home and out of uniform. A suspicion of this came to me when he chose to walk through the main office where his staff were, instead of going into his own office through his own private door. This little ceremony over (in later years this trait of his was able to irritate and embarrass me seriously, and in the war years Wilfred as well), he hastily made some pretence at signing a few papers, and, slamming home his desk drawers, said: 'Come along now, or your mother and the others will never forgive me for being so long.'

We set out at his usual quick short-stepped speed for home. On the way, a difficult silence fell between us. I was longing to tell him that I was sorry I had made such a mess of things.

He himself was longing to hear from me every detail of my experiences, but neither of us could start and the most we could do was to break the embarrassing silence with stupid trivialities far removed from our thoughts. Matters were not really helped when my father, probably trying to get a lead, asked me about my Hindustani. I was a bit uncomfortable about this, for I had not tried very hard to learn any and felt very guilty, so I mumbled that I had not managed very much. He looked disappointed and cross about this; whereupon, to save the situation a little, I said I had picked up a few words. At this, my father immediately ordered me to recite them. I said my odd phrases and was miserably drying up when inspiration flashed into me and I remembered my fine flow of riverside and fo'c'sle Hindustani. Thinking my fluency would impress him, I let it pour out in splendid spate. The result was not at all what I expected, for it pulled him up dead, flushed with genuine shock and real anger. Almost inarticulate with mortification and rage, he waved his arms about in an effort to stop me, but I was going too gloriously to be stemmed and it was not until the very last of my lineal descriptive obscenities and curses had chattered themselves out that I stopped.

I knew at once that my father was extraordinarily angry. 'Very well, my boy, I shall talk to you about this later on. I can only hope you have no idea what you are saying. In the meantime, not one word of Hindustani in front of your mother and sister—or even in the house. I will have neither them nor it defiled by such foulness.' I was tired of this 'mother and sister' business and resentful of my father's unrelenting parental attitude. I wished he would grin a bit instead of looking so shocked and worriedly savage. If only at that moment my father had rolled about helpless with laughter over his small son spouting atrocities, an understanding and mutual confidence would have been born between us and given us both many more years of companionship than we did have.

But, true to his own form, after a hundred yards or so of stern and silent parental disapproval, he changed the subject—he never once referred to it again—and became the genial father pleased to have his young boy home again.

But I knew he did not really understand and a doubt crept into me if he really did know what went on in ships and seaports. I made one further stumbling effort to explain that this was no more than a seaman's technique. Had he heard me out, I would have told him—with excusable exaggeration—that, without it, I should never have got across the river to my ship that night on the Hooghli but, instead, would have been a nice pink little naked corpse on the muddy bed of it; but he would have none of this and silenced me with peremptory elderly severity. I decided I would have to be careful about what I said to him in future; and, for the second time, I glimpsed with realism and sympathy some of Wilfred's difficulties and misunderstandings with my father. I was disappointed for myself that he did not seem to think of me as somebody more grown up, now that I had actually done a voyage.

However, diversion—as it always was in our family—was at hand. As we neared the usual turning we always took to reach our house when walking from the station, my father laid a restraining hand on my arm and said: 'A surprise for you, Harold' (I was glad he had dropped the harsh 'my boy' and was using my name in his friendly, kindly way again)—'we have moved to a bigger and better house since you went away.' My first thought was a hope that my watercolours and drawings were not dispersed or damaged in the moving. But I was instantly reassured in my mind that my mother would have taken great care to see they were all right for me; after that thought, I was pleased and excited.

It was curious coming back so unexpectedly to a fresh house, but so strong was the feeling of family that in a few minutes I did not feel

I was in a strange house at all. The excited warmth of affectionate welcome that was effervescing from them all agitated me into an emotional state of well-being and brought out in me a love and pride in my family to a depth which amazed me. I felt how very good it was to belong to them all and curiously inflated with a lifted-up sensation over their demonstrations of happiness that I should be safely home with them again. My mother had prepared great masses of food, every bit of which in some form or another was one of my favourite dishes. I saw a shadow of consternation blur her eyes as she took in the significance of the gaunt thinness of my face and, sliding her hands in loving concern over my body, felt my protruding bones. I detected, too, an air of quiet triumph that she had got me home again, as she fondly thought, for good. My father, I think, detected it as well—as he was meant to—and 'pooh-poohed' rather irritatedly over her avowed plans for 'feeding me up' and restoring what in her eyes was the only thing that mattered, the physical damage.

Careers and ambitions and future plans were not worth a thought to her until this was put right, but my father with tremendous joviality overthrew his irritability and refused to rise; he wanted to make up to me in some way, without really letting me see it, for his over-anxious, sharp harshness over my too-fluent Indian curses. He wanted my first day at home to be a happy one for all of us and straight away set himself and us to a job which he had actually saved up for this occasion. This trivial diversion—how desperately hard-up for pleasure he was—he had reserved so that he could have the double excitement of my return and the special job, which was the burning out of a barrel, on the same day.

He was a great hand at turning such trivialities into major operations, and would have the whole house stirred up to assist, but he would take no advice and brook little assistance. If his carefully laid plans went awry, he did like to have us about to shout excited orders to and he liked to be able to parcel out the blame afterwards. The barrel-burning to-do came about through our need for a new wash-tub. In order to economize, my mother, instead of sending our soiled linen to a laundry, engaged a woman to come to the house once a week and wash all our clothes in a vast tub and do the mangling; the drying, airing, and ironing would be dealt with later by herself and Mary. Somebody had told my father that the best and cheapest way to make a wash-tub was to buy an empty oak tar-barrel and burn it out with fire. This would leave it both clean and with a finely charred inner surface impervious to water.

Accordingly, on this pleasant afternoon of my return, my father with considerable discipline mustered us all on the extremely small, flagged back-yard of our new house to watch and admire the operation.

As I was helping him to roll the wretched thing from lower down the garden, I could see by his hesitancy that he was dubious about the safety of the business and really rather frightened he might set fire to the house. After some moments of deep pondering, we decided to put it in position on the stone yard and then see how it looked. It did not look at all safe, and I think my father had decided not to risk it for I saw him looking anxiously at the woodwork around the house. We were all peering into the black and sticky depths of the barrel when Wilfred, straightening himself up and looking solemnly and steadily at my father, said: 'You know, Father, if you try to fire that thing you will burn the house down.' And he proceeded to give us all a little lecture upon the extremely volatile combustibility of burning tar. This was all that was needed to cause my father not only to throw away caution but to become instantaneously highly combustible himself; and with irate looks and many snorting trumpetings thrown towards Wilfred, he immediately proceeded to hop around collecting newspapers and other dry rubbish exclaiming as he did so, 'Can't find a spark of pluck in this family, everybody frightened of anything I try to do. Nonsense, absolute nonsense, no danger whatsoever, nothing to be afraid of. No use being funky about these little things.' Turning directly to Wilfred he said, 'I am quite capable of doing this job without any scientific disquisitions from you. I don't care tuppence what it says in your confounded chemistry books, if only you would all of you stop talking so much we might get started. . . .' With this, he set about soaking newspapers in paraffin. My mother's frantic pleas to be careful and that he would only set himself and us on fire, and the house as well, only made him more determined than ever. He would at that moment have preferred to set the house on fire rather than be thwarted and, pouring in a great can of paraffin—'for luck, and just to show us'—lit his paper torch and tossed it in.

At first, nothing much happened; then smoke came up, thickening all the time until great clouds and twisting spouts of oily blackness poured up. This seemed harmless enough, and my father was looking jubilant again, until, with a crackle, the mass burst into orange flame. The eddying wind whipped this about in all directions but mostly towards the house. My father, frightfully red in the face, was prancing about like an intoxicated bantam cock, throwing water about in all directions and shouting to us in no uncertain way to do the same. Actually, he was enjoying himself immensely, and now that there was no room for argument so were all the rest of us. All at once the whole thing seemed extremely comical, so that we could hardly run for laughing. Wilfred was enjoying it all, too, and shrieking instructions with the best of us as we rushed in and out to the tap for water with tremendous agility and infectious excitement. When the trellis work caught alight, it was he, Wilfred, who concentrated on the flames and subdued them. When the paintwork on the house door and windows began to blister and sizzle, my father, grabbing hold of me, yelled: 'The clothes props—the props! We must get the props and tip it over and roll it away from the house!'

Watching our chance with the wind, we dashed past the flames and coming back with the long poles jabbed at the top of the cask until it toppled over, to burn more fiercely than before; luckily it fell the right way and with the whole family manning the props, we lunged at it until we had it on the roll. We all cheered it madly as it trundled its flaming way through flowers and borders. For one moment, it looked as if it would come to rest against the highly inflammable bicycle shed, but with more shouts and lunges we steered it safely past, letting it come to rest in the middle of the much-prized square of newly-sown lawn, and left it there to let it lessen its fierceness, for it was still exploding with gushes of burning pitch and paraffin.

The thick black smoke and the laughing excitement had brought some neighbours running. It was Wilfred who reassured them, telling them it was just our Saturday afternoon fun, and it was he who stopped the most panicky ones from rushing to break the glass of the nearest fire-alarm. My father was still hoping to save his cask from total destruction, and when the fire started to subside in it, he hooded himself with a wet sack and, armed with a garden fork, somehow juggled it back on to its base again. But of course it was no good, it was too-well alight, and one by one the staves fell in and the hoops fell down. But what did an old barrel matter! We had had a glorious afternoon of fun and excitement, and all of us were well-pleased with one another and the parts we had played together; it was in the gayest of spirits we trooped back into the house—to make splendid inroads into my home-coming tea.

The next morning, my father proposed that we should all of us walk over to Uffington Church for the morning service. I was very pleased about this suggestion, not because I wanted to go to church but because I wanted so much to see my village again and find out if it would still be the same to me now that I had been away so far and seen so many strange places. I had an unhappy presentiment that I should find it different and that its power to satisfy me might be gone.

There was the usual to-do before we set out, with none of us agreeing with the other. What amazing capacity for fuss was generated in us if a proposal my father put forward involved the whole family; trivialities loomed up as large as mountains. My mother, who really wanted very much to come, began to wonder if she was really feeling up to the long walk. This irritated my father and made him stalk off—in something of a pet—to borrow from a neighbour a bath-chair, which was sometimes available; and, of course, there was the usual dispute as to how the lunch could be prepared, if both my mother and Mary came with us. No sooner were these irritations and difficulties straightened out, than Wilfred, coming half-way down the stairs, announced that he was much too busy to come. This set everything a-flutter once more; his last-minute decision upsetting my father all over again. Exasperation all around followed. My father expostulated and my mother pleaded that as we were all together, how nice it would be to go to church. Wilfred, with very bad grace, muttered: 'Ah, I see—to offer up thanks for the return of the sailor! Yes, yes—I'll come.'

When we did finally manage to evacuate ourselves, my father was in a rare temper and set off at a terrific pace going great guns with the bath-chair, so that my mother had real difficulty in steering anything like a course. The chair itself was rocking from side to side splendidly and bouncing magnificently on the loose stones. Gentle remonstrances from my mother only brought forth fresh bursts of speed and choleric ejaculations about 'you people'—he was fond of addressing his family like this in such moments: 'If only you people would get up earlier in the morning, all this rush could be avoided.'

Wilfred, not unwisely, being in bad odour this morning, had dropped behind and was quietly strolling along, dipping every now and again into his pocket and pulling out a book. He had set himself a task of memorization to be achieved before we reached the village. Colin and I, tiring of my father's speed, fell behind to keep him company and see if there was any fun to be got out of him this morning; but he waved at us impatiently with imperious gestures to go away.

He would have none of us or of our idle chatter and with apt quotations to emphasize the unprofitable nature of our idle high spirits, drove us away from him. My father, having cleared his mind by his violent exertion, had slowed down and was talking quietly with my mother and Mary and by now for the first time that morning enjoying himself. His frowning and fussy severity had all gone, and in its place—as if to make up for his earlier nervous commotion— had come a gently smiling tolerance and a mood of self-effacement which, as it was always able to do, endeared him to us all very much.

As we neared the primitive ferry that would take us across the river to the village, Wilfred caught up with us, his book safely hidden from my father's sight; and as we boarded the leaking, groaning punt and the ferry-owner, an ancient countryman, hauled us hand-over-hand by means of the taut wire, the steel strands humming and singing pleasingly against the iron rollers, a tranquillity descended upon us all which was good to feel.

The square-ended craft, with a plopping gurgle, slid on to the mud banks, while my father with immense care and solicitude steadied my mother against the jolt of impact.

The stepping out of the ferry safely negotiated, Wilfred joined my father in what amounted to a ritual—the aiding of my mother up the very steep rough path which led from the river bank to the village. My father taking her by one arm and Wilfred by the other, slow progress would be achieved, with many pauses for her to regain strength. Sometimes one of us younger ones would be seized with an access of helpfulness and, placing our hands upon her shoulders, would add propulsion from behind.

Although at this time my mother was so slight a figure she did find great difficulty in walking any distance and suffered seeming distress when climbing hills. However, on this morning our family serenity preserved itself. My mother was in one of her sweetest and most lovable moods, my father retained his smiling tolerance. Wilfred had lost his preoccupied resentment at having been made to come with us and had become gay and easy, arguing light-heartedly and pleasantly with my father. How ready my father would always be with conversation when Wilfred, losing his tenseness, relaxed to normal reactions. As we wandered along, I became aware that my being away from home had sharpened my perceptions very much; so much so that what I had so far accepted and taken for granted about my family as fixed and unalterable, I now began to see in a different light: for perhaps the first time I realized that change was inevitable and was able to reflect—and feel a little disconcerted about it—that I could now see them from an impersonal angle. Up until now I had, I think, only realized them as a part of the structure of myself; now I discovered that I could see them as something separate and individual. Because of this I looked more closely at them. I remember that my father and mother, as we walked slowly up the flagged path to the church porch, were in the lead, side by side—my mother's hand on my father's arm. My mother, I thought, looked specially lovely. The long full-skirted dress gave a slightly majestic air to the slow-moving walk. My father in a dark church-going suit, high stiff white collar and stiff shirt-cuffs, carrying gloves and cane, carried himself proudly enough, the deep red-brown of his face showing startlingly against the snow-white collar. Wilfred was more loosely clad, his tumbling dark hair adding to an air of careless-ness which I admired very much. He looked just what he was—a serious-minded, intent young student. Mary walking demurely along-side him—Bible and prayer-book tightly clasped—was freshly pretty, her frailty making Wilfred look taller and heavier than he really was. I was the least conventional and odd-man out, for I had not yet acquired a civilian long-trousered suit and I had been forced to don the once nearly discarded knickerbocker suit and stockings, which, with much letting out of braces and clever adjustments by my mother with needle and iron, had been deemed passable, anyhow for Uffington. I was not so sure about this and not at all pleased. Colin was attractively juvenile in grey school flannels and brightly-coloured barred silk tie that my mother had knitted for him.

Walking along with them like this the thought came to me, what a nice family it was that I belonged to; I felt very proud and happy to be with them, and simultaneously a realization came over me of what a pity it was that we should be so short of money all the time. It was this I saw that made everything so difficult; except during moments like this when our general appearance of comfortable well-being helped us all to forget and smothered a little the everlasting anxiety my father and mother had to contend with, we were in a state of perpetually living on the borderline of poverty. It was the constant necessity for make-believe, I thought—our very appearance of prosperity on this Sunday morning as we walked up the path to the little church was nothing more than designed make-believe—which made my mother lethargic to ambition for us and my father hopelessly despondent about any projects which were not immediately wage-earning. I suddenly knew that if only we had just a little more money, my father's intolerance of Wilfred's reading and of my own plans for painting and the arts would disappear. I wished very much that I knew how to make some money.

It was perhaps the mingling with a few obviously rich families outside the church which put these thoughts into my mind. If I looked a little enviously towards a boy of about my own age, whom I knew to be at Dartmouth, it was only with a sincere envy that had no bitterness in it. I thought how much I would not change my family for all the opportunities or riches in the world

During the walk home we split up, my father going off along the river bank to peer for motionless weed-camouflaged pike and basking chub; I, to make for the river in the opposite direction, for I was thinking about the other Sunday morning when I was taking my craft manned by Lascar boatmen down the Hooghli and wanted to experience the spice of comparison. Coming around a bend of the river and seeing the low mud-bank on the opposite side, I was suddenly and very vividly reminded of the blindness of the little brown girl-child I had watched standing in the yellow sear of the sunlight, so motionless in the hammering heat of the Indian midday sun. In some curious way, I was able to project her image on to this English riverside, so that I could clearly see her standing there.

My absorption with this curiously intense imaginative recollection was so deep that I had not heard Wilfred coming up behind me and it was with a start that I swung around to meet his slightly sardonic question:

'What is it the one-time mariner sees that gives him such an appearance—mark, my dear Harold, the qualifying word—of deep thought, unusual even if unreal?'

Nettled by his tone, and disappointed by the interruption, I retorted: 'Nothing you have ever seen—or would understand if you did.'

'Oh, I see; some more of your seafaring vulgarisms. What is it now?

Stung to unwariness (as Wilfred had well-intended I should be), I answered back with sincerity: 'No, I was looking at a lovely little brown girl without any clothes on.'

I had shocked him, this time out of his bantering humour, and he came back with, 'I understand one thing, the sea has started to ruin you, and it's a good job for all our sakes that you can't go back again —to be completely ruined.'

Not to be outdone, I said: 'I'd rather be ruined, as you call it, than stagnate like you!'

'What on earth do you mean—"stagnate"?'

'Only that if you don't get your nose out of your old books, and your body out of your mouldy old vicarage, and stop pretending to be a parson, you will soon start decomposing.'

With one of the sudden changes of mood which so often came over him when his own career was in his thoughts, all his mockery disappeared and in its place came an almost sad seriousness. The malicious ferocity fled from his eyes and into them came a depressed look of forlorn humility, a withdrawal into himself, with a drooping of the shoulders. This always had the instant effect of making me feel mean in myself and wishing so hard that he did not force me to say unkind things back to him. Looking at me with a softly dark gaze, he quoted: '"Out of the mouths of babes and sucklings . . ." Yes, yes, as you so unpleasantly put it, perhaps I am decomposing in my wretched village. Why, why couldn't I have gone up to Oxford? Just think what I could have done with three years there!'

I nodded sympathetically, and thought to myself what I could do with three years in a painting school.

'We both seem a bit stuck Harold, don't we? I think I shall try for a tutoring job in France. If I have got to live in poverty and extreme discomfort, at least I would prefer to do it in a civilized country rather than over here. I will not go into the Church; so a garret on the Continent seems my only hope, that is to say if even this can be managed.'

'I shall go back to sea again, when I can get a ship.'

'You don't deserve it, Harold, but in return for your useful insinuation concerning my mouldering and mock parsonizing, I must tell you that you won't go back to sea because Father has given in, and is going to get you on to the Railway as a junior clerk—that is, if you can be scraped through the infantile test papers, which I very much doubt. But shut up now, here he comes! And for goodness sake, Harold, do be more careful of the things you talk about while you are at home.'

My return home from the sea, I can realize now, caused no little consternation; my unfortunate habit of coming out with what I was thinking had certainly spread some alarm. My father had no doubt given to my mother an account of my fluent use of the foul Hindustani that had surprised and shocked him so much on our way home from the station and Wilfred's concern, like my father's, had no

doubt caused him to go to my mother and with genuine anxiety
confide to her his own fears about me. As ever, her solution of these
anxieties was to provide her pet off-set, known to the family as a
'steadying influence', and so on this same day after lunch, my mother
suggested that Wilfred and I should go for a walk together. I was not
particularly surprised, for she was very fond of suggesting any little
plan like this which might occur to her, but I was surprised at the
coupling of Wilfred in the suggestion, and even more astonished over
his ready acceptance of the idea. I was not pleased about walking at
all, for I very much wanted to collect my old drawings together and
to spend the afternoon gloating over them with the refreshed eye that
I knew my absence from them would have given me; still, I thought,
old Wilfred was going back to his vicarage that evening, so I consented without much fuss, wishing all the same that it was Colin I
was to go with and not Wilfred. With Colin I could have made some
fun or 'adventure' of some sort. With Wilfred I knew I should
contrive neither but instead have to suffer lecturing and possibly
downright fault-finding.

Our walk was not a success. I soon sensed from Wilfred's tutorial
manner that I was to be catechized and led back to the straight and
narrow path, that is, if it was found I had ever left it, which they
rather blindly comforted themselves was perhaps extremely doubtful.

With great nervous effort, he managed to ask me if I had done
anything 'bad' while I had been at sea. My cheerful retort 'not to be a
silly old ass' although not making him understand in the least,
satisfied him, and after muttering again that I must not go about
talking about 'girls with no clothes on, or repeat bad language—even
in a foreign tongue', he gave me a quick flashing smile which, I could
see, had quite a lot of envy in it. I was gratified to see this and
thought how much I could entertain him if only he would drop his
elder brother nonsense and let me do so. But my story was never
told and we were back again to our elder and younger brother
association. What might have been our moment had disappeared.
Wilfred maintained a silence for some time, after which we fell into
some desultory conjecturing about our futures; but our conversation
lacked any sparkle and had no inspiration in it.

He was very depressed about everything now, which was perhaps
dispiriting for me and would have been more so if I had not, in a
juvenile and inexperienced way, realized that he was never able to
put himself into my thoughts and ambitions; that even when con-
senting to talk to me at all he was all the time applying everything

to himself and not to me. I thought to myself what a queer, savage, gentle Old Wolf he was, but I knew that I could look for no help at all from him. But in spite of this I loved him just as much all the same. As we turned to walk home again, he cheered up a bit and becoming ordinary again put it forward that I should be good and reasonable and agree to accept the Railway job.

Wilfred, now that he was living in Dunsden, found that his work as the vicar's unofficial curate brought him wider and more varied social contacts; he was perturbed to discover as well an awareness creeping into him of the shallow meaninglessness of much that went on around him—a great deal of it hallowed by the name of religion. Young as he was he thought he realized that here was orthodox non-sense and conscious insincerity masquerading as true religion. In a letter to me a little later he wrote bitterly of this, and with youthful fire denounced the Established Church as a complete divergence from the teachings of Christ, at the same time counselling me to read the New Testament and perceive for myself—adding in brackets, 'if your limited capacity will allow you to do so'—the true poetry in the Man and his life.

On this Sunday afternoon, as we walked slowly towards home, his mood seemed black and hopeless and he was talking more to himself than to me, making despairing conjectures about the future. I was feeling rather helpless and outside his one-sided conversation and wishing so much I could think of some brilliant thing to say that would shake him out of his moody introspection; for, although I had been piqued by his earlier superiority, his present gloominess gave me the feeling of being somehow harder and more able to deal with difficulties than he was. For all his scorching tongue when he was in the mood to castigate, once he fell into low spirits, he seemed pathetically defenceless; all his acidity and scathing denunciation seemed never to have been; only the lonely vulnerability remained. At my age at that time I could not formulate into thought what I felt. I could only numbly realize his intense unhappiness and as always when this happened, feel older than he was and long only to somehow comfort and cheer him. The more I sought for something to say, the more inarticulate I became. We lapsed into an uncomfortable silence.

We went into the house for tea, a hurried and violent affair, scrambled through in something of a flurried atmosphere, for my father was expressing his disapproval of our unpunctuality—we were very late—with glowering annoyance. My mother's over-attention to Wilfred and her fussing care that he should eat a good tea before setting out on his journey added fuel to his silent irritability. Wilfred, scorning the carefully prepared meal and impatient over my mother's insistence, gulped down some scalding tea and dashed upstairs for a final look around his books, and to sort out one or two he wanted to take back with him to Oxfordshire.

My mother soon followed him up with fresh tea and a loaded plate, which caused my father to jump up and down—like a jack-in-the-box —with suppressed fury and to make infuriated prognostications as to the outcome of this 'confounded molly-coddling' and pampering of Wilfred's unpunctuality and general carelessness of time and procedure. When he could stand it no longer he leapt out of his chair and, flinging open the door, raced with splendid agility up the first flight of stairs, to stand there roaring to Wilfred and my mother to come down at once—or the boy would miss his train.

My father was perfectly right; it was always difficult to get Wilfred started off from home and there would always be the last minute rushes to the top of the house for some book or papers that he had forgotten. He was usually nervously composed himself, and this outwardly cool nonchalance only served to whip up further my father's ire. He really was getting late for his start and, as well, it was pelting with rain, so my mother hurriedly organized me to go along with him to help carry his bag and to make sure he got himself into the right part of the train.

As we made our way to the railway station, using a trotting-walk to try to make up lost time, for without extreme speed he was likely to miss his train, he kept up a quick-fire, running string of questions about the places and ports I had seen. I did my best to answer intelligently, between the splashing downfalls of rain, but it was an uneasy effort. As well as the streaming rain, I was being dragged over on one side by the weight of his bag. I was managing well enough, but as we jogged along, panting from our trotting spells, I realized that in his questions I myself did not count at all; he was not interested in my relationship to them; they were quite purely academic. He would not let slip a possible chance of gaining some factual knowledge— even during an uncomfortable and hurried rush like this. I could sense how little I came into it at all, and that he was in no way thinking about me as a brother or as a person, but only as a possible— certainly very improbable, but nevertheless not quite to be ignored as a possible—conveyor of information which he might be able to turn to his own scholastic advantage.

It made me feel very separate from him, but as it was he who was going away I was in the mood to try and please him, and answered his tricky questions seriously enough.

All went well, and I was congratulating myself upon a good acquittal, until I mispronounced Malta: I had spoken of it as though it was spelt 'Mollta', which was the way I had heard it spoken in my ship and the ports. This brought down upon my head vivid vituperation and many allusions to my 'donkey-like cerebral mechanism'—an expression which he was fond of substituting for 'brain' at this period. I was a bit bored with all this and told him—with no uncertainty—to shut up; and I suggested he might carry his own bag for a bit, which he immediately seized with genuine contrition and condemnation of himself for what he called 'his crass thoughtlessness'. We were nearing the station now, and increasing our speed we sped along without further speech.

The train was running in as we reached the station. Wilfred quickly boarded it and after a warm smile and an affectionate embracing wave of his hand he pulled up the carriage window.

Walking back from seeing him off, I cogitated a lot about my queer old brother, and pondered with unusual seriousness over his strangely changing moods, which flickered over him with such jumping uncertainty from extreme ferocity to tender humility and not quite disguised affection. As always when I had just parted from him it was the softness I recalled and never his baiting assumption of superior wisdom and knowledge. Thinking like this, I would always wish I had been nicer to him. However, the sting of his invective would remind me healthily enough that he really did not give me much chance. Just the same, I was always happier if, when we parted, it was he who had had the best of our encounters. I always hated it if, by some rare chance, I was victorious and he retired consciously defeated. At these times his saddened deflation always made me miserable and left me with another uncomfortable realization that, physically and mentally, I was made of a tougher and more resilient fibre than he was. I felt how much I should like to put my extra hardihood between him and any hurt.

For a day or two after Wilfred's return to his vicarage, nothing much was discussed about what I would have to do now instead of going back to sea. I knew some decision could not be delayed for very long. Matters were brought to a head by a letter to me from the Shipping Company ordering me to report to the Head Office in

Liverpool and another one to my father asking him, if possible, to accompany me so that the question of my indentures could be talked over and settled. My father was terribly worried about all this and showed his extraordinary simplicity over business matters by his failure to recognize for one moment that it was the Shipping Company who were anxious in case he, my father, should decide to lay a claim for damages against them for negligence, which on account of my extreme youthfulness and inexperience would have undoubtedly been sustained.

My father and I kept the appointment in Liverpool, and (I think to my father's surprise) were immediately shown in to the office of the two senior partners. At first the atmosphere was tense and noncommital while they reconnoitred their ground and parried for an opening. My father was quiet, courteous simplicity itself, but this was belied by the hard, steel-blue of his eyes brought on by nervous tension, which gave him a fierce look. This nonplussed them a bit, as it did most people, but they were extremely astute business men and quickly sensed that a negation of any claim on the indentures on both sides would satisfy my father. With almost indecent haste this was carried out, signed and sealed. After this everything became extremely friendly. The senior partner chatted to me and drew me out about my experiences in their ship. I liked him very much indeed and thought him most friendly, especially when he said that the Company were sorry to lose a promising young officer. I did hope so much that my father was hearing this, but I was afraid he wasn't as he was talking away twenty to the dozen to the junior partner about Bombay. After more affability all round, we took our leave, but before we left the senior partner turned to me saying that in view of the good reports about me from the Captain and Officers and our present happy settlement of my unlucky experience, he wished as a token of good wishes to present me with three months' pay; and, ringing for a clerk, he had the cheque made out. As the pay was only a few shillings a month, the amount—although large to me—was of course very trivial. The gesture gave me more pleasure and heartening than anything else that had happened to me for a long time and as I walked away from the offices with my father, I felt somehow that this cheque, made out in my own name, in some extraordinary way put a lot of things right that had been wrong before.

It was with a gay and confident sensation that I stepped along beside my father through the streets of Liverpool, thinking to myself that perhaps after all things would work out all right somehow. I remember thinking that as well as some funny sort of people, there did seem to be quite a lot of very nice people in the world. I was remembering the senior partner, with his genial behaviour towards me, and liking him again very much indeed. My father, too, was in high fettle and filled with relief over the outcome of our interview.

Stopping suddenly in the crowded street on our way to the Birkenhead ferry-boat to catch the train, for which we just had time, he exclaimed: 'I'll tell you what, Harold, we'll miss this train and go and have tea somewhere to celebrate.'

While we were having tea, my father brought the talk back to the Shipping Office. He expressed his surprised astonishment over the fact that the firm must, after all, have thought quite well of me; and I noticed that he was glancing at me in an unusual way—as if, for the first time, he was seeing me differently. This curious trait in my father, of always rating all of us—except my mother—at such low estimate, had nothing to do with his affection and love. It was, and always remained, a question of regard. He just could not bring himself to look upon any of us as showing the least real aptitude, let alone promise, in any direction; neither could he visualize any of us securing success through anything of value inherent in ourselves; so that it was perhaps not unnatural that he should take the view that our only hope lay in diligence, good character, and hard work and the securing of the good opinion of some firm or person who would, for these reasons, overlook our lack of real ability. It was a terribly thwarting attitude to hold towards us; it affected us all with varying degrees of discouragement.

Still, his frank incredulity on this occasion was offset by the puzzled glance he had given me and the manner in which from time to time he looked straight at me, with so much conjecture. This gave me hope that at last he might be thinking of me as another person and forgetting his parental prejudice—that I was only his own somewhat unpromising son. After ruminating a little, he turned to me and said: 'What a pity you had to mess up your first voyage like this. Really, the firm seemed to think quite well of you. You might have had a good chance there.'

I said: 'Yes, Father, it is a pity.'

'Well, my boy, you have made your bed and you must lie on it'—he was very fond of using this depressing proverb—'and it's no good crying over spilt milk.'

'Yes—I mean, no.'

'You've had your chance, and I shan't be able to give you another. You understand that, don't you?'

'Yes, I suppose so.'

'What do you mean, "suppose so"?'

'Only that I would still like a chance to go on with my painting.'

'Now, Harold, it's not a bit of good your starting that again. I should have thought your voyage would have cured you of that—if it did nothing else.'

'It hasn't; nothing ever will. And I should still like to go on drawing.'

'Now, my boy, it's no good talking like this. You know very well it's no good. Here I've got Wilfred still on my hands, getting on for twenty and not earning anything larger than shillings; writing poetry so your mother tells me. And now, if you please, he wants to be a poet or write books or be a newspaper editor. Anything, it seems, except something sensible and fitting. Now, you keep talking about wanting to draw and paint and be an artist. Just pleasant nonsense, my boy. Just pleasant nonsense. Next thing, I suppose, Mary will want to be a doctor and Colin a sculptor or something.'

Dropping his voice to a quieter level, he went on: 'You know, my dear boy, your mother has set her heart on Wilfred having his chance somehow; and, after all, he is much more talented than you are and it does seem a shame if all his reading and knowledge should go to waste. Anyhow, as I say, your mother has set her heart on it and we must see what can be done.'

'Yes, Father, of course he must. We all know and want that. I only thought you might be able to help me to get some work where I could use my drawing and painting, like designing wall-papers or textiles— I am quite good at it really.'

'Once and for all, you must put this foolish idea of painting or any professional art away from you altogether and try and remember that your father and mother always know best what is good for you. I thing you are becoming very much inclined to forget this lately. But come along—or we shall miss this other train. We must catch it, for I want to tell you on the journey home the plans I am making for you.' He paid the bill and we rushed off to seek out our train that was waiting in the familiar soot and smoke-filled caverns that made up Birkenhead Station. My father had of course had a compartment reserved for him, so we were all alone, and he was soon telling me that he had arranged for me to take up work on one of his railways. It appeared that he had got busy and secured for me—always provided I could pass the examination—a temporary junior clerkship.

He had apparently only been able to do this in his own area and, worse still, only able to secure a post for me on his own staff. He made no bones at all about the grim foreboding with which he viewed this unfortunate arrangement, for he had less confidence in me as a prospective railway clerk than even I had in myself; and he warned me that any sign of inefficiency and consequent embarrassment to himself would mean the instant withdrawal of me. However, he hoped this could be avoided, and if so when I was old enough he would be able to get me on to the permanent staff and appointed elsewhere. In the meantime, I should be earning—I forget what it was—round about eight or ten shillings a week, which would enable me to live at home.

He proceeded to give me a bad-tempered lecture upon what I must do and more especially what I must not do, when I started work on his Railway in a few weeks' time. I could see very clearly that he did not like anything at all about the arrangement, especially as I would at first come under his own indirect control. He finished up with the remark that, having sworn that no son of his should ever take a post with the detested Railway Companies, it was galling to see it actually happening and exclaimed, 'What a poor exchange it was for a life at sea in a fine ship such as the one I had just left.'

I was thinking so too, but I was not unduly concerned about everything, for I knew then that I had no intention of stopping with the Railway or any other office job. With this in mind, I wasn't averse to trying it out and seeing for myself what this sort of work was like; it would be something new anyway. In the meantime, I should be at home for a bit longer and so gain a breathing space to think things out.

18. *My Father's Offices*

About a week after this I took up my railway clerking. It meant just nothing to me and I went along with my father for my first day without the least suspicion of trepidation. I was surprised about this, for in all my previous interviews and appointments and for all those yet to come, I had been—and was for ever to be—plagued with sick stage-fright and nearly intolerable nervous agitation. This episode stands almost alone for the completely unflurried state in which I accompanied my father, accepted the necessary routine introductions and climbed on to my allotted high-stool to commence work. In all my life I have never had less trepidation about any happening. My indifference was so extreme that it afforded me my first experience of complete nonchalance —an experience I found so strange that it was wholly pleasing.

I was, of course, in one of the outer general offices, wedged in with some dozen or more other clerks. It was a dark and dreary place, sour-smelling from the stale engine smoke and soot that seeped up from the platforms underneath. The windows, which looked down on the station approach, were covered with a sort of wire gauze, which prevented any of us seeing anything that might be going on outside. I thought this was a pity—I should have liked to have seen what was going on.

I was set some triviality or another in the way of a task; I can't remember what but something to do with forms and copying something from them into a ledger. It was certainly easy enough but awfully monotonous. I kept looking at the huge clock to see how the day was going but its alteration seemed unbelievably slow. I began to think that if every day was going to be like this one, the span of life could indeed be endless. However, a stroke of fortune was to come my way, and in a day or two I was to get a move from the main offices. Apparently these were overcrowded and the Company had decided to open up the ground-floor of some official's house which belonged to them but was now empty, and use it for a subsidiary office for a small department. This house was about a mile away from the main offices. My father, who had the organizing to do, sent down a fairly senior clerk and was quick to jump at the chance of appointing me there too, as this man's so-called assistant. He was very pleased about this arrangement, for he thought it embarrassing for his staff to have his own son working with them. The staff thought so too, as I had been quick to realize.

I was pleased as well at the idea of getting away from the main offices and more so over escaping from under my father's nervously critical eye. I was genuinely concerned in case I might—with one of my usual stupidities—let him down in some way or another. He was himself alarmed in case this should happen, mostly I think in fear that my unknown clerical gifts would fall so far below the standard he demanded of his other juniors. When he took me down to the house, I had a most pleasant surprise for I found it was right on the river. It also had a considerable patch of garden waist-high in weeds but nice to look at and the room we were to use was quite a pleasing one with french-windows leading out to the overgrown garden. It was furnished with an ordinary large table and chairs, instead of desks and stools.

I had not yet met the official who was to be my senior. I think his name was Harker or it might have been Harris or Harrison. When I did so I was agreeably surprised to find he was a largish man with merrily wicked eyes and genial expression. His appearance gave little indication of his occupation: he was dressed in loosely fitting clothes, altogether unorthodox for an office worker. I think I knew at once that here was another of the staff whom, like myself, my father was not sorry to relegate to a distant office. For the first day or two there was considerable restraint and formality between us, which surprised me as it so very much belied my first impression that he was a jolly sort of man with a free almost gay manner. It was my asking him if he would allow me to smoke a cigarette which at last dissolved this; after some tentative fencing on both sides, he came out with a burst of confidence and told me of his disappointment—that having had the luck to secure for himself this 'plum' of a job, where he could smoke all day long, all on his own, it was only to find himself saddled with the boss's own son as assistant, and ended with: 'Pretty bloody, isn't it—if you see what I mean?'

I agreed it was more than 'bloody', and assured him that indeed I did see what he meant and, returning his confidence, told him I had just come back from a voyage at sea and that I hated this office work and had no intention of remaining at it for long; and I went on to tell him that if any time he fancied setting fire to the place—as far as I was concerned, my father would be none the wiser as to who had done it. Whereupon, in magnificent high spirits, he lit up an enormous great pipe and blew clouds of smoke all over the room.

After a bit, he said to me: 'You know, young Owen, your father is quite the nicest old cock I have ever worked under but he's a devil for finicky discipline and if he knew I smoked in office hours he'd have the skin off me.' I assured him with some feeling that I wasn't keen on being caught smoking myself and we agreed to keep 'cave' for one another, for it was likely that my father or some other 'high-up' would pay us surprise visits from time to time. 'Right, young Owen, give me your hand on it, mon ami.' (He was very fond of introducing bits of French into his conversation, now and again.) 'And now, to celebrate—for I haven't told you the darkest and deadliest secret of all—but I'm going to—come with me.' Leading the way into the garden, after carefully looking around to make sure we were not observed, he walked to the deepest clump of weeds and with a dramatic flourish parted them to disclose six bottles of beer, shining like a nest of black babies. Even this was not all, for tucked away inside the office room were pounds' weight of excellent toffee.

Having finished off a bottle of beer, with a cry of 'Dead men tell no tales' and a fine overarm flourish, he sent the empty bottle sailing through the air to land with a smacking plop in the middle of the river. But he was conscientious in his own way, and never skimped his work or allowed me to do so; instead, he put into practice a theory which he told me he had long held that the average day's work of any routine office worker could, with intelligent application and very fast working, be accomplished in two or three hours instead of the usual ten.

We certainly gave this idea a try-out with a vengeance, and found ourselves with lots of time in hand for beer, tobacco, the toffee, and racy conversation. The man was chock-full of theories, a pronounced one being that the simultaneous consumption of alcohol, tobacco, and good sticky toffee, while not only being the height of bliss, produced such a prodigious flow of saliva that it became extremely beneficial to the working of the alimentary canal thus leading to good health in general. I often thought he must be storing up considerable quantities of future health at a great rate. I shared in the tobacco and toffee, but I was still shy of embarking on the beer. So, to be companionable and not take the edge off his rollicking good humour, we laid in bottles of lemonade for me.

Everything was working splendidly, except for the question of 'cave'. This we had been neglecting and by so doing taking unjustifiable chances. We had one breath-taking experience and had nearly been caught with bottles and glasses in array and the room full of smoke; we had only saved the situation by pitching everything— glasses and bottles, bags of toffee, pipes and cigarettes—out into the weed-beds and violently fanning the smoke out of the room with the door-mat. We knew after this that we must devise some sort of safer look-out. It was while we were delving about when the immediate danger was over, trying to retrieve our beer and tobacco from the tangle of weeds, that Harker, straightening up, let out a yell of: 'I've got it. I've got it. Why the hell didn't I think of this before?'

But he refused to tell me what it was he had 'got'. Instead, he bade me wait until tomorrow morning when I should find out quickly enough.

Without doubt I did, for, approaching the office early next morning, I was greeted with the most frightful baying and savage barking. It seemed as if there must be a wild beast loose in the room. I could hear chairs being knocked over and the slithering sound of someone being towed about.

Opening the door, I beheld Harker being dragged about by the most enormous Airedale terrier—throwing slaver and spume all over the place.

'Quick, shut the bloody door and keep out for God's sake. If he gets loose, he'll kill you.'

I thought so too, and needed no second bidding to slam the door shut and get myself to a safe distance. After some more bangings and thumpings, things quietened down, and Harker—dishevelled and breathless—came out to find me and tell me it was all right, to 'come in now, and make friends.' He had got the dog chained up in the garden. I was glad to hear this, but dubious about my conciliatory powers.

The sight of me sent the brute off into fresh fits of paroxysmal rage. With his bloodshot eyes and slavering, frothing mouth he was a fearsome sight.

Rubbing his hands with satisfaction, Harker said: 'Now, we can't be taken by surprise again.'

I agreed that with such savage alertness chained up, there was no possibility of that; but imagining what my father's face would be like when he came to inspect us and found the snarling beast, I thought my friend Mr. Harker might be having a surprise of another sort coming towards him and ventured to suggest as much. But I had underestimated friend Harker, for winking casually he contented himself with saying: 'Oh, well, with all these suspicious characters hanging about, it doesn't seem right to leave Railway property unguarded. When I've told your father the tale, he won't really believe it but it will be enough excuse for him to agree. You just watch, and I'll have "Lion" here eating out of his hand in three days' time. Your father's all right, you know.'

Lion never did eat out of my father's hand, but otherwise Harker was right—or we thought he was—and the dog was allowed to stay.

Harker was something of a specialist in the breeding and guard-training of these animals. Lion certainly proved a most sagacious creature, and gave us ample warning of approaching seniors and better still, discouraged many of their visits altogether. There was something about the angry beast lunging and snapping at the end of his chain which made them work out uncomfortable mental calculations as to what the breaking-strain of the chain really was—all that is, except my father who in his bantam-cock way 'pooh-poohed' any idea of attack if the dog did break loose and remained happily convinced that he would with his walking stick be more than a match for any Airedale that ever breathed.

For the first week or two, all this seemed quite good fun, but after that I began to feel the irksomeness of the routine; the clerical work I had to do I found dull and uninteresting. Harker helped me out generously when he could, but since the arrival of Lion, the volume of work sent down to us had increased by ever larger amounts—my father, who was so often his own fool, was never anyone else's—until we were hard put to it to finish by six o'clock. It was when we had to stop late day after day that Harker finally protested to my father. My father listened carefully to what he had to say and ignoring the details about the work, only said: 'Yes, yes, Harker, but does it not occur to you that barking dogs can be a great distraction to work? Think it over, think it over. Shall we say that if it wasn't for the disturbance of this idiotic animal here, you might get through the work not only by finishing time but possibly half-an-hour before.'

'Would you like me to take him away, sir?'

'Not at all, Harker, not at all. We are most grateful to you for safeguarding our property like this.' He stamped around as if to leave but, half-turning, said: 'And these suspicious characters you thought you saw hanging around, what about them, eh?'

'I don't think I have seen any about just lately, sir.'

'In that case. . . . But there it is, Harker. The dog is yours, and you have my permission to have him down here—but think it over, just think it over. . . .'

With this, he strode out of the room, shaking his cane in a challenging but friendly manner at Lion.

As soon as my father was safely out of earshot, Harker, rubbing his hands over his face, turned to me and with a wry grin, said: 'Well, well, young Owen, what do you make of that? The clever old so-and-so, piling on the work all the time and then comes down here as bland as butter, with'—and mimicking my father—'"Not at all, Harker, not at all. We are most grateful. . . ."'

This time it was my turn to wink, and I gave him one full of meaning and unsaid things. I was very proud of my father.

That evening Lion went home, and never came back again.

It was a peculiar month or two that I spent in these Railway Offices and during all of it I felt a complete misfit, as of course I was. I can recall no great pleasure or provocation happening to me; on the contrary, from the day I started this clerical work everything seemed to go dead. It was, I think, killing the vital interest which had so far invested for me even unpleasant happenings with a quality of excitement. Compared with this the hospital in Calcutta took on a glamour that I found nostalgic. In these weeks I could raise no enthusiasm for the work whatsoever. The dreary routine began to pall. Harker, with his beer and toffee, absurd theories and French phrases—which had started off as fun—was becoming tiresome and inane.

I was disliking my work in the Railway Office more and more, and could only apply to it a weary disregard—often flippant—which annoyed my father very much indeed, and created an unpleasant sort of official barrier between us which was very unfriendly. A mounting restlessness overtook me and a persistent urge that I must somehow put an end to my prosaic, unpromising situation.

My father probably noticed something of this, and one evening purposely stayed on late in his office, so that his walk home would coincide with my own later release. He told me we would take the riverside way. After beating about a bit he suddenly said: 'Why don't you resume the night-classes at the School of Art? I dare say Mr. Weaver might take you back again if we asked him nicely and it would be a nice hobby for you again.'

I was overdue for a boiling-over of exasperation and the misinterpretation and misunderstanding implicit in my father's question immediately brought this about. The vehemence of my retort surprised myself, and my father more so. I reminded him that when, so recently, I had wanted nothing better than to stop on at the School, he had insisted that I could not do so; but now, when I had no intention of ever going back, he suddenly wanted me to do this. Why was that? I asked. And, anyway, I didn't want a nice hobby; my painting was real, not a child's toy. And what did he mean, 'ask Mr. Weaver nicely'. With a flood of boastfulness, released by indignation, I demanded why, in any case, there was any need to ask Mr. Weaver 'nicely'. Hadn't I got 'firsts' in half my subjects already, and hadn't Mr. Weaver told him himself I was his best student? I said this and much more aloud to my father. To myself I said 'Hell, hell, and hell.' Was I to be for ever just someone of little account in my father's eyes?

As usual with me, when once started off, I could not stop my words tumbling over themselves in nervous bad temper. Stuttering away in great form, I told my father quite definitely that I just would not go back to the night-classes, if for no other reason than that having left the School as a full-time student and taken myself off to sea, with all the attendant enhancement this had given me, I just scornfully refused to go back, especially for evening-classes only—more especially in the guise of an underpaid local Railway clerk—and by doing so to admit defeat.

My father, whose eyes were snapping angrily, had stopped and was banging away with his walking-stick, striking the paving stones great blows which threatened to shiver the stick and his hand as well, and barked away at me, calling me 'a silly boy'—which infuriated me still further—and telling me I was 'ungrateful and dissatisfied'. Both of us calming down somewhat, we strode along in uncomfortable silence. Presently—'You know, my boy, I want to get you settled down.'

'But I don't want to be settled down.'

'Now, now, it's not a bit of good talking like that. I can't afford to have you at home much longer, and I can't keep you on as a temporary clerk, but I know that the Company will take you on permanently if you want to make a career of it; but understand, if you do this you will have to stick to it. I won't have any changing of mind, and of course you will have to go somewhere else—not stop in Shrewsbury, I mean.' After a pause to let this sink in, he went on,

'Do you see what I mean, my boy?'

I very much thought I did. Here it was, once again, the grim foreboding of miserable cheap lodgings, dragged back once more to the slums, or back-streets at best, and the stagnation of life in a Railway office, stretching—as I saw it then—away to dreary endlessness.

My father was still talking away in his stilted and official voice but I was paying little attention to what he was saying. My mind was back to the waterfronts, seething about amongst the turbulence, the hot blazing colours, the breathless crowds—never too breathless, though, to cease their perpetual volubility. I was sufficiently aware of the tone of my father's voice to know that a crisis had arrived in my affairs; and without listening much, my mind was made up—let come what may I would have no Railway office.

Abruptly, I said to my father: 'Father, I am going back to sea.'

'But I've just been telling you all this time that I have arranged for you to get a permanent post on the Railway.'

'I'm sorry, Father, but I won't take it.'

'But, my boy, you must. And you're lucky to get this chance, I can tell you.'

'I am going back to sea.'

'Just as you like, my boy. After all, you must decide for yourself, and I think you would be better off there. For one thing, you don't seem to be very good at this railway work; but of course it would be a living for you—of sorts——'

'Yes.'

'Of course, if you get another sunstroke, you won't get over it. You know that, don't you?'

'They told me often enough. But couldn't I get a ship not on the Indian run, perhaps?'

'You mean the Mediterranean, or Northern Europe?'

'Yes, or the South American run.'

'Pretty hot there; full of tropics, and crossing the Line, you know.'

'The Western Ocean, then——'

'Humph, humph—bit difficult to pick and choose, and always the risk that you might be sent somewhere else. Gulf of Aden, f'rinstance. A bit dangerous all round, you know, but I won't stand in your way, if you like to take a chance.'

'What d'you think, Father?'

'It's your own responsibility, my boy, and you must decide for yourself. I'll help you what little I can to find a ship, but it won't be much.'

'Thank you, Father.'

'But you must make up your mind soon, because I must let the Company know if you are taking on permanently or not. But here we are almost home.'

As we turned into our own pathway, my father, with what was for him a rare demonstration of friendliness, gave my shoulder a squeeze, and said: 'I shall go fishing this evening. Would you like to come?'

'Yes, please, Father, and let's take Colin with us.'

Weeks had passed since we had been out for an evening together. I knew now that he had thrown off his 'official office' manner and that we were once again father and son. As we fished that evening his relief that I was about to take myself out of his own offices and go to sea again showed itself in his merry lightheartedness and wrinkling smiles, as we tied on our 'cockabundies', 'coachmen', and 'bloody butchers' in desperate efforts to rise a fish out of the darkening waters. . . .

Immediately I had written my letter of 'resignation' to the Railway Company, I set about getting myself to sea again. I knew this would not be easy to do; vacancies for apprentice officers were never profuse and the waiting lists—without influence—were formidable. I did not want to go to my uncle again, and if I had wished to do so my father would not have allowed it. For he was nagged pretty badly by the thought that I had still to repay the seventeen pounds ten shillings I owed to Uncle Edward Quayle.

I was afraid, too, that explanations about my previous voyage would be a difficult stumbling block, but here I was wrong and I soon found that properly handled this was easily turned into an asset. I think the partner in my old Line must have played up well; in any case my already having sailed a voyage was considered good ground for priority. In quite a short time I had secured an offer from another Shipping Company to sign indentures, this time with the official rank of Cadet, a term which was coming into use to distinguish an aspiring sea-going deck-officer from the countless other land-bound occupations that worked the apprenticeship system. Applied to young boys learning the craft of seamanship in the capacity of junior officers, although honoured by tradition by seafarers, the name 'apprentice'— to those outside the profession—had always been misleading and something of a misnomer.

This company had a Line of ships trading to many parts of the world including the coasts of France, Spain, Brazil, Uruguay, Argentina, Patagonia, Chile, Ecuador, and Peru, with the possibility of occasional trips through the Panama Canal, which had just been opened, often taking in the West Indian Islands on the way through.

I had been quite unable to get a ship on the Mediterranean run or to any of the other more temperate climates. When the chance came to me to take the South American Line, we, as a family, to buoy me up connived together to prove to ourselves satisfactorily that these places would only prove of moderate heat—not like India, anyhow; Ecuador and Brazil took quite a lot of talking down, to say nothing of Guayaquil, but we managed it somehow and it was decided that I should take a risk and hope for the best. I signed the indentures, was immediately appointed to a ship, and a week later I was back at sea again, heading south for Cape Horn and the Falkland Islands; eventually to pass through the Straits of Magellan and so up the west coast of South America to tramp the ports of Chile and Peru.

19. *At Sea Again*

It must now have seemed to my mother and father that at least one of the brood was safely flighted out of the nest, with a future determined for the next three and a half years, provided of course that I did

not go down under the heat again. I had not forgotten this risk nor
the warnings of the doctors in Calcutta as to what would happen
to me if I did. I thought a little miserably that in either case I was
certainly 'settled'; the neatness of this thought momentarily pleased
me and brought me a forced mental grin, but in spite of this I did not
find it very pleasant to think about and the depressing threat caused
my grin to crack rather badly. But I was not yet sixteen years old and
so able to thrust out gloomy thoughts and make up my mind to forget all about such things as fevers and tropical diseases.

But no sooner had I gone off—not safely but most unsafely—to sea
again, than Wilfred arrived home with proposals to throw up his
puny security—the religious scheme which he had himself been
against, anyhow. He was obviously tired and looking frightfully ill,
and with no plans as to how he expected to earn a living. He was
depressed and savagely bitter, and tormented himself continuously
with an obsession that he had somehow failed to achieve anything
and—what was much more distracting to him—was under the
conviction that he had failed to get on the right path towards
achievement.

He would proclaim continuously to my mother of the necessity for
achievement in the youth of any poet and would quote the work of his
favourite poets, bracketing the age of the poet at the time of inspiration. He was writing, thinking, and living poetry prodigiously at this
age, and condemning and destroying most but not all of what he
wrote. He developed an obsession not only to write poetry but to be
a poet, to be known as a poet, to be in a professional sense a poet, and
above all, to be recognized as a poet. He day-dreamed and longed
with all the passion of his taut intensity for this and this alone.
That he must earn a living he knew, and to further his poetry he knew
he must earn a reasonable one; even his youthful passion for a degree
was instinct with the knowledge that if he obtained this it would
ensure for him the means of earning a living in such a way that
his poetry could live too. From the age of ten years, until he was
killed, this passion to be a recognized poet burned in him continuously; it gave him no rest, nor did he want it to do so; all other
things were secondary.

His decision to leave the vicarage was not to be lightly taken, or
suddenly come to, and the turmoil of his indecisive thinking about it
had enlarged his perplexity and added to his state of over-anxiety.
Having contemplated this step, it was not now the thought of his
future which was bringing him so much despondency but that being

at home once more, he felt he was back again to where he was when he went away. His obsession with time was extraordinary; the morbid thought of the lack of it possessed his mind until it became a monstrous threat; he was shaken with panic and fear that he would not have time, time, TIME. How greedily he wanted and demanded this. And how desperately he disbelieved that it would ever be his to take and use.

After a while he brought out his plan that he would like to find a post in France. My father was in favour; he was deeply perturbed about Wilfred's depressed states and brooding attacks of morose intolerance, alternating—as they did—with short spells of gay, bright-eyed, often nonsensical hilarity. This unreliability of mood puzzled and distressed my father. In his worried way, he was realizing that Wilfred was not fitted for the usual occupations generally allotted to 'well-educated' young men born and reared in provincial towns, and had abandoned hope of his finding a suitable occupation in England; and with the renunciation of the student-curate work in Oxfordshire, the myth of his going to university was finally exploded (though Wilfred himself was still determined to read for an outside degree). Perhaps France and new surroundings would help.

Eventually Wilfred received a reply to an advertisement he had answered. It was from the Berlitz School of Languages, offering him a rather indefinite sort of part-time post to teach English in their school in Bordeaux. The pay was pathetically small and, under the system, precarious, and after working it out, it seemed almost impossible that he could manage to live on it. But he was excited and keen to take it up; it was a chance to get to France, and the very nature of his work would be the best possible way to fulfil a minor ambition—to speak and think precisely as a French-born national.

So it was that the summer of 1913 found Wilfred in Bordeaux preparing to take up his post with the Berlitz School of Languages and me outward bound for the South Atlantic. For my part, on our outward leg, we were to take in the ports of France, Spain, and Portugal to load cargo.

My new ship was a dirty, coal-blackened freighter, of some 4,000 tons, old, or anyway past middle-age, and in her blowsy squatness looking even older than she was; the once white upper-works fouler-looking in their sliming coat of fog and coal-dust than the painted black of her streaky hull. She was lying heavily down in the water, loaded down dead to her plimsoll marks with coal. There was an inertia about her, as if the dead-weight of her load was pushing and straining against her over-taut belly-skin. There was an animal-like lethargy about her, which at first I could not place, until the thought came to me that she was like a black-and-white sow too heavy in litter to do more than sink lower and lower into black slime, fouling its white markings as it abandoned all effort and submerged to supine settlement.

What I really saw was a single-funnelled tramp steamer, the funnel colourless in its coat of black paint, so thin and high that it looked more like an alien iron chimney than a part of a ship; and two masts painted a sickly ochre colour. Of rake to funnel or masts there was little, and the straight-up-ness of them accentuated the square, box-like superstructure comprising the bridge and quarters; amidships, pronounced fore and aft well-decks broke up any vague suggestion of ships' lines still more. Her bows I saw were blunt and ugly, with no flangeing over-hang or fineness of cut-water; the stem itself rose up perpendicular. Her counter was entirely graceless and noticeably gross in fat clumsiness. No, I saw at once she was no beauty, and noting her sullen under-balanced dead-weight, I thought to myself how she would roll like a long dead pig in any sort of seaway.

But so great is the power of the seas to transmit life to the craft that sail them, that as soon as I stepped aboard I knew this ugly, square-ended, chopped-off iron box, sulky and resentful as she looked, was not a dead thing and that once away from the hated land, she would revive and in her own special ungainly gait wallow along with gallant refractoriness.

I joined her alone this time; and sorting my way through the cluttered decks ankle-deep in coal-dust, I reported to the First Officer, after which I found my way to the apprentices' quarters. I was disappointed with these, for they were well below decks. The cabin had been a lazaretto at one time. The access to the quarters was dark and tortuous. The airlessness of the alleyway and the room itself was heavy with a dank fetidness, and lying in layers in the dust-laden air was the putrefying, unmistakable smell of rat mange. I knew she was a 'rat' ship; evidence was everywhere. It was too dark to see them, but I could hear the scurrying multitudes as they squeaked and pattered with tiny sharp-nailed toes within inches of my feet. Here and there, an evil red spot of light would flash for a hundredth part of a second as a rodent's eye caught a stray beam of light and threw it back—magnified and malignant and most incredibly evil.

As I opened the door of the room and switched on the dim electric light, I saw swarms of rats—mad with panic at the sudden light, flowing in grey-brown rivers in all directions, running over one another's backs and biting and snapping in terror.

The ship's rat colonies were in a state of flux. The loading of the bulk cargo of coal had driven them out of their secret and well-used stronghold. With uncanny telepathy and astounding prescience of approaching threat, rodent intuition and cunning had spread the intelligence that the vessel's holds were filling up with uneatable impenetrable black stone and that to be trapped meant death by thirst and starvation. If this happened, the colonies would not die by single units but by gradual elimination; in the fight for survival the strong rats, turning cannibalistic, would attack the weaker and live by consuming the dead bodies. The ghastly elimination would go on and on, but never to the point where not one rat would be left alive. Always there would be the few survivors, foully diseased, not by ordinary rat sickness but through their desperate resorts to cannibalism turned into living embodiments of deadly viruses which, breeding with fearful rapidity, yet did not swiftly destroy life in themselves, but instead with frightful menace transformed them into escaping hosts of plague.

Ten thousand rats, even although ring-tailed with mange, if finding sufficient access to food and moisture to prevent cannibalism, were less dangerous contacts than ten 'survivor' rats, replete and gorged on the putrefying corpses of their fellows. These last were latent with menace and could spread death with every footstep. The rats I was treading through were emigrating from their old haunts, to seek, with military acumen, fresh quarters where their communicating lines would not be cut off and their chance of existence assured. As the rats hurried and scampered all around me in the dark strangeness of the ship's corridors, I happily reasoned to myself that as we were loaded with an uneatable cargo they would leave the ship. What I did not know, but was to learn before this voyage was over, was that not only would they remain in the ship but driven to the last stage before cannibalism overpowered them, in their frenzied desperation of hunger, they would feed from sleeping human beings. Before we reached Peru and frontier fumigation, I had no hard skin left on my heels or the soles of my feet, and my toe-nails were gnawed back to the quick.

Exhausted by the hard seaman's work—for it was a hard-working ship for apprentices—carried out in the killing spells of watchkeeping of four hours on and four hours off, we would flop into our bunks and in our extremity of tiredness fall into sleep, which became near anaesthesia with its absolute lack of consciousness. In this state we were fine rich feeding-ground for the rats.

They would run over our bodies and with uncanny intuition seek out only the insensitive parts of us. If one, maddened beyond fear, bit me to half-wakefulness, I would find myself brushing a stream of living foulness from off my face and chest; and at my feet would be a muster of rats, one to each toe. Even my head was not immune, and I would find on my blankets gnawed off tufts of my hair. It was some little time before I realized that it was not the hair itself they wanted but, crazed by lack of fats, were devouring the Macassar hair oil I was using. When I stopped using this, they left my hair alone.

Their desperate boldness was incredible and frightening. If I did start up in horror at the feel of their horrid feeding, to throw them frantically off, they would only dive away with squeaks and wild leaps in somersaulting falls; but they would not leave the cabin, instead would crouch in rows and clusters, beady-eyed with expectancy, until once more my body slid back into insensitive sleep.

But I did not know anything of this as I opened the door of my quarters on my first day of joining. All I knew was that the breath of the old ship was foul and gaseous from too long land imprisonment.

We sailed that afternoon. As we cast off and our tug moved us away from our berth through the dock gates and headed us into the murky river, the old ship—as if resenting the pull at her straining old body—groaned and belched complainingly until her own pulsing innards came to life, shaking her into a violent shuddering tremble as her slow propeller gripped hold of the water, kicking meanly at her old stern as it jerked her into an unwilling forward gait. Protesting with warning creaks from ten thousand groaning rivets, and moaning from every deck, she ambled into obedience to helm, and she commenced to roll until she had eased herself into a five degrees starboard list, settling herself down to this as we wallowed into the open sea, and with the bite of salt water she found her confidence and regained her courage.

She refused to accept our persuasion to give up her comfortable list and, except in dock, never ceased her rolling.

The bitter sleet-laden gales, blown straight off the ice-floes of the South Atlantic, cleansed and toned her up and before we made a landfall at Tierra del Fuego she was rejuvenated and the impact of the northers off the coast of Chile made her almost skittish. I was to make two voyages in this oldish ship, and more in others like her, but the others were always a bit younger and never quite so disastrously lacking in line and shape.

As all seamen are always prone to do, even very young ones, while I was sailing in her I upbraided her without mercy. As I came down dead-beat from the flaying icy work on her decks and struggled with lashings to secure myself in my bunk, knowing full well that if I did not she would roll me out while I was helpless with sleep, and most likely crack my skull for me, I would think of her as a 'she-pig' and call her 'a dangerous old sea-cow'. Once, when five hundredweight of chain sling and fifty pounds of steel hooks—after falling thirty feet through space—whistled past my head with only inches of clearance, because it was my own carelessness, and not she who was responsible, I cursed her for a 'killer' ship. When she nearly drowned me in her own struggle to keep afloat, I did not though feel resentment against her, only kinship with her in her own distress. Before I left her, I knew her and understood her floundering stupidities, and I was sorry in an affectionate way to say good-bye and with my regret came a realization that although the profit-searching shipowners might throw together these freighters and ocean tramps, it could not prevent these ships—once they were afloat—from becoming alive.

My voyagings embraced all the ports of Chile, Ecuador, Peru, Colombia, Patagonia, the Argentine, Uruguay, Brazil, the Atlantic Islands, and the West Indies, with one passage through the Panama Canal. During that time I developed outwardly into what I longed to be—a hard-case ship's officer. Inwardly, I do not think I changed much, except in the obvious way from a childish naïveté to more adult address, together with a detailed knowledge brought about by the intimate rubbing of shoulders with seaport vices. The foulest and most detailed obscenities of the world flowed about me and shared the air I breathed; but deep inside me I kept a secret core to which neither the hard-fisted young mate that I became, nor the surrounding atmosphere, ever gained admission. I was in the best school in the world for building up an outward shell of hard toughness. It was a tough coast we tramped up and down, the last resort of the sailing ships and their hard-bitten crews seeking the nitrate trade of Callao or the grain and dried peaches from further south. Outwardly, I moulded myself to it and sought to excel in ship-work. I was soon in

charge of holds and took pride in either getting the cargoes broken
out and unloaded, or picking up freights from the bobbing, swinging
lighters that rode the rolling Pacific swells—the swells which so often
kept us miles offshore loading odd consignments.

Once having touched at Coral or Coronel, which were usually our
first ports after working our tortuous passage through the Straits of
Magellan and clearing Cape Pillar, working ship would become
excessively hard. We would frequently make port in the early morning, deal with cargo all day, and make another port that night, work
there all through the night and sail again immediately. Quite often,
of course, there would be longer runs; but mostly it was entering and
leaving port with no watch below in between. As it is not an easy
coast, from a seaman's point of view, all this was exceedingly good
for my navigation and almost better for ship-handling. At certain
times of the year, northers and the coastal fogs were menacing or
made navigation tricky.

These northers could be especially dangerous, and we would often
have to secure with slip-rove hawsers, and with steam up ready to slip
and run. To be caught on a lee-shore with a sudden norther springing
up meant losing a ship. If one of these sudden winds sprang up it
would do so with little warning, causing gigantic tidal waves to sweep
inland; these had been known to scoop up full-rigged ships and cast
them half a mile or more inshore. Looters and driven sand would
strip them to ribbed skeletons. But before they fell apart the destroying sand, to make amends, would with swift driftings bury them and
preserve the relics for ever.

I was working hard in my spare time to master the rudiments of
navigation. To begin with, on account of my very limited grounding
in mathematics, I found it sticky going but once over the first hurdle,
it came more smoothly; deep in the intricacies of logarithms I began
to sense the fascination in the exactitude of figures and precise com-
putations. The paraphernalia connected with it helped—the easy
working, sliding parallel rulers and the dividers: the first sliding
smoothly over the chart and the second walking primly across it
picking off sea distances with such neat precision. From simple
transit bearings, which came in the way of duty on anchor watches,
I advanced to azimuths and working out positional sun-sights. It
was mostly a case of finding out for oneself, but occasionally an officer
would go out of his way to proffer definite instruction, though not
very often. However, to make up for this we were never obstructed
and had the run of the charts and chart-room. I soon found out that

if I puzzled over a navigational problem long enough, one of the officers sooner or later would casually come along and set me on the right track, and for short periods become interested in my progress. But with or without instruction, we were expected to become competent navigators, able reliably to take sun and stellar sights and plot the ship's position with accuracy, and—surprisingly enough—we for the most part did do so. Just quite how I have never been very sure. As cadets, we were of course given many intermediary officer chores to do, any duties which would not immediately jeopardize the ship: patent log-reading, deep-sea soundings and, outside of officers' work, acting as leadsman when entering shallow water—this last only after clear proof of ability, and therefore much coveted. I always found it most extraordinarily exhilarating and somehow magnificent to be 'in the chains' of a ship entering harbour, heaving the lead with fine flourishes and calling up to the bridge with grand seaman's intonation, 'By the deep four' or whatever the tiny bits of coloured bunting denoted. I most especially liked it when I found really shallow water and felt the ship urgently alter course and the engine-room bells would ring, always excitingly, for half-speed, or —the cream of all—full-speed astern. At these times, I felt powerful and splendidly responsible.

All this sort of thing, although it was as it were negative instruction, added up and I soon discovered that the more competent we became the more inclined were the watch-keeping officers to hand over watch-keeping duties to us. This delegation of duties encumbered them with responsibility for so doing, and I was quick to notice—as we became useful to them—how keen they were to make us more so, and thereby gradually ease their own minor duties on to us. It was clearly a technique of not giving something for nothing, or more likely a sea mannerism of sorting out the interested and the uninterested. I found myself taking every advantage of this. Finding how well this worked, from my own point of view, I made the best use I could of it. From time to time cadets would come and go who thought this only a mean way of 'putting on them', and resented it. I could never see it like this. Anyhow, I I was madly keen for responsibility and ability, and meant to get it the quickest way I could. The practical seamanship looked after itself. The rough and tumble of constantly entering and leaving port; the breaking-out and loading of mixed cargoes by night and day often necessitated the special rigging of booms and tackles, jumbos and general derrick work. Our cargoes would vary from locomotives—

dead-weight only, and therefore easy, and their thousands of railway lines, these last vicious with springing whiplash and dangerous to sling and hoist—through the gamut, including livestock and fear-crazed horses, to the innocuous small bags of dried peaches from Coquimbo.

On the longer legs at sea we would be put to work before the mast and with the sailors, and were expected to hold our own with them, splicing heavy wires and in general seamanship. As well as this we were detailed for all boat-work in port, sailing and rowing not as coxswains but as oarsmen, and would often row the Captain two or three miles from an anchorage to the port mole in hot sunlight and be sent again to bring him back aboard in pitch darkness at one or two in the morning, often through heavy swells.

In this way, we never lacked for practical experience. What we lacked so often was sleep—and at times this became excruciating. I became horny-handed and sun-burned to the colour of a coffee berry. Out of it all I came to appear arrogant and—I think to myself, now—slightly swashbuckling; and, although I was still a cadet, I gained a name for myself on the coast as 'a young officer who was a hard driver'. This genuinely astonished me, for I felt anything but hard inside me, indeed I was often worried by my internal softness.

Although I was surprised, it did nothing to lessen my enjoyment of this reputation; it fitted well with my ambition to be a 'hard case'. This bit of fanciful thinking that spun itself around me originated, not from my association with our own crews or the crews of other vessels, but from my over-keenness when working cargo to get more work out of my own hold than anyone else would out of theirs. We always employed port labour for this—gangs and gangs of local stevedores. Of moral values they had no inkling whatsoever; their enormous resources of cunning in perpetrating crimes of every description were unbeatable; they were thieves and liars, it seemed, not so much from circumstances as from design and wish. It is perhaps little wonder that the perpetual vigilance which was necessary to control these gangs, case-hardened us and turned us cadets into veritable little toughs.

It was always a case of ourselves or them, and we took great care that it was never ourselves.

I found myself donning my armour of hardness with the greatest of ease and driving hell out of my foul-minded gangs. In actuality, they were quite impossible to lead, and they would stop working automatically immediately supervision was withdrawn.

But it wasn't all coast work, and we would often have long legs at sea between ports and quite long spells in port when weather or the Pacific swells prevented cargo working. At these times we would get shore leave more frequently. I welcomed these breaks for the time and opportunity they gave me—not only for escape from the dark airlessness of the reeking holds and relief from the sweating crowd of strong-smelling labourers—but to be working on deck again, which always seemed like a holiday after the imprisonment below.

It is true that at first these sand ports of Chile and Peru and the coastal strips of bleak and sterile desert threw back an impression of sere desolation, especially accentuated in the tiny ports of which there were so many strung out along the coast. Approached from seaward these looked depressing in their solitary isolation; most of them comprised only a handful of rough buildings of unpainted corrugated iron, interspersed with sand-blasted wooden shacks. There was something about these derelict small ports with their ramshackle array of hutments squatting insignificantly in the vast surrounding desert of sand that breathed out extreme loneliness.

Just the same, after the first impact of desolation had worn off, there was also something about the hard treelessness which became attractive, especially in the early mornings and evenings, when the burning, obliterating glare of level sunlight transformed the irritating sameness into marked undulations and detailed wavelets of riffled sand, intricately patterned by the wind and thrown into clear design by the purple and pale green shadows that receded in lovely graduations until they were lost in the vagueness of the foothills that in great sweeps swept towards the coppery-coloured mountain ranges. Out of this belt of spectrum dust alive with refrangibility would emerge the great-sided slabs of the precipices, washed with sliding colour from palest brick to burnt purple; still further behind this, the peaks of the Andes themselves would sometimes glisten fugitively with milky whiteness.

At times I would see it like this, but at other times it seemed I could not see past the stark ugliness of the broken-down moles, the dilapidated shanties, and the strewn dishevelment of the rusting iron drums and broken oddments of stranded floatage. When I was in moods of this sort I could sense the loneliness, and, feeling very far away from home and familiarity, I would sometimes be a bit cast down. However, there was never much time for contemplation and whenever I was not required on board I was eager to get ashore—so much so that very often, having worked cargo for fifteen hours during the day, I would with or without a companion, jump aboard the last lighter going shorewards and spend the night walking around whatever port we happened to be in. There was no need to walk more than we wanted to, for in the bigger ports there were water-front 'dives' and cafés where we could spin out an order for coffee for hours if necessary. Quite often we would run into cadets from other ships; when this happened we would gang up and do the rounds of the dance-halls intent upon light-hearted diversion. If one of the party, overcome by the heady atmosphere showed signs of falling by the wayside, he would be pinioned by the rest of the party and dragged out to cool off. If he were too long coming to his senses, he would be frog-marched down to the harbour and pitched spread-eagled into the water. These sorties were not without some risk. It was this which lent to them the spice we needed to satisfy our high, salt-laden spirits. There was rarely trouble unless we had to carry out this evacuation of one of the party. One of the girls, perhaps having entangled a member of our party would—immediately we commenced our forcible extrication of the too-willing victim—raise the house, shrieking her indignation, and hellish uproar would follow and free fighting commence all round. This was good for our generalship, for to avoid casualties—which we were not always able to do— meant quick thinking and even quicker movement.

This form of diversion soon palled, most likely on account of the similarity about each incident, and after the first flush of excitement I gave it up entirely; but I never got tired of spending the night ashore and would 'jump the last lighter' on every possible occasion. Getting back to the ship was always a gamble, as of course there was no boat laid on for us at two or three in the morning; police boats were our best hope, and if the ship was lying any distance out, our only hope; if she was close in, failing a friendly police launch, we would strip and, belting our clothes across our shoulders, swim for it. As we swam we were all the time hoping most anxiously that the quartermaster on duty would be awake to hear our low hails and throw us a line up which we would 'walk' the side of the ship palm-tree fashion.

But mostly we got a police boat and I soon discovered the one technique that would nearly always work. This would take the form of an entirely fictitious recounting in local Spanish and international mimicry of the tremendous efforts of gallantry we had expended upon their delightful ladies of the town. It always worked like a charm. I became quite expert at the mimicry, able to reduce them to drooling at the lips with envy and amazement over our gallantry. Full of

compliments they would wrench away with their arms, if it was a
pulling boat they were using, or, if a power launch, would rev up
full-speed in order to get us aboard quickly so as not to waste a
moment of our well-merited revitalizing time. With delighted grins
and head-shakings they would put us aboard and with black moustaches waggling—like demented semaphore arms—their real arms
gesticulating admiration, wave us 'a restorative good-night' and with
more winks and leers, promise to lay in wait for us the following
dawn.

I think I enjoyed the nights ashore in these Chilean and Peruvian
coastal towns and cities more than anything else. They never seemed
really to sleep; the cafés were open all night and along the water-
fronts there were the sailors' dives and hide-outs, these last always
mysterious with dim lights and tortuous secret-looking passage
entrances. From them would come crude music from accordion,
mouth-organ, or banjo, as half-drunken sailors beat out a dance tune.
Inside a motley of seamen and girls stamped with their feet in time to
the rough music, swaying crazily in drunken efforts to dance between
the jigging tables. Over everything hung a heavy pall from the fumes
of the cheap red wine and strong black coffee. Broken glasses lay
everywhere and empty wine bottles danced amongst themselves as
they bounced and cavorted to the jump and sway of the trembling
floor. The table tops swished with red and black pools, which,
cascading now and again to the floor, took with them their load of
cigar and cigarette ends to be pounded and squelched by the thumping feet.

I liked wandering around in and out of these places; my insatiable
curiosity and determination to find out everything for myself recognized no bounds and this led me on to treacherous and always
dangerous ground. I can see now with what hideous uncertainty my
traversing was fraught, for I was certainly reckless in my eagerness
to visit the shanties, wine-shops, and dance-cafés and to seek out for
visitation all the lowest and roughest waterside haunts and vice dens
where sailors foregathered; but I was actuated by the romance of
these places, the smoky semi-darkness, the rattle of the cheap pianos
and the general atmosphere of men, the sea and ships. There was a
rhythmic pattern running through it all, which brought into high
glittering relief sensations of action and adventure and a reality of
living which I had never experienced before. It was a correlation of
ship work and seamanship, of strong competent seamen—crude

and violent but immensely able—of Conrad and Stevenson, the sailing of leagues of ocean and, above all, the visitation of strange lands, unknown cities, towns, and ports, which wove itself into a tapestry of such infinite allure.

It was my somewhat detached outlook which allowed me to run the gauntlet of the seaports without coming to any harm, and to wander through the dark streets of Callao, Valparaiso, Bahia Blanca, Antafagasta, Pernambuco, Taltal, Pedro Miguel, Talchahuano, Guayaquil, and a hundred others with similar magic names that crystallized for me so much of what I sensed was the fullness and rich ripeness of existence. My frequentings and preference for night life built up around me a reputation for being a 'hard case', which was in no whit true and certainly never earned. But all of this was only a fractional part in time out of the life at sea in a merchant ship. For the most part, it was hard, monotonous work with only short spells ashore and only a matter of days at home in England between voyages.

But I was liking it well enough, and at times my life seemed full and even meaningful. I was painting. I was not neglecting my navigational mathematics and was paying more and more attention to my civilian education, which I had begun to realize was so seriously lacking. I was, of course, quite tutorless, but I found that by some chance I seemed to be picking up bits here and there which I soon discovered had a way of binding themselves together with the cement of my—by now—heavy reading. Classical or scholarly concentration was, through lack of guidance and time, out of my reach; but I was finding out the satisfaction of acquiring knowledge and practical learning in some small way, and, perceiving for myself this fascination, began for the first time to enjoy the feeling of gain which came with it all.

Not only was I painting but I was producing my water-colours exuberantly in these pre-1914 years. I was selling a great many of these paintings and sketches in different seaports abroad, but only rarely in England. I sold them, unframed, for small sums, mostly around the same price, which ranged from five to fifteen shillings— an advance from my fourpences and sixpences of the Uffington days. Half-a-guinea was my stock price, but I was always quick to judge my prospective buyer's mood and would make lightning mental adjustments up or down in order not to lose a sale and yet to get as much as I could for the sketch. Occasionally I would get a guinea. Those that I sold were only the ones I did not care for myself very

much. I was still adamant over the ones I thought good, and refused
—often to my own future detriment—to sell them at any price. This
being so, I enjoyed these transactions very much indeed and although
the sums I received were small, they were large compared with my
miserable cadet pittance and made all the difference to my night life
ashore, enabling me to drink coffee often and to buy a seat occasionally in the theatres of the larger seaports.

But this water-colour drawing did more for me than to ease a little
the perpetual money-shortage: it built up around me another sort of
reputation so that I became quite well known amongst the ships and
in many of the ports. There was a curious contradictoriness about me
in all this: on the one hand a tough young seaman, on the other a
young boy madly enthusiastic over the creation of delicate drawings;
but I found the duality immensely intriguing and hardly ever
embarrassing.

In nearly all my ships I had some adherent to my cult, and in one
ship I ended by running quite a painting school in which competition
and emulation ran at fever heat.

In this particular ship I had amongst others the Chief Engineer, an
elderly, disgruntled, and very disagreeable Scot; the Purser, a man of
middle-age; and the youngish Second Officer. The first two became
madly keen, especially the huge shaggy old Scottie, who with infinite
patience would laboriously copy every painting I did; it entirely
changed him: from a churlish old man he became youthful in his
ardent eagerness to learn from me, surprisingly humble as he begged
for instruction and happily good-natured in his importunings as he
strove to extract from me explanation and hints that might quicken
his skill.

At first he would only copy a painting I had already done, and
resisted—with childish diffidence—all my persuasions to attempt an
original effort. It was not until I refused to lend him something of my
own to copy that he was driven to make an original sketch, but when
he did, it turned out such a surprising success that afterwards there
was no holding the—as I thought of him—'old cock'. His passion
for painting became a byword throughout the ship and it was no
unusual sight for the crew to observe two or three of us sitting on
the hatch-combings in the dog-watches, drawing away with tremendous absorption some land- or sea-scape. Before we got home the old
Chief had quite an interesting collection of his own of which he was
inordinately proud.

When we returned to an English port, I was bidden to a tea-party in his cabin, first to help arrange the exhibition of his drawings, and then to meet his wife and of course witness his triumph. In all my life I have never seen a more surprised and incredulous woman.

Until now he had been dreading the day when he would be 'beached', for his retirement was imminent; now he could hardly wait to get the news—so anxious was he to settle down and paint the hills and lochs of his beloved Scotland. As I was taking my leave, his wife, a big raw-faced dour-looking woman, inveigled me out of ear-shot of the cabin and whispered hoarsely in my ear with barely intelligible Glasgow accent: 'It's only a bit of a boy you are yourself, but it's a surprised woman I'll be if I don't live to be grateful to you for this thing you've done to my big Jock.' She embarrassed me still further by smiting me not only with affection but with painful force as well about my shoulders.

This painting of mine in foreign places might have led to something of serious import to me and I was beginning to see that a sea-faring life and painting could go well together, and how it might be possible to divorce the two later on. In the meantime I was determined to qualify at sea, as a safeguard for my bread-and-butter.

I can see now that these years just before 1914, in spite of the homesickness, the considerable hardships, real privations, indifferent food, and physical exposure to cold and heat, were nevertheless successful ones for me, within of course their limited scope. I was keen and ambitious: I think too the stars must have been set favourably for me; I was lucky: minor successes seemed to come half-way to meet me. My bit of painting was a financial asset, and seemed to be quite a general acquisition all round. As a professional seaman, too, good fortune seemed to be watching over me in a smiling way so that bits and pieces of luck fell to me.

The first of these: the Shipping Company I was serving with had, at that time, a small coasting ship, used only for coastal work on the Chilean and Peruvian seaboards. I had, of course, quite often seen her fussing in and out of the ports. Actually, she was something of a joke amongst us blue-water ships, but I had always liked the look of her, with her long, low awnings stretching from stem to stern. She was incredibly ancient, and some romance of the very early foreign river-boats seemed still to cling to her. She did a moderate trade in small consignments of odd cargoes and a roaring one in saloon and deck passengers; hundreds and hundreds of the latter crowding her decks for standing room only. These would be very poor people, often in whole family units, complete with all their worldly goods and live-stock—donkeys, ponies, goats, pigs, and chickens. The small animal traders would have their canaries and parrots stacked around them in tiny split-bamboo cages, not much bigger than the birds or small animals themselves. They brought all their own food and water, bedding and cooking utensils, remaining on deck night and day throughout the short passages, building for themselves little separate homes by piling their goods and baggage to make partitions. The decks had the appearance of an immensely overcrowded zoo.

Seen, though, from a distance she looked a welter of life and live-liness, all tidied up nicely by the long stretch of sun-bleached awning. I always thought she was a trim and attractive-looking little craft, and the idea of handling her had often intrigued me. My chance was to come along quite soon and with it I took my first forward—and professionally lucky—step.

An epidemic of some sort of mild coastal fever had swept through the little vessel and temporarily decimated her deck officers. To my enormous gratification and delight I found myself seconded to her, temporarily, as a fully-fledged officer. Bursting with pride, I packed my sea-bag and boarded her, and with great joy watched my own ship steam past out of harbour to commence her gruelling port-to-port tramping.

It was a pleasant prospect to know that for some weeks I should have no cadet's duties. I was to rejoin my own ship for the home-ward trip when she returned south again. In the meantime I would only have watch-keeping and navigational duties to perform, a cabin to myself—and what a splendid vista of freedom for thought and action this conjured up—and, above all, recognized authority and sea-going responsibility. I was made Fourth Officer of her, and revelled in what appeared to me such an immense advancement from being a mere cadet. I was accorded the marks of respect and mode of address usual to a fully-fledged officer, which made up quite a lot for my bitter disappointment in not being allowed to keep the bridge alone for a complete watch at sea: I would be left in sole charge for short spells only, when conditions were favourable, but these were everything to me and as I paced 'my bridge' exacting the utmost accuracy of compass steering from my Quartermaster I felt—if not a very important one—at least a small Conrad: it was the little ship herself though, her gallant age and noisy engines, and her splendid air of courageous—much painted—dereliction; and not myself, which in her isolated romanticism made me think vividly of Conrad.

My best piece of luck, however, was to come along in a few months' time. In the meantime I enjoyed my temporary promotion. When I rejoined my own vessel, the Captain sent for me and told me I should rank as Fourth Officer of our own ship from now onwards. In an ocean-going ship, such as mine, this did not really amount to much, except as additional status, for it was complimentary more than actual, but it excused me from the less dignified jobs usually delegated to apprentices. It entitled me as well to the 'Sir' from the lower deck and the much-prized sea courtesy 'Mister'—the traditional appellation given to watch-keeping officers—from the Captain and senior officers.

Altogether good fortune did smile upon me in this my practical career; but this was only one side of myself and for a boy it was a coarsely rough life, often brutal in its stark rawness. Nevertheless I seemed capable of dealing with this aspect of my life satisfactorily and it seemed more or less successfully, and without undue nervousness.

The other side, the highly nervous and sensitively perceptive side, reacted differently altogether, often bequeathing me legacies of misery and dissatisfaction, and the ensuing unhappiness—unlike its counterpart in the rough seafaring business—never seemed to nurture aesthetic satisfaction. This left me feeling lonely and somehow cheated. I was disappointed that my everyday life sped along so satisfactorily, and jealous that it should outstrip so easily my aesthetic yearnings and hopes. I was, of course, dissatisfied with my progress in painting.

In a somewhat desperate endeavour to find a preceptor, I, with a spontaneity unusual in myself, wrote a lengthy letter to Wilfred in Bordeaux, trying to tell him something of my difficulties and the phase of tangled thinking through which I was passing. I knew that I could not get a reply for some months, but as the time drew near when a letter from him would be possible, I scanned eagerly any mail that came for me at our ports of call, looking for his characteristic handwriting.

It was at Punta Arenas that his letter eventually caught up with me, and it was with some impetuosity that I tore open the envelope in haste to discover if I had drawn anything of help or value out of him. I had hardly hoped or expected to do so, but this did little to lessen my furious disappointment when, running my eyes quickly over his clear writing, I found neither of these things but only the same tutorial and distant elder-brother tone, with all the prosaic, maddening admonitions and enjoinders, which I knew so well and was so heartily sick of. The letter ended affectionately enough in a stilted, guardedly unequal way. In a passion of disappointed rage, I tore his letter to shreds and cast them over the side to leeward. I watched the white specks drift down on the black, ice-laden waters.

All that day, as I stood tallying on the fore-deck in the blizzard that was mounting with vicious force, my thoughts kept turning to Wilfred, wondering vaguely what would be the outcome of his passionate zeal for learning and his tentative essays into poetry. Out of my thinking I clumsily arrived at the conclusion that he was so absorbed at this period with his own creative thinking that he was impervious to the immediate difficulties of his surroundings, and this blinded him to much that was passing in the minds of the other members of his family.

As I stood on the freezing deck, automatically tallying in cargo, my thoughts travelled elsewhere, and flitted about and around my professional contacts and casual acquaintances; my mental meanderings left me wondering where I could look for—much less find—any indisputable opinion. And thinking of the stupid bantering chaff and all the repetitive inanities of double-meaning that passed for conversation in our daily shipboard life, I felt despondent and wondered whether, perhaps, I was just being priggish and superior in my wishing to discover deeper and more subtle meanings in things; but I did not really believe this and in my heart knew that what I was seeking by instinct was right and true; and, as always when I was thinking like this, I became overwhelmed and hot in my hatred of the various board schools that had so ill-prepared me and, with unusual bitterness for my years, half-realized the demarcation of the instructed and the uninstructed, and knew that I was on the wrong side of the fence.

In my untutored way of thinking, I had little quarrel with this glaring fact; what really made me unhappy was the startling realization that both my mother and father could accept so easily and even foster the idea that 'the wrong side of the fence' was the proper place for me, and that in some way a humble contented acceptance of our lot was noble in itself. How I hated humbleness and humility and acceptance. While I was decrying these things to myself, I suddenly realized just how much Wilfred hated them as well, and saw too with what vigour and ruthlessness he had set about combating them. In his quiet, silent way he was determined to keep himself free of these fetters; instead he was determined to arm and equip himself in the only way he knew—by reading and unremitting study.

Even as hatred for meekness was hot in my heart, I felt another wave of admiring envy sweep through me as I saw how much farther he had taken himself than I had. I envied his singleness of purpose. At least he knew now where he wanted to arrive; the details and the manner of his travelling were still obscure and difficult, but his beacon was lighted and clear and he was by his absorbed preparation of himself gaining the means to reach it.

How much I envied Wilfred's clearness of vision. Materially, perhaps, his prospects at the moment did not seem as good as mine. There he was, somewhere in the purlieus of Bordeaux, almost jobless and nearly as penniless. But he was writing his poetry and ever striving after knowledge. Even his way of earning his few shillings a week was—by perfecting his languages—advancing him towards his desire for mastery of letters. Whereas I myself was off at a tangent, and for the life of me I could not see how, in spite of my few sketches, this seafaring life could possibly advance me technically in the craft of painting. I could not feel I was doing anything like this: I had neither of these things, and knew my course to be hazardous and unmarked. I wondered unhappily if, in the turmoil of ships and the sea, foreign ports and whore-shanties and the troublous business of being a tough young 'hard-case' ship's officer and my irresistible love of exploration up every tortuous path, I was not indeed already lost. Even if I wasn't, I knew myself to be lonely and bewildered. Still, I thought to myself, this life at sea—in spite of its crudities and hard-ships—was much better than being an office-boy in some obscure Midland town. Anyway, I had no choice now. I would get my sea-going certificates. After qualifying I promised myself I might be able to see things more clearly.

20. *The Hulk*

The first wintry days of 1914 found my ship loading wool in the Patagonian port of Punta Arenas in the South Atlantic. We were under orders to proceed to another wool port to finish our loading. I remember this mostly for the sense of depression which gripped me for a few weeks while I was in these extreme Southern waters, and for an experience which will rank perhaps always as the one out of which was to come to me the naked consciousness of what stark terror could be like. So far, I had had my fears, my pains and accidents, and my narrow escapes, and with them had gone through the normal fears and misgivings with almost cheerful nonchalance.

Day after day and week after week we had seen no sun and felt no warmth, only the everlasting grey wastes of white-flecked water. It seemed, indeed, that we were in a world of water; cloud pressed close down upon and around us, and the air we breathed was heavy with cold wetness.

The fury of the wind, when it came upon us, gave us no relief from the maddening sensation of living in a different world, bounded everywhere by black or grey menacing waters; I became unhappily conscious that below this grey waste of meaningless surging swell, as I watched it cream in mile-long troughs, lay hideous depths of cratered sea-bed; I wondered what it would be like to be sucked down through the tumultuous broken surface to the unmoving stillness of the weight of black water that lay beneath me: when I thought like this the thin shell of the ship seemed only feeble separation.

The wind in all its power was unable to thin the wall of vapour that pressed in upon us, driving the Cape Horn sea-fogs before it, its own impetus creating fresh blanketings of atomized sea-water as it tore at the tops of the curdling waves to shred them into globuled vaporous spume.

Steaming our easting down to make a landfall in the Falklands, we rolled with drunken abandon and pitched to wicked strain, until it seemed to me the old ship would break her back or her ataxic propeller would shudder her entrails out of herself.

Clinging on to the flying bridge as we careened down into some deep dark trough riven out of the solidity of the water, I thought again as I saw the liquid walls speed past me how tiny and fragile the ship looked. I felt so minute myself that I could sense my own entity slipping into insignificance. As we shot down to the bottom of these dark vales, even the wild shrill triumphant trumpetings of the wind would be muted and for an unbearable fraction of infinitesimal time silence would smite us and stillness would hold the ship, it seemed with deadly intent, until she staggered into movement again and fought her way to survival and fresh struggle. The screams of the tortured wind after the deathly silence of the troughs seemed friendly and strangely warming in contrast to our diving into the divided waters and our glimpse of the frightful immobility and eternal solitude of a cold sea grave.

It was neither misgiving nor fear that bothered me, but there was something about these cold, metallic-looking expanses in the South Atlantic that often filled me with unhappy, rather dreary searching thoughts. I was not alone in this. It was generally noticeable that after weeks of buffeting, perpetually wet bodies, poor food, and the discomfort of continuously being awash—our quarters and bedding always soaked, often knee-deep in water—that depression was liable to descend and settle with heavy oppressiveness to clog the spirits of the whole ship's company. It was the inertia brought about by physical exhaustion and the constant wailing shrieks of the pounding wind; low-spiritedness was perhaps a better definition than actual depression.

It was after a battering of this sort that we groped our way through a thick, blinding snow blizzard into the inhospitable harbour of the lonely Islands, let go both anchors, and prayed God for holding ground. The next morning, as so often happens in these near-Antarctic latitudes, broke clear and bitterly cold. We prepared ship to take in cargo.

As I looked around me, I could see what unrelieved desolation lay about our anchorage. The port itself lay some distance across the bay; small clusters of houses and buildings all low-lying, flat, and uninteresting. It was, perhaps, the flatness which gave the whole place such a drab, colourless look. There seemed some undulations but no hills that I could see; the place seemed completely treeless, the only vegetation being the salty-looking scrub grass that stretched away in bare flats. A few ragged-looking sheep browsing discontentedly completed the dismal picture, so that I turned with relief to look at our own deck cluttered with debris from our hammering, at our twisted rails and stanchions plaited grotesquely like a child's string puzzle gone wrong, at our smashed bridge and boats and the gouged-out spaces where other boats had been. On the whole, in spite of her lacerations from her fearful beating, I thought she looked more friendly than the severe, prim-looking island. I wished very much to be out of this horrid world of snow and swirling mist, and had a bad attack of wishing I was at home and near warmth and friendliness.

We were to take in wool bales; it would be a lightering job, for we were to load from the old hulk that I had noticed with the first of the daylight as I came up on deck. It would have been impossible not to notice her, for her grim dereliction dominated the scene.

She must have been a three-masted ship, for I saw that although grossly amputated her fore, main, and mizzen masts were still standing; on the main mast, starkly disproportionate, hung a huge spar, by the look of it her original lower main yard-arm. She was used

as a wool store hulk. I saw she was rolling unpleasantly to her over-
sized moorings, showing off her streaked and naked-looking body.

There was always too much swell to run alongside and load direct
and on this day it was running too high to ferry with lighters; but
next morning with a moderating wind and decreasing swell we commenced the work. I was detailed to the hulk to break out and check
the wool.

I remember, as I climbed over her side, an unaccountable extra
sensation of lowness of spirits caught hold of me. It may have been
due to the intense cold or, more likely, the effects of the thumping,
bruising passage we had just run down; or perhaps it was just the
effect the hulk had on me. Whatever it was I reacted to her with
strange disquietude immediately I set my feet on her deck. I became
possessed with a violent antipathy to everything about her.

All that day I remained peculiarly sensitive to a hostility coming
from her and could not rid myself of a feeling that in some strange
impractical way she was dangerous to me. I tried hard to overcome
this unpleasant hyper-sense of sinister and worryingly undefined
threat, but it was no good: so like a practical little seaman I ran my
eye with extra intent over all the running gear and tackles, in case my
sensations were precursors of some serious running rigging accident
—the sea, I had found out, made seamen very attuned to this sort
of warning. But I was convinced it had no connection with everyday
happenings. Anyhow, I found everything in good order: at the
bottom of my heart I knew it to be something altogether different.

The day's work went off with no unusual happening; yet all day
long I remained acutely aware of a most discomforting sensation of
being in too close contact with something inimical—I did not know
what—which was strangely alien to me. Nasty ripples of chill were
running through my veins; I tried to put these down to the intense
cold but somehow they would not fit in quite as normally as that. It
was with a feeling of release that, having finished the loading of the
last lighter of the day, I jumped aboard her and headed for my own
ship.

We had another day and a half of loading to do and I was more and
more disliking the idea of another spell aboard the old hulk. I made
up my mind that if I could, I would somehow get out of it. Once on
board my ship I felt better and consequently a little silly, but I did
approach the Third Officer and asked him to change places with me
for the next day, so that I could stop aboard instead of going to the
hulk; but he did not want to make this unnecessary rearrangement

and would not agree. On account of my growing feeling of silliness, my request was only tentative and lacked persuasion. When he asked why I wanted to do this I had no answer. I was feeling foolish, but not nearly foolish enough even to hint at my real reason—my vague unease; we passed over the matter good-naturedly enough but my curious dread remained with me.

The next morning, the port, the hulk, and ourselves were enveloped in a driving scud of snow and fog vapour, so that we were in an eerie yellowish world of our own which spasmodically turned lurid as odd gleams of washed-out sun found a tear in the curtain of gloom. I had hoped that the conditions might stop our work, but they didn't, and too soon I was in the sea-boat being rowed to the hulk, the creak and scrape of the oars making ghostly rhythmic accompaniment to the mournful cry of the seabirds. We could not see the hulk and I was trying to make her on a compass bearing. I had little faith in my boat compass but knew with uncanny surety that even if I turned my boat about the hulk would still draw me with unholy magnetism directly towards her. She did. I heard her before I saw her—heard her sobbing moans and the sluicing swish as the black water ran back from her rolling flanks. In a few seconds, I veered and was alongside her. I had fetched up dead amidships.

The muttered compliments from my shivering boat's crew upon my compass reading brought a twisted smile to my mouth and an uncharacteristic sharp rejoinder to my lips, which surprised them.

All that day my depression mounted, so that I almost began to hope that a sling would part or a lighter sink, to break the tension. Nothing happened though; and as darkness quickly began to fall we secured derricks and prepared to leave. I had been given permission to go ashore that night. A young Customs Officer had invited me to spend the night at his home, and I was much looking forward to this.

The last lighter we had loaded was to be towed to our own ship and would be tied up alongside ready for the morning; I would go ashore from the hulk with the last launch taking the stevedores' gang off. I had made arrangements with the launch-man about this and thinking of the cheerful fire and supper ashore, I watched our ship lighter wallow off with some freshening spirit. I had to go down the hold for a last look around to make sure that everything was secure for the night. I slid down the ladder with some gaiety, and finding everything all right, I climbed to the deck again and made my way over to the shore side to go down into the launch. As I looked over the rail, a horrid shock of panic pierced my chest. The launch was not there.

Gripping the rail, I peered shorewards. Disappearing into the foggy blackness I could just discern the frothing wake of the launch. Filling my lungs, I let out a terrific hail, but even as I expelled my voice I could hear it caught and flattened, to scream past my own ears; the tearing wind was in my teeth. I knew it was hopeless. As I stared, the wake itself was swallowed up by the marching wall of darkness.

The hulk had got me.

My own ship would think I was ashore. On the Island I would not be missed; my Customs Officer friend would naturally think I was aboard my own ship unable to get shore leave. The coxswain of the launch must still be under an absolute misunderstanding; he would never have left for the shore if he had the least doubt of there being still a man on board. I was miserably certain that it could not be forgetfulness. In this small community a visitor from a vessel was an event, and hopelessly I realized there was no chance of the boat returning for me. With frightening clarity I knew that for the next sixteen hours I had no possibility of contact with the outside world: from now on the struggle was joined, it must be a battle between the hulk and myself. The hulk had got me; I felt the clutch of her, as her evil spirit eddied and swamped around me.

In the ordinary way, this long lightless night was not much of an event to befall anyone; there was, of course, a large degree of discomfort—no light, no food, no heating. The cold, while intense, was not for a sound young boy actually dangerous; exposed on the deck it might have been dangerous but down in the hold I knew that the heavy stowage of wool would generate a certain degree of feeble warmth and act as a barrier to the bitter cold.

After some minutes of stunned and appalled fear at my predicament I became unpetrified and released my grip of the hulk's rails. As I did so, I was surprised to realize that in my passionate wish to make my plight known I was still sending powerful hails to the launch; but with the release of my hands my mind began to work again and I ceased my desperate cries knowing them to be useless.

A dreadful feeling of terror took hold of me as I thought of the long hours of dark aloneness which lay in front of me and panic surged and scrabbled for outlet through my throat; but I choked it back and forced my lips into a quavering whistle. It was a feeble effort but I felt better for it; anyway, it held back the gag and gorge that was struggling in my chest to reach my throat.

Turning away from the rail, I looked about me, measuring up the degrees of darkness and cold that were surrounding me. I saw there was still a slight radiance of grey light, just enough to distinguish the gaunt, sawn-off mast stumps and the main outlines of the deck hamper. The cold was increasing and I felt a numbness creeping over me which warned me that, no matter how much I disliked the idea, I must get below decks before exposure clamped hold of me.

Feeling my way towards the scuttle, which I knew led by companionway down to the next deck, I fumbled down it. I was hoping that I should find sufficient shelter here to make my headquarters for the night and save myself the ordeal of a blind descent into the yawning depths of the black hold. I quickly discovered that I could not, for the wind was finding its way in and the space itself was bare and empty, but it was sheltered and dry enough to let me pull out my nearly empty box of matches and count how many I had—oh, dear Jesus, only six. . . . Little sharp pings of panic tattooed up and down my spine as I thought of the sixteen hours of black blindness in front of me and for several moments I was tempted to light a fire to attract attention. Fortunately, all my instinct rebelled against such an action; all my seaman's horror of fire at sea rose up in me. A small signal fire would have been difficult, most likely impossible, to control and the thought of such a risk in a wool ship smothered any temptation; in any case, through the wall of driving vapour and snow, nothing less than a conflagration would be seen.

I worked it out that two matches would light me to the hold ladder; the ladder itself I knew I could descend easily in darkness by feel alone; on the floor of the hold I would use two more to find some crevice between the bales for warmth. My brain was working well now and I was pleased to find I could visualize clearly just such a long narrow corridor where we had broken out a deep tier of bales that afternoon. I knew if I could reach this place I would anyway be safe from dangerous exposure and might even find some warmth; I immediately felt in my pocket to make sure that the great hooked pocket-knife that Colin had given me for my last birthday was still there. Feeling its rough strength in my hand I knew that once I gained my retreat I could rip the sacking of a pressure-banded bale and work out some of the oily, greasy raw wool and wrap it around my feet and hands and thaw them out.

All this time, I had felt the hostility and threat of the hulk and I was dreading the fumbling descent into her gaping interior; but with enmity declared between us—and the first round to her—I was feeling better and combative once again.

All the same, I was very frightened, and standing in the dark 'tween decks counting my matches by finger feel, I felt lonely and horribly deserted. The wind was rising and drumming with horrid howls which to me in my frightened state took on the high-pitched screaming wail of an animal hysterical with pain. The gale was working itself up into a savage tempo, alternating its wild shriekings with uneasy silences; the stillness of these hiatuses struck at me with more menacing force than the wild, more normal, thundering blasts. There was in them a quality of unearthly quiet that, in the solitude of the old ship, wrapped about me apprehensive chills.

It was during one of these eerie, soundless spells, while I was bracing myself to climb down into the black hold, that some of my cold-spirited loneliness melted away; I found myself tensed with listening, and presently from out of the void—and yet not of it— came floating to me the thin thread of muted shrillness that I had heard at other times like this . . . the last time in India . . . the long sweetening cry, the song of the family. Transfixed and strangely warmed, although I knew I was still bodily alone, I knew also now that I was not any longer quite alone. A spiritual assurance was threading down out of infinite time itself, and physical aloneness did not seem to matter.

Trembling a little from my tensity, I listened again for the vitalizing reeded song, but it did not come; in its place I could hear only the infuriated tearing, rending sound of the gale as it hurtled back, hitting the sodden old ship with vicious rage and heeling her over. I could feel the deck under me rise up as the wind lifted us and the fearful shuddering as the mooring cables snatched her back.

The realism of the violent impact brought me back to actuality. The ancestral cord was bellying with straining vibration somewhere out in the immensity and black howling void of the oceans. But it was there and unbroken. With renewed heart I waited for another lull—not to listen this time but to act, to risk two of my precious matches and with them find the ladder top and, if I found it, creep with feeling toes and clutching fingers, down, down, down, until my feet should signal to me the bottom tier of wool bales. While I waited for the abatement which would let me start on my match-flickering journey, I put my hand in my pocket and savoured the friendliness of the rough-hafted knife and thought with what relish I would drive it into a bale, ripping the hessian until I could drag out tufts and spirals of warming wool.

The rough, friendly feel of the huge knife took my thoughts to Colin and home. How dreadfully far away it all seemed. And, in the black darkness of my plunging prison, how separated I felt . . . until I remembered the thin piping that had been borne down the ages to me, to enter my being and bring me comfort and courage . . . the song of my family and their forebears orchestrated together in vibrating waves of sound. . . . Still gripping my knife I waited for another lull and when it came, with steady hands now, struck my match and commenced my treacherous crawl to the ladder head.

It was strange and eerie down there in the bottom of the groaning hulk and the darkness had an oily pressing thickness which had not been present on the upper decks; but I felt at once that it was many degrees warmer. I thought to myself that if only I had a whole box of matches it would not be so bad after all. As it was it had taken me four matches to find my retreat in the alley-way amongst the wool, two to reach the top of the ladder, and two more to find my way from its foot to where I was now—in the crevice I had visualized when forming my plan for the night. I knew that I must keep the two matches I had left for a long time yet, one for when I woke up if I I went to sleep—I did not think sleep would come to me but hoped it would—and the other until daylight came to release me from darkness; the last match I knew I must not use but keep only as a promise of light and by so doing make it into a talisman against fear and the panic of aloneness.

Fumbling about in my niche of wool bales I could feel by stroking about with my hands that I was nicely enclosed and would I thought be able, if I could once get the circulation going again in my hands and feet, to keep safely warm; but I was not very hopeful of keeping comfortably so. Taking out my knife I set about slitting a bale and working out some of the raw wool. It had been baled under such heavy pressure that this was not easy, and in spite of its oily nature my finger-tips became sore and aching as I tussled to unravel enough to wrap my hands and feet. Even as I worked, I felt the repugnance, innate in all merchant seamen, to breaking into cargo. Although I was unable to see even an outline in the pitchy blackness, I yet found myself working—by the sense of feel—to make neat incisions and do as little damage as possible.

Twisting some strands around my wrists, I felt a suspicion of warmth running up my arms; so, lowering myself down, I stretched out my legs and leaned my back against the wall of wool and closing my eyes tried to sleep. But it was no good; my brain was racing and I knew, too, that not far from me, lurking fear—horrible, trapping fear—was waiting, to plunge me into panic. Instinct told me that with fifteen hours of this dark solitude still to go, I must erect an encircling insulation of thought around myself through which fear could not pass. Thinking like this gave me an armoured feeling so that I was able to relax and even start to do a bit of my whistling. But I did not get through all my ill-assorted airs and tunes; the feeble sound of my whistlings seemed only to bring the darkness closing in on my body with more pressure than ever and accentuate the battering dirge of the wind as it yelled and tore across the decks overhead.

The whole vessel was rolling and plunging, and lying as I was near her keel, I had the uncomfortable gyroscopic sensation of spinning up and up, always higher and higher until, snatched up short by her shackled cable chains, she shuddered to a fractional stillness before starting again her screwing descent. At these moments the wind would hammer at her straining sides and with vicious spite, in revenge for its thwarted desire for destruction, throw pockets of water and frozen rain to beat a frenzied tattoo on the upper decks, the main body of howling pressure sweeping on until its sounding violence thinned out to graveyard wails and deflated moans.

Lying listening to its approach and demented savagery of attack as it hit my reeling hulk, I found myself following its hurtling self-destructive course as it sped past me and in fearful imagination followed it over the leagues of black water—so cold and deep and avidly hungry. Giving myself a shake, I forced my mind out of this dangerous absorption with the patterned movements of the storm.

My breaking away from mentally following the path of the wind brought closer to me the uneasy labouring of the old hulk. I began to listen too intently to the racking groans, the creaks of springing timber which—it seemed to me—were interspersed with cracking rends and splitting ribs. It was while she was still lying over to her port beam into a trough that she jagged more savagely than ever to her jumping chains. As the chains, springing into bar-tightness, snubbed her leaping bows with rending shock, she shuddered with dreadful violence and with drunken reaction suddenly went torpid and heavy with lifelessness, careening through a horrible swaying arc to lie dead-weight to her starboard beam.

Terror gripped me and ran with an icy prickling flush all over my body. I thought she was foundering and, starting up, ran—with the miraculous surety of deadly fear—to the foot of the ladder and found

myself gripping the rungs, braced to meet the inrush of black water.
Even as I waited, I could see myself being torn from my hold and
swept into the awful unevenness of the limbered obstruction of the
'tween decks, to be forced upwards into the trap of the deck-head. I
saw myself spread-eagled on the flood, with only my head free, to be
bounced and splintered against the deck-head as the volume forced
me upwards.

But the rush of water did not come; instead, there seemed to be an
easing of strain all around me and once again there came to me the
familiar jerk as she rode to her cables, but this time with play left in
them. I sensed we were still moored and as she righted and steadied to
a normal roll I knew she was not foundering.

When this knowledge came to me, I was mid-way up the ladder.
Actually, I had stopped climbing to try and ease the irritation of my
forehead by wiping away the dew of fear which must have sprung out
on me; as I met the colder air it condensed and turned to ice; the
irritation was maddening, but so violent was the surge of the ladder
that I dare not let go a hand, but pausing, rubbed my brow against
my gripping wrist. This simple action brought a quietude upon me
and swinging in mid-hold—only able to feel the ladder and not see it
—a sensation of confidence swept over me, as I sensed the fine
strength I had in my hands and legs. Although the sway and swing
was nearly as great I could certainly feel an easing; the movement
was altogether smoother, the spasmodic dangerous snatching was
less violent. The jerking strain on the moorings as she rebelled and
fought the stiffening cables had nearly gone out of her. I felt she was
riding better to the bighted weight of them. All the same, I thought
that before I went down again to the trap-like unpleasantness of my
dungeon in the lower hold, I would climb to the upper-deck to
satisfy myself that there was no real danger.

I groped through the 'tween decks towards the companion hatch
and as I opened the scuttle doors I was hit by the sustained pressure
of the wind as it streamed across the hulk; out on the deck I was
seized with a dreadful feeling of bleak loneliness as I peered about
me with stinging eyes into the curtain of driving snow and rain and
frothy spume. It seemed greyer and lighter up here after the density
of the inside; I could dimly make out the black shape of her heaving
carcass and the gaunt unsightly threat of her sawn-off mast. As rents
were torn in the wall of speeding wetness, I could see the vast
stretches of awful grey water and every now and then a pear-shaped
gleam of unearthly light where helmeted crests of whiteness were

torn free from the waves and sent racing—like pale, disembodied spirits—to streak about in the welter of bitter water and uncanny desolation that swirled above and below me. I had a feeling of unreality, and felt disembodied myself and highly nervous about the ghostliness of it all: I thought of drowned sailors and wondered if, perhaps, these horrid formless streaks of grey were not the ghosts of them escaping for a few delirious moments from their eternal entombment in the wet fathomless depths. I did not at all like the supernatural affinity these formless grey shapes stirred in me. The whining shrieks, the long drawn-out moans, and the shrill demented whistles of the wind had a tormented sound of things inhuman yet human . . . long dead, yet living . . . seeking escape and never finding it. When a flying scud of grey spume struck me in the face with slinging feathery froth I felt enveloped by the unknown and staggered back as if from some foul embrace. Recovering myself I spread my hands over my face and hair to wipe away the horrid wetness.

I was trembling from the cold and shuddering from my fantastic imaginings and the feelings they brought of unrelated desolation; my teeth began to strike against one another uncontrollably. Knowing I must get below to shelter immediately, I gave myself a reassuring shake and dived quickly back through the companion hatch. With the feel of the black darkness underneath me my nerve for the return to the hold nearly left me; I managed to hold on to it just long enough to start my slow downward journey.

When I got to the bottom and felt the wool under my feet, I crawled along on my hands and knees thinking to try to find my recess again without using one of my two remaining matches, but I had not gone far when the painful blackness and gyration of the vessel lost for me all sense of direction; I found that the utter darkness was hurting my eyes in much the same way that too strong sunlight or snow-glare can do, and every now and then I had to shut them to find relief in the swimmy purple that came when I closed my lids. Striking a match with enormous care, for they were Chilean matches and not to be trusted, I took a good look around to find my direction, and before the match went out lit one of the spills I had made out of pages from my tally-book. In the strong air-currents, this was not very good but just enough to help me to find my way back to my hole. Teaseling out some more wool, I re-wrapped myself and lying back tried to sleep.

I could feel the weather moderating to a strong gale, but with this the ordinary groans and creaks from the straining ship became more noticeable and from far distant parts of her came muffled rendings and now and again sharp reports as she complained and threatened. Lying there in my cubby-hole, I felt again the hostility and as the mysterious noises gathered force, I began to have a terrible feeling that I was not alone. I knew there was nobody else on board, but my imagination was leading me on to explore in visual thought the cavernous, dank emptiness of her other holds and passageways; as I did so it seemed to me more than ever that although I was certain there was no other human on board, nevertheless I could not be free of the feeling that everything in the ship was not inanimate. My imagination was racing; it seemed to me that something was closing in on me with unspeakable menace. I felt the uttermost need to guard myself from some dread discovery which might with blinding speed penetrate my healthy armour. I felt the drag of horrid invitation from this unknown beastliness and fought against the evil entice-ment, for I knew that to pursue my search held unnatural danger. I was, I sensed, on the brink of discovery and suddenly felt enveloped with deadly fear and knew that I was encompassed all about me by something so mysterious and remote that if I perceived it clearly I would cease to live.

In my plunging prison I sensed the despairing urge for headlong physical flight and leapt to my feet for the second time this night to make a blind rush. I somehow managed to strangle my cry of fear . . . yet again through the roar of the gale, from immeasurable distance, came the thin ancestral message of courage, to hold me safe. . . . Relaxed, but weak and shaking, I tumbled back into my half-lying position and let the song bring me ease and confidence. As I did so knowledge came to me of slow recession—unwilling in its withdrawal —of the pressing danger. Nevertheless everything in me cried out for light. How much I needed light—I must use my last match . . . only light had meaning. . . . Trying to master the icy shake in my hands and body, in ecstasy with the promise of light I fumbled with scrabbling delving for my last match. Even as I did so, I knew that if I struck it I would destroy the last margin of safety which just this one unstruck match would give to me; but so great was my urge for light that I determined that whatever it cost me in the long dark hours ahead, I would have light now. I was in the act of willing my hands to steadiness to coax my flame when, our of nowhere, afar off, and from a great distance came a renewal, stronger now, of that shrill piping —the song of the family. . . . Once again I felt I was not really quite alone. . . .

Tension went out of me; comfort flowed into me, and putting the unlighted match back in its box, I wrapped the whole carefully in my handkerchief and packed it safely into my driest pocket. Leaning backwards, I lowered myself down again, easily now, and felt a tingling flush of natural warmth play over my cold body; with this came a slightly triumphant pleasantness of power in me to combat this threat from my dark prison. I think I must have drifted into a sort of reactionary coma, half-way between sleeping and wakefulness, and as usual with me when in this undefended state, I was assailed with great gusts and rushes of loving affection for my family, my thoughts speeding back to them in remorseful solicitude.

21. *The Dream*

As I twisted about on my hard bed of baled wool, marooned in the South Atlantic, vignettes of our family life kept jumping across the years and to and fro across my mind. My thoughts refused to leave them. I think it was instinct which told me to think of these things and using this absorption defend my mind against the threat of the shadowed living blackness of the hulk.

I saw again the attic Wilfred and I had used as a bedroom, with its undersized bed which we had to share. I remembered how, having been ordered by him to go to sleep, I would be unable to do so and would lie restless but not daring to move about, looking now and again towards Wilfred, whose dark round head I could see bent low over the improvised writing-table, ceaselessly writing and muttering to himself, the single guttering candle by which he was working throwing a grotesque and huge shadow on the steeply sloping ceiling. I did not mind so much when he was writing but when he was reading I found myself waiting, with held breath, for the turning of each page. From time to time I could lie still no longer; Wilfred without turning or stopping what he was doing would exclaim with savage irritation: 'Oh, do go to sleep, you stupid boy. I cannot work unless you do.' On other nights, he would pace the eight feet or so of the minute room, declaiming aloud or memorizing in a mumble. Hours later would come the painful business as he inserted his cold and shaking body into the bed; his chattering teeth would keep me awake after he himself had fallen into exhausted sleep. I felt again my seven-year-old sensations, when I lost my way going to school; or I was back again in the streets of Birkenhead being hunted by the gangs of little toughs.

Coming to myself again, I realized with startled surprise that I was still, of course, in the old hulk, thousands of miles away from where my thoughts had been taking me. With this realization I recommenced shuddering from cold and emptiness. I felt tension return as the unearthly noises from the creaking timber impacted afresh upon my senses and with the sound came an increase of the frightening sensation that I was not quite alone . . . with something like desperation, I drove my thoughts backwards . . . perhaps now it was the connection of intense cold which flighted them back to the cruel walks that my father made me do with him on bitter winter Sunday afternoons when I was a very small boy—those long treks deep into the country lanes and fields. The going outwards I liked, enjoying trotting along by my father's side, stamping on the cat ice in the puddles and ruts, smelling the rich sharp tang coming off the dunged fields carried by the winter vapour, the warm breathy smell of enclosed cattle as we skirted around stockyards and cowsheds.

Thinking how jolly and young he could be when he wasn't harassed, took me back to our skating expeditions which he would immediately start organizing if there looked like being the least possible chance of the ice bearing. Somehow or other he fitted all four of us up with skates. There was always great ado about matching them to boots, with borings and screwings and wedges here and there to make them nearly fit. His own pair, real beauties, of nickel-steel, were always brought out with great ceremonial—followed by the story of how he came to possess such a pair, then by the serious business of removing the protective Vaseline, the oiling and polishing until they were silver-bright, and finally by the *pièce de résistance* when my father would permit us, one by one, to run our thumbs along the plates and marvel at the fine accuracy of the cutting edge.

This excitement of the skating always galvanized Wilfred into splendid high spirits and if my father gave the word that ice was holding somewhere he would jump and rush about, cracking his fingers, laughing and working himself up into a fine and infectious joy, calling out to all of us for hurry and speed. It was, perhaps, the only thing for which he would readily and immediately drop his books—and, with them, his serious and abstracted air, becoming as hilarious and spiritedly youthful as the rest of us, deferring to my father's wishes and suggestions without his customary difficulty. My father, delighted over this genuine enthusiasm of Wilfred's, would respond spontaneously and we would all become immensely happy.

Best of all was the night skating when in the evening we set off by train for some more distant place. The bearing ice nearer home was all on ponds or pools or the canal, but when we went further afield it was always to a mere. From earliest remembrance, this name 'mere' —compared to pond, lake, or pool—had always enamoured me and lent to these expeditions a magical air: the short train journey, the walk down the country lanes, the ringing tune of our slung skates in the frosty darkness as they struck against one another, the uncertain journey across the mysterious fields until at last from deep in the bowl of the hills would come to us the thin-drawn whine and sharp resoundings of the complaining ice; and presently through the trees and woods we would catch sight of the gleam and twinkling glitter of the bonfires crackling and glowing on the mere's edge. If I could find a deserted part of the ice, I used to like skating slowly along with my head thrown back, just staring into the fathomless intensity above me. Then I would shoot off to find Colin. When I found him, we automatically linked hands and raced across the mere towards its swaying middle, giving froglike ungainly side-kicks as we did so to try to pick up the fastest possible speed, which was all we cared about. . . .

It must have been while my mind was back speeding across the frozen mere with Colin that troubled sleep took hold of my flagging body. I remember hearing distant sharp reports as the wind struck afresh at the straining hulk that was imprisoning me; but I could not be sure if they were the sharp, snapping sounds of the ice splitting on my Welsh mere at home or if they were being torn out of the entrails of the senile old vessel by the mad fantasia of the shrieking wind as it hurtled and blasted its uncontrolled and diabolic course over my head. The roaring of it all was bludgeoning my brain and just before hypnotic sleep gripped hold of me, I knew that I did not care.

In my sleep, phantasmal dreams came to me. I soared up to immense and terrifying heights only to be plummeted down again into unspeakable depths. Cold horrors crept close about me. I felt the thresh and struggle of my legs and arms as I sought desperately to regain my wakeful body; but I could not waken and presently it seemed that I slid away from myself and in fearful loneliness found that I was isolated in a strange bleakness—a bleakness which was veritable and in it no life lived; all around me was cold hard rock, split and riven into deep fissures and vast celestial craters; a desolation and feebleness of spirit encompassed me and I knew I was utterly alone in a dead and petrified world. With mounting fear I could feel my body hardening into icy paralysis. If help did not come to me, I, too, would petrify into this world of unreality and become drained of all vitality. My eyes—seeking everywhere—roved over the lifeless desolation until, with a tiny shock of hope, I thought I heard straining through to my numbed hearing a flutelike call coming from infinite distance. My whole entity seized on this with hungry compulsion and gradually I felt the power of it drawing me until my eyes held fast to the most distant and highest mountain of rock. I saw mid-way up the hard, shining slope of this, a dark oval blotch and, still under my strange compulsion, I sensed it becoming clear to my gaze and, as it gradually focused into minute detail, I saw that it was the dark overhung entrance to a cave familiar to me in every way, so that I recognized every stone and every bit of loose rock and the smooth, sole-worn track leading down into its friendly, warm and smelly darkness. Between me and this cave I could feel a uniting cord stretching, straining and tense; my eyes became avid to hold and keep this invisible vibrating connection in this strange cold land of lifeless solitude. Presently in this dark hollow smudge, I saw movement, and out of the cavernous mouth crept two figures. At first, I could only recognize the movement, for with their emergence the whole mountain and its dark mark receded farther and farther, so that I began to fear that my tenuous bond with it would stretch and stretching too far—break; but, just as I knew this strange communication must give way to the fearful tension of the withdrawal, it held again and with this easement I could feel life and warmth coming back into my body. The two figures were specks now, but I could discern movement and I saw that they were climbing and sliding over the undulations of the mountainside in a frenzy of speed to come to my aid . . . and all the time the comforting, warming sound of the song of the family floated across on high-strung notes to put courage into my heart that was icy with desolation. . . .

As my straining eyes stared towards the tiny figures, diminutive with immense distance, they neared and grew larger and with this enlargement came familiarity which at first, except for its sense of succour, I could not determine until suddenly I saw they were my father and Wilfred. One of them was young and slim and the other old and thick and tough. The old tough one I thought was my father and the young short slender one was Wilfred. At the same time, I knew that neither of these small people was really either of them in actuality, for these two figures seemed centuries old and I knew that my father and Wilfred were young, as I myself was young and new. As they swiftly closed nearer, I could feel behind me some deadly approach of cold and diabolical evil. I knew that these strange figures who were my father and Wilfred—and yet were not my father or Wilfred—were racing towards me, pitting their speed and strength to intercept and fight this evil and save me from utter extinction . . . I sensed the extremity of my jeopardy but I could not move. As the two forces sped towards me I could feel a precursory shock as I waited for inevitable impact. From immobility I turned to rigidity: I was helpless in paralysis of terror. When they were nearly upon me I saw that their faces were queerly distorted and crumpled and although recognition remained with me they were yet strangely unfamiliar. Desperate for the comfort of absolute recognition, which I knew ought to be there, I sought the eyes of the elder and found in them the eyes of my father—fiercely narrowed, kindled with concern, and behind the flinty hardness a terrible anxiety. Seeking the younger, I caught for a fleeting second the warm, brown smile that was in Wilfred's eyes and the flash of his brilliantly white teeth. . . .

As I felt the evil behind me blow cold with nearness on my petrified spine and knew that devastating wickedness was closing upon me, the four arms of my father and Wilfred shot out to grasp me. They themselves were so close that I could feel their heaving pantings blowing on my cheeks. It was at that instant that a rending explosion tore up with splintering force from under our feet and with the noise of doom the rock beneath us opened up leaving a swiftly widening rift between us. In my sleep, I heard myself cry out with fear as the gap widened. I saw my strange father raise his hand in a spasmodic gesture of frightful warning; his mouth opened but no sound came to me. I saw my strange brother run backwards and I knew he was going to try to leap the awful ravine. My father did not move but I knew he was aware of Wilfred's intention; and as Wilfred came hurtling along to throw himself off his edge of the gulf to try and leap the impossible distance and land on my side, my father, still unmoving, waited; as Wilfred came abreast of him, about to hurl himself towards me, my father with a reflex action sprang and threw him to the rocky ground. Placing his foot on Wilfred's neck he braced his powerful short leg to pin him down. . . .

All this time he had not moved his eyes away from me. The

statuesque group they made was receding away from me now at an awful pace and as the distance grew so did the width of the black bottomless abyss which was opening between us. They were in one world and I was in another. I was riven with mortal disappointment and great stabs of fiery pain struck through me as I felt the loneliness of this tearing separation. I was tortured with the apprehension of catastrophic, unendurable loss and strove and thrashed to loosen my locked body from its thrall of paralysis. I cried out, but no sound came; only with my eyes could I follow them. It was with the coming of the instant in time when I knew I was about to lose them for ever and that the tensing thread connecting us would snap for all eternity, that I saw the minute figure that was my father, and yet was not, straighten up with a galvanic effort—which hurt me as I felt his strain; I saw his hands go up to cup his mouth in an agonizing effort to magnify a voice that was not there; his head went back, and obliteration came down upon him, but our thread of communication was twanging madly under the frantic exigence and pulling strain of separation, and down this thread from incalculable distance—not reedlike or faint, now, but strong and powerful, its euphony muted only by the immense distance of its source—came to me the song of the family which, gaining momentum as it swept towards me, trumpeted with shrill ecstasy, triumphant in release, victorious with its message of strength and life and power. As it cascaded about me, I felt its strength unlock my bonded body and life flow into me. With its high-pitched intensity ringing madly in my brain and blood, I knew that I was safe once more from the cold and deadly menace that had thrust its groping fingers so close about me. . . . In that instant I awoke and putting my hand out I was not surprised to feel the rough hessian of the bales of wool that made my prison bed in the reeling hulk.

I was trembling uncontrollably and very cold, but I was not afraid; deep fear had gone out of me and I could sense the recession of evil about me. The hulk was impotent now and with this absolute knowledge my immediate discomforts began to crowd about me. I longed intolerably for food and warmth. Visions and scents of steaming, savoury dishes tantalized me wretchedly and I longed to plunge my frozen body into heat and to feel the prickle of returning circulation.

I lay supine now, triumphantly savouring the exquisite relief of my escape from the demoniacal bondage of my dream; I sensed that the figures in my dreaming had receded far away, far out of reach of recall. I could not, now, hear the song yet strangely, without hearing it, I could still feel the deep music of it about me—the far-flung reeding, the strange ancestral cry—and feeling this strong about me, triumph drifted away from me and, as realization came upon me of just how little my own puny efforts had contributed to the conquering of the unknown fear of the hulk, awed humility took the place of my boyish pride and I started yet again to wonder about the strange choric communication which, travelling through the ether, could give to me such pure and powerful succour.

Lying down here buried in the heart of this black darkness and cradled in this eerie wildness, my thoughts jumped to another plane altogether; and, as I remembered the fluting calls that had come down to me along the aisles of time, I felt receptive and was, I think, acutely susceptive, so that I became conscious of a difference of thinking and with it came an overwhelming distaste—a distaste not for the work of the sea but for the crudities and conversational banalities that eroded deeply enough to stultify my everyday thinking. For a second or so I had another flash of alarm that I might be becoming priggish and intolerant, until a glow of realization warmed through me that this was not true and all that was really happening was that I was awakening from my environment and that perception was coming to me; and with this perception perhaps even some power of original thought and the infinite range of delicate mental adventure which this opened before me. This brought about in me a feeling of urgency—that time was passing too quickly—that I must do something about this, but just exactly what I did not know. I at once thought again of Wilfred and doing so thought I understood better something of his own pre-occupation with this frightening escape of time and his constant self-flagellation in his efforts to harness the fleeting moments to his needs; I wondered for some seconds if I was myself catching his disease, until with a wry grin I remembered my reputation for obtuseness. No, no, this did not seem quite likely. Immediately after this, reaction set in and I became dissatisfied and out of sorts with my thinking and my uncertainties. I fetched up a sigh and with some anger thought to myself that what I needed to allay these disturbing ideas was a trip to Rio or Valpo and a run around the streets of the whore-shanties, slapping the girls' thinly-clad tails as I went. Even as the thought formed itself, the very phraseology of it hit me hard as I realized how painfully synonymous it was with my seafaring environment. I could not—so short a time ago—have thought in words like this; it surely must be the result of the continuous banal quippings that constituted shipboard conversation. Whatever it was, I felt shame and distaste for myself and disgust to be any part of such vulgar pretence for conversation and thinking. What was happening to me? . . . were my nicer Uffington thoughts being suffocated by all this pornographic banality which I knew now was an integral element of shipboard life? I wondered again, was I becoming priggish? I still did not think so, it was something altogether different. Puzzled, I could not make up my mind. I only knew that sour revulsion pervaded me. Another reaction set in. I became conscious again of my immediate discomfort and started to shiver and shake with physical misery for it was still grim and horrid down here cooped up in my black hole with the utter darkness pressing against my eyes all the time; but I was easier now, with my wool wrappings and my curled-up position. I found I was generating a little warmth around me. I could feel, too, that the wind and sea were moderating and although it was still blowing hard the note of uncontrolled imbecility had gone out of the wind's frenzied escaping; the old hulk, although moaning and grinding under the surging stress, was riding more easily; the groaning crackings, dangerous shudderings, and snatched-short jarrings were much less frequent. I had no doubt now that she would ride it out without parting from her moorings or tearing open her ancient carcass. With the slight comfort I was feeling real sleep came upon me and dropped me into oblivion.

When I awoke, I knew that it was near daybreak. It was still dark but no longer black. Into the darkness had come a thinning, hardly noticeable; it was really only the release of the pressure on my eyeballs that told me that morning had come. As I rubbed and flexed my stiffened body, I could feel gentleness all around me; the hulk herself was almost still, only swaying with a cradling motion. Faintly from above me came the petulant screaming of the seabirds. I felt contented and lay idly waiting for the first glimmer of greyness that would release me from my blindness.

As I waited, it became increasingly important to me that I must not share this strange experience. I could not rid myself of the feeling that to do so would be a violation, and I determined to keep the bare fact that I had been benighted in the hulk a secret with myself alone.

It did not take me very long to realize how easy this was going to be. All I had to do was to time things rightly, so that when I showed myself on deck I could mingle with both the gangs that would soon be boarding the hulk for the morning's work. The gang from the shore would think I had come off the ship, and the crowd from the ship would think I had come aboard with the shore lighter. In the half-light and general early morning bad temper and confusion, I would pass unnoticed; so if I was careful to keep quiet and say nothing, my whereabouts during the night would—I was quite certain—never be questioned.

Into the thinning darkness of the hold a greyish light was stealing, so that I could dimly sense the bulky tiers of the stacked cargo. In a little while I was vaguely able to see. Partly by feel I found my way to the foot of the ladder; grasping it, I shambled up slowly for my muscles were stiff and aching and my hands had little feeling.

It was fine to be on deck again. Looking around me I saw that I was surrounded and shrouded with a white sea-fog, and for a few seconds I felt again the pierce of isolation; I found myself tensed and listening as I heard all about me an unnatural silence. No sound, now, of a quarrelling gull or any sad piping of the stormy petrels, only—besetting me—the impenetrable, soundless sequestration of the sea-mist. Glancing up to gauge the depth of the white pall, I saw spanned above me the incredibly motionless form of a splendid albatross. It was only his grey stillness that outlined his glorious wing stretch and separated him from the camouflage of the pearl-grey swirl of the sea-fog. Only his wicked head, out-thrust with the projection of his long, cruelly down-curving beak, showed any movement of the living and this only with infinite minuteness. The brilliant yellow of his mandible, as it quested almost imperceptibly, disassociated itself in an extraordinary manner from the wraithlike shadow of his body as he hung suspended above me, supported by moveless skill. He was altogether spectral, so intense was his emanation of independence of animate effort. His pale, white eye stared malignantly through me, so that something about his ghoulish unwinking regard made me uncomfortable and I longed to drive him away. But seafaring superstition was strong in me and I feared to offend him; instead, I moved across the deck. When I looked up again he was still over me, in exactly the same position. I wondered if he had been there all night, his all-seeing eye penetrating wood and iron to lay me bare.

Across the ghostly waters, with sudden sharpness, came short fussing hoots from a tug. Moments later, came the long-drawn, melancholy roar from my own ship. I knew that my release was near at hand. In a few minutes I would be out of my strange, ethereal world and back again in the bustle and blasphemy of ship-work. I looked up to bid my weird companion the albatross farewell but without sound he had vanished. I had the feeling that I was looking pinched and white about the face, and set about beating my arms and stamping my feet to try and make myself more normal-looking before the working parties came aboard. Timing my appearance with some thought, my plan worked as I expected it would, and by mingling with both crews my presence passed without comment.

Only the Third Officer gave me a second look, and, as he did so, remarked:

'My God, young Owen, you look awful. What have you been doing? Making a night of it? I had no idea you could in such a god-forsaken port. What did you find? A bloody fat little Tierra Del Fuegan, I suppose.'

Edgy with fatigue and in order to change the subject, I snapped back:

'Shut up, for Christ's sake, and give me a cigarette.'

'Certainly, certainly—no offence meant, so don't get all touchy. If you could only see yourself—all big-eyed and white-faced—I mean to say, anybody might think you'd spent the night adrift in an open boat or something. Here, take a cigarette. Damned if I can fathom you sometimes, Owen.'

'Thanks.'

'Sorry, but I haven't got a match. And I'll bet you haven't either.'

'Oh, yes, I have. I never, never leave myself without a light.'

In a nice attempt to cheer me up, he struck a facetious note with:

'Ha, ha. Our tough young Fourth all afraid of the dark, maybe. Ha, ha.'

'Maybe, Third, maybe. Quien sabe. Quien sabe.'

'Well, well, get out of sight to smoke that cigarette. And for God's sake don't set us all on fire. Perhaps your night ashore has made you forget you are in a wool ship.'

Scrambling down to the next deck, I made my way for'ard, well out of sight of everyone, and with the match-box in my hand, fingered for the solitary inmate. For a moment I studied its bright pink stalk and yellow head; then, with glorious abandon and a fine nonchalance, I struck. As it spurted into smoky flame, I savoured to the full my little self-made conversational drama with the Third a few moments ago. With exquisite pleasure, I drew the smoke of his cigarette deep into my lungs. As the smoke slowly escaped from me, so did some of my curious sensations evaporate with it. Taking my time I finished my cigarette and when I had carefully stamped it out I sprang for the ladder. Once more, I had become the uncomplicated young Fourth Officer. I shinned up the ladder at great speed and with enormous gusto set about hazing up the work of the cargo gangs. My driving brought about a remonstrance from the Third but I did not care; I was determined to get this last bit of cargo broken out—even if the speed of the hemp running through the blocks brought smoke from the sheaves. Quite soon the men themselves were infected and enthusiasm ran high. As we slammed and rattled the last bale over the side, a little cheer went up. We had cleared cargo in record time.

That evening in our own ship, after battening down hatches and securing all round, we shortened anchors and in the dying light from an unseen sun, slid out into the grey wastes of water, our thumping engines and churning propellor making a comforting sound against the cold whistle of the rising wind. I had the watch below going out, but something—strangely impelling—made me go up on deck for a last look at the old hulk.

The walling darkness was enclosing everything quickly, but I could just make out the heaving wallow of her lifeless body and the grotesque truncation of her mutilated masts. Every now and then, as she lurched more heavily, her single great spar would point upwards like some thin black finger of doom. As she righted herself again, spar and amputated mast would combine to form a freakish cross, unmoral in its disproportionate and stark ugliness. With a shriek the wind swept between me and this monstrous emblem, laden with snow and frozen rain, blinding me as I stared through the driving whiteness. I blinked hard to clear my vision, but I had seen my last of her. She was gone.

I groped my way below to my quarters and, as I went, the smells of my own living ship smote at me—the pungency of burning fat and bad cooking, the reek of hot engine oil, the tang of singeing waste as some fireman caught his sweat-rag on the white-hot fire-bars, and the indescribable odour of drying ship's paint.

Staggering to my cabin, I threw myself on my bunk and, as the pulsing throb of the engines stole my consciousness away, I knew that their rheumatic grindings were driving me out of cold seas and snow and blizzard, and that we were heading for the sun and blue water— Bahia Blanca, the glory of the lovely Rio de Janeiro, Santos, Buenos Aires, and Pernambuco, later the Canaries, London, Swansea, Liverpool—and home.

22. Panama Zone

I was looking forward very much to the excitement of going through the Canal and thought what luck it was to have hit a ship bound through so soon after it had been opened.

I had heard tales of the great heat sometimes encountered hereabouts, and now and again a qualm or two would grip me. The Calcutta episode was still very fresh in my memory and sometimes, if I was very heated and over-tired, my imagination would run riot with me and I would dread with liveliest horror any possibility of a recurrence of the semi-conscious nightmare experience which I had gone through in India.

However, it did not bother me overmuch, and I was able to reassure myself by thinking that no ill-effects had come from my walks through the burning afternoon heat of the streets of Havana, Puerto Rico, and Jamaica, or of my long days on blistering iron decks in other ports with no degrees of latitude. I rather welcomed the idea of the Canal Zone and afterwards the trip to Guayaquil in Ecuador which I knew was bang on the equator and, in the everyday patter of our ships, reputed to be the hottest spot on earth. Although I was pretty confident and not really giving much thought to it all, I did somehow feel that if, as I knew I should, I could survive these tests, I would then be able to forget for ever all about temperatures and possible consequences.

I liked both Colon—chiefly perhaps because it contained a strong American (North American that is) influence which I had not encountered before—and its twin town of Cristobal where we docked in readiness for our entrance into the Canal. I did not have long ashore here. I got the impression of mushroom growth, mostly I expect through the extraordinary juxtaposition of extremely modern American-type square, box-like houses planted down, as it were, in the middle of bush and jungle. Great palm trees and smaller, over-luxuriant jungle growth remained or shot up in most unlikely places; the roads were unfinished, and there was much dereliction everywhere. There were not, I think, any big buildings except the Government structures and the great pile of the uncompleted Washington Hotel, standing isolated in open space.

Cristobal was altogether more colonized, and here it was that the immense army of Canal employees and railway workers had their thousands of dwellings and lived their lives. Colon impressed me most, I think, because of its conglomeration of framework buildings; everything it seemed to me was constructed in squares and rectangles; nowhere could I find a pleasant curve or a rounded surface. I kept on being reminded of the skeleton-cube that I had drawn so often in the Shrewsbury School of Art. The Aveneda de Paez was perfectly straight and, looking up the built-up side, the impression was of hundreds and hundreds of perpendicular posts running up from the outside edge of the pavement to the eaves of the three- or four-storied buildings. This was due to the system of verandaing insisted upon in the architecture. It all gave me the impression of perspective gone mad; this was accentuated by the formal iron railings which ran along the opposite side enclosing some sort of plaza.

Cristobal's Third Avenue was entirely different and as soon as I saw it I burst out laughing; it reminded me so much of a collection of gigantic meat-safes. Actually the houses were constructed just as food-safes might be, with everything enclosed. The outer shells of all the houses were constructed of fine wire mosquito-proof metal mesh. The effect was further heightened by the fact that every building was raised a foot or two from the ground and supported by brick or concrete blocks here and there. This hitting symmetrical severity was, however, rapidly being overcome by the return of the bush and everywhere it seemed to me there was evidence of the jungle's determina-. tion to overwhelm the work of man. Suckers from felled trees sprouted between cement cracks; gross coarse-leaved pulpy looking plants flourished in the oddest places; strangling vines put out their indestructible tentacles with rapacious swiftness and, towering over all, palm trees top-heavy with attenuation swayed with a gentleness that was almost indiscernible or drooped over in stupefying lethargy —statuesque in their absolute stillness. To stare at this immobility was surprisingly disconcerting.

There was an airless humidity about Colon and Cristobal which I did not like, so I was glad when orders came for us to get under way. Leaving Cristobal, we steamed across Limon Bay and, taking aboard our Canal pilot, entered the great Gatun Lock which was to raise us bodily eighty-five feet above our present sea-level. I was not mechanically minded, and the gigantic engineering feat which screamed out its triumph all about me left me vaguely interested but without any thrills of technical excitement. In this I was unlike our engineer officer who talked of and speculated on nothing else. I did, though, like very much the idea of the ship being lifted up wholesale and the sensation of proceeding through a continent by means of a narrow, water-filled cut only about one hundred yards wide, channelled through the mountains.

For eight or nine miles, near Culebra, I think, these mountains lifted themselves to such heights that the whole effect of the great engineering work was dwarfed; so that, to me anyway, the whole thing had the appearance of a child's set of constructional toys—an effect absurdly heightened by the electric-powered 'mules'. These fussed up and down with much the same action as a clockwork plaything, all of which was further exaggerated by the unfinished untidiness which was evident everywhere—broken masonry, scattered railway lines, and a general strewing of disorder, which was astonishingly reminiscent of a children's nursery; only the mountains seemed real.

It was not the marvels of construction that gripped me, but rather what was still left, untouched, after the engineers had had their way. Most especially I was intrigued by the floating islands which slewed about in the lakes and larger stretches of water, so that we had to attend carefully to our navigation and frequently had to alter course to avoid running into them. These floating islands exercised a strange fascination over me, especially when they bore down on us in the golden, dust-laden glory of the setting sun. As they loomed up in the cloaking light, they took on themselves a luminous detachment which was beautiful. There was something altogether enchanting about these masses, disassociated as they were from sea or land; I had the feeling of sliding through fairyland. They varied from little more than smallish lumps of grass-covered earth and low half-submerged areas of water-logged weed and scrub, to large pieces of land with great timbers and palms still growing on them; some of these appeared to be disintegrated bits of forest, dense with trees, which in their turn were entangled in their own parasitic ropes of jungle vegetation. Watching them drift and sidle about in the oily-looking, slightly steaming water, I had a sudden queer realization of their complete disassociation from the world of man. Here were moving, growing, living masses, entirely independent of humanity. As the nearer ones drifted closely past, the living silence of them impinged on me acutely and an uncomfortable realization swept over me of the minuteness and inconsequential insignificance of my own self. In my untutored way, I was savouring the proportionate lack of importance, and indeed lack of need for the existence of human beings in the vast universal scheme.

I remember being slightly startled by this extraordinary revelation.

It was the first time that any thought had occurred to me to disturb my conception that all existence and the presence of the seas and the mountains, the volcanoes, the rivers, the vast concourse of animals, the mute but virulent life of vegetation could be anything except dependent upon, and in all ways secondary to, mankind. I had no unpleasant sensation of insecurity but, rather, a great marvelling and wonderment.

As I stood the middle watch that night on the bridge of my ship, landlocked midway between the grey Atlantic and the blue Pacific, pleasantly freed from responsibility by the presence of our Canal pilot, I was able to stare around and upwards into the smoky loveliness of the tropical night; and, staring like this, something of the utter profundity of great space and distance wrapped itself about me; so beautiful were the stars that night that I felt a most profound sensation of insignificance but I could not look away from the lacy cobweb veil of glittering fire that filmed the immensity of throbbing blueness. As my relief came up and I turned to go below to my bunk, I had a curious tingling sensation of being nothing at all. Perhaps my disturbance over the proportion of things may have biased my outlook; whatever it was, my original lack of feeling for the grandeur of the monumental engineering achievement remained, and with it the extraordinary impression I had about it all persisted—of a child at work with its bricks, toy gantries and trains.

We did not get through without mild misadventures for our ship, and one or two personal ones for myself. The first one of my own happened—it was a Sunday morning, I remember—when for some reason or other we had had to drop anchor in the middle of the Gatun Lake. We were encased in a windless, steaming heat, with the temperature soaring towards the 120's. Bored and limp with listlessness I suddenly thought it would be nice to swim. The water, in its stillness of surface, looked like hot oil, turgid and coppery-red with discoloration from the infiltration of disturbed sun-parched sub-soil. It did not look at all inviting but anything, I thought, was a better alternative to this slow broiling on the decks. Climbing down the pilot-ladder, I struck out, thinking to swim lazily around the ship—a pastime I was much addicted to whenever we were anchored. This custom of mine always caused considerable derisory comment and much good-natured banter from the ship's company. Mostly some of them would follow my course around on deck, shouting ribald encouragement or rude remarks about my graceless plunging for, although swimming anywhere at any time was one of my chief delights, try as I would I never achieved much dexterity.

At first I did not notice the warmth of the water; after the yellow scorch of the sun that had burned me on deck, the liquid lave of the water seemed pleasant. It was not until I was half-way round that I began to realize that the water was not only warm but hot—much hotter than a hot bath. A cooked sensation overcame me; my breathing, from being laboured, rapidly turned to painful gasping and all my strength drained away. I was now on the wrong side of the ship for the ladder. All I could do was to let out a feeble squeak for help; but looking up the sheer black iron side I saw that the deck was deserted. I knew, then, that my only hope was the anchor cable. It was half the ship's length away by now but I was just able to turn towards it and as I turned I knew at once that I should never be able to reach it.

Again I looked up the black smooth cliff that was the ship's side in the hope of seeing some movement on deck that I could hail for help, but desertion was complete; the impervious lifelessness of the gaunt ship was alarming and little darts of fear were starting to strike into me. I was exerting all my remaining strength to tread water, but in spite of this my head was dipping below the hot oily surface. Soon the fear seemed to be slipping away and in its place a warm, contented lethargy engulfed me in extreme lassitude. I remember a strange green luminosity prevailing all about me and a gentle fading of all reality. I realized I was happily conscious of the absolute unimportance of anything that could now happen. . . .

It was the wet, slapping sting of a heaving line cutting across my face and a voice above screaming at me 'hold on for Christ's sake,' that gingered me into actuality and sufficient galvanization to make a frantic effort to wrap the line around my chest before I melted to limpness. In a few moments I felt myself being bumped and flopped like a dead fish up the iron plates of the ship's side. This and some very inexpert artificial respiration, which amounted mostly to angry cuffs and buffetings from the Chief Officer, brought me out of my daze. Actually I had taken very little water into me; it was the heat of the lake which had affected me and not a near-drowning condition. In five minutes I was myself again. The Chief Officer—perhaps to make up for his over-rough handling of me, for we were good friends—told me afterwards that I had bent a good seamanlike bowline around myself. This bit of unusual praise pleased me so much that I felt, on the whole, the escapade was not to be regretted.

In half-an-hour, in the excitement of getting under way again, I had forgotten all about it.

We did not get very far through the Panama Canal before we got seriously stuck: just ahead of us a landslide roared down with a rattle of splintering rock. Our ship was completely trapped; we could neither go ahead nor astern. We were to remain landlocked like this for thirteen or fourteen days. It must I think, have been in or near the Culebra Cut, most likely between San Pablo and the Pedro Miguel locks—I can't quite remember.

It was fearfully hot, but all the same I thought it rather fun that our ship should be so tightly jammed up like this, especially as I saw chances of getting ashore at nights. Nights of dark loveliness that I could perhaps possess and make my own—away from the ship and the men in her—long hours by myself of wandering about hoping for small adventures; or if these did not come along I should always have the fine uplifting sensation of complete freedom that I knew would come to me, and with this the release that I could never find on board. If nothing exciting or even interesting happened to me I could, I knew, always enjoy the simple silver beauty of the tropical sky. There was a lot of talk amongst the ship's company about shore leave not being permitted, due to the strictness of the United States Zonal supervision; I saw for myself evidence of this around me.

I write this from memory only, for I did not make notes and neither then nor at any other time did I keep a diary.

Not intending to be incarcerated by the United States of America for fourteen dreary days I began casting my eyes about me and reconnoitring my chances of getting ashore to explore the country beyond. In my young English way I had little respect for formalities and regulations of any sort—and none whatsoever for frontiers. I set so much store upon these solitary expeditions that I was quite determined, if we were going to be stuck here for some time, to get myself a night or two of freedom ashore. In the day-time I readily accepted my role as the young hard-case ship's officer and indeed rather revelled in it but I had found yet again that I was coming more and more to rely for peace of mind upon these nights ashore when I could be entirely alone; it was only in them that I could find release. I looked forward with intense delight to these sojourns, savouring the solitary tranquillity that I knew would come to me immediately I was away from the ship and quite alone.

At these times I had the strangest sensation that everything about me really belonged to me, the luminosity of the night, the blaze of silver and gold from the throbbing sky, the clean sharp cold lights of distant cities, or the nearby glow of warm, foreign, friendly villages, all made lovely by the rich and gleaming cloak of tropical darkness, the creamy sibilance of warm seas washing over hot pebbled beaches . . . all of this and much more I found was mine for the taking; but I also quickly discovered I must never allow any other person to share this enchantment. If I did, the magic—so entwining was it with solitariness—disappeared. These nights had to be something which I must always keep for myself.

I soon, however, made another discovery; that it was necessary to explain what it was that I did with myself when I went off so much alone. In this ship, we were I remember an unusually hard-case crowd and like all such ships every member was expected to give some account of his doings, most especially of any adventures of the night. This at first presented itself as a real difficulty. In a crew such as this any attempt to explain that I just liked walking about alone would have been met with hoots of derision and the merest suggestion of an attempt to explain the magic enchantment of it all would not only have bewildered them but made them all quite certain that I was rapidly going out of my mind. I knew that something must be done and done quickly if my delight in these solitary excursions was to be safeguarded. This difficulty remained until I hit on the splendid idea of always returning ready prepared with the narration of some adventure which they would understand, the more sensuously told the better. With practice I found little difficulty and as time went on became more graphic. This constant dissembling was an irritating nuisance to maintain but to ensure my freedom at night I thought it well worth while.

Presently confirming news came through to the ship that we would be stuck where we were for an indefinite time, probably fourteen days or more. I was hoping very much that I should not be allocated to night duty; if this happened I should only have the insufferable day-time to idle through and none of the plans I was so carefully laying to explore the country outside the American Zone would come to anything.

Nothing much stands out of the monotonous boredom of this heat-soaked inertia, except my successful escape out of United States occupied territory which gave me my night of penetration into the wild country of the Indians. In order to while away the welter of burning idleness during my first day of day duty, for we could do no

ship's work, I spent my time spying out and forecasting my chances
for a night ashore in the forbidden Columbian Indian country lying
outside the American Zone. As I paced up and down the hot well-
deck my roaming eye made short work of actually getting off the
ship. I possessed the supreme physical confidence of my age; I was
not to know until many years later, that the innocent enough action
which led me to cross over the guarded United States demarcation
line might have led to international tensions. When my opportunity
came along a few days later I was quick to seize my chance. All my
previous planning of the subterfuge necessary to get me out of the
canal zone focused itself most obligingly. I found I had only to put
into practice what I had already rehearsed.

The sun gone, I went below to await my chance to slide like a
shadow and glide as I hoped unseen off the ship. My plans worked
out very much as I thought they would and I slid ashore without
difficulty, the companionship of the blue-black darkness giving me
friendly cover. Creeping along silently on plimsolled feet, moving
noiselessly into the blackness, I heard the heavy footsteps of what I
thought might be a United States patrol; a momentary pause in the
measured tread made my heart miss a beat. I held my breathing and
froze. In a moment or two the reassured pacing continued again and
with a noiseless expulsion of my caught-up breath I went forward
into the cloaking obscurity of the night.

I had a fine feeling of freedom, pleasantly prickled with excitement
over walking into this forbidden ground. I was inside the Indian
territory; how I was to get back to my ship in the morning must be
left to itself. It was enough for me at this moment that the night was
mine. It was hot and dark but the glitter from the stars was just
beginning to give a luminous transparency to the darkness; I thought
that quite soon I should be able to see fairly well. Finding what felt
like a trodden track, I wandered along it enjoying the sensation of
not knowing where it might lead. One path led into another in a
most confusing way but one of these gradually drew me into a
deepening bush forest; as the density increased, I noticed the track
itself widened and underfoot I could feel deep ruts made by the
wooden disc wheels of primitive carts.

It seemed to be getting lighter all the time but perhaps my eyes were
adjusting themselves to the darkness. Presently I became unpleasantly
conscious of sounds coming from the forest—barely audible rustling
pad-paddings—which seemed to come from close inside the edge of

the bush parallel with me, but just a little in the rear. I began thinking rather hastily what wild animals might inhabit this part of the world and to realize that this was something to which I had given no thought at all. I stopped and listened but as soon as I stopped the following steps stopped too; walking on I heard again the rustling steps synchronizing with my own; I wondered if it was some freak echo but I could not convince myself for I could feel I was being followed; every ten yards or so I would abruptly stop, and motionless I would listen, but always the same thing happened—immediately I became still the shadowing padfalls ceased. . . . It was eerie walking through the strangeness of the night; the gentle following of the two animals one on either side only just behind me sent little prickles of disturbance through me, but I did not feel really alarmed. Although I disliked being followed like this I did not feel it was dangerous. I had been walking for an hour or two still accompanied by my unseen companions when, stopping to listen, I felt little puffs of forest wind come tumbling along behind me. Borne on them I could scent the strong odour of cat. I instantly recalled stories I had heard of some species of large jungle cat whose curious habit it was to stalk human beings through the bush for many hours on end. I was certain now that my unseen followers must be two of these harmless creatures; I felt friendly towards them and grateful to them for their proffered companionship.

A little later, I saw through the trees the diffused glow from a fire. I knew this must be either an Indian village or an encampment of one of the nomad tribes of Spanish Indians. I stopped, assailed by momentary qualms about going forward. I suddenly remembered I was very much alone but as so often happened with me my intense curiosity and eagerness to meet strange peoples overcame any temerity; I walked on. After a few minutes I noticed something was different . . . my friendly escort of cougars had left me. I listened for retreating padfalls but no sound came. Silently I raised my hand and waved them goodbye.

I did not want to come on to the village unheralded, thinking this might not be wise; so I scuffled my feet and started up my whistling. As soon as I did this some mongrel dogs rushed towards me barking madly but not, I thought, resentfully. Coming into the firelit clearing I saw that I had walked into a small community of Indian people; they were squatting in a circle around their fire. I stood hesitant on the fringe of firelight; if they were surprised to see me they showed little signs of it. Instead with exquisite courtesy they rose up and with beckoning motions made it unmistakably clear that they were inviting me to join their circle. They were, I saw, in the middle of a meal, eating from a communal cooking-pot which was simmering on the glowing wood ash. Making room for me they motioned me to be seated. One of the women produced a calabash bowl, filled it with food from the pot, and with grave diffidence offered it to me; to express my appreciation better I took a piece from the bowl and commenced to eat whereupon they all set to again, unhurriedly eating from the steaming vessel with their hands. I was entranced to be sharing their meal with them, but I was disconcerted by their extraordinary gravity. I tried out my bits of Spanish and while I got polite responses they were quite unsmiling; suddenly I felt rather out of things sitting there with my solitary calabash while they were fishing away with their fingers. Making tentative signs I sought their permission to join them and eat like them from the skillet. At first this was not understood and only resulted in more food being put in my bowl, so presently with much diffidence I stretched my hand over the stewed food and looking around to be sure I was committing no breach of etiquette I picked up a bit and made signs to my mouth. The effect was magical, excited chattering broke out, smiles rippled and spread all around the circle, they stopped their own eating and vied with each other to delve and fish for choice morsels which they carefully swam to within my reach; satisfied that I was well supplied they recommenced themselves. Now it was a feast full of gaiety and rollicking humour; the small children—whom I suspect had been driven into the bush at my approach—were recalled. They came tumbling in, their oily little bare brown bodies glistening in the firelight as they wriggled between us waiting for scraps to be thrown to them. They were not at all shy and were soon clambering all over me eager for the legs of lizards or fillets of frogs and parts of other small creatures that I thought made up the bubbling stew, but it was a savoury mixture mostly of herbs and roots; I was enjoying it all immensely. When we had finished eating, the women and children withdrew. I did not see the women again but as it transpired later three or four of the children—from three to six years of age—were to sleep with me all night. The men one by one went off, to come back again with home-made musical instruments, and after heaping brushwood on to the fire they started making rather pathetically sweet, soft music. I was completely enchanted by this and entranced with these small brown people's simplicity and niceness; I was sorry when I felt I ought to say good-bye and leave them. Making the necessary signs I prepared to do this but they were insistent that I should stay with them; they took me to a freshly constructed bivouac of branches with a bed of forest undergrowth.

I was afraid though of going to sleep because I knew I had somehow to get back to my ship in the canal. Our tremendous conviviality had broken down our language difficulties and with signs and mimicry together with odd Spanish-Indian words we were able—if not to converse—to understand each other. I conveyed to them somehow the importance of my returning unseen to the ship, and they in turn promised to awaken me and guide me back almost to within sight of the canal. We ended up with enormous laughter, for to underline what would happen to me if I was caught going back, I used the universal sign of drawing my finger across my throat. This for some reason they thought extremely funny and in between staggering bouts of laughter kept on using the sign on themselves. When they recovered they gently shepherded me into the bivouac. I lay down and before the men had left, the three or four little naked children crawled in to share my bed. I pointed to them but with friendly grins the Indians only shrugged and opened their palms wide to show me they could do nothing about it. I lay down and with a baby across my chest and two or three more across my body, I was soon asleep. Before the light broke the Indians came for me and after gently removing the sleeping infants led me through the forest to a point where I could safely make my attempt to get aboard again unseen.

I succeeded.

23. *The Madam*

I suppose it was around about now that another stroke of professional good fortune came to me. We were I think in Bahia Blanca or Rio de Janeiro; in the ship I was in at this time we were carrying a Third Officer, a Scandinavian, a first-class seaman with a square-rigged Master's certificate. He had served many years in sail, at one time commanding a full-rigged ship. Physically he was without exception the toughest man I have ever met. He was not a big man but just to look at him gave an astonishing impression of enormous strength; in some curious way he emanated an astounding capacity for toughness and endurance and this was especially noticeable in his hands which, even when idle, gave out this almost frightening

impression of unnatural strength. He was rough and in every way
unpolished, yet in some odd way this not only did not seem to matter,
but became entirely lost sight of when sailing in a ship with him. So
powerfully was this impellent strength of his forged into his personality—it seemed for the sole purpose of discharging this aura of vital
physical supremacy and unquestionable bodily courage—that his
simple but obvious uncouthness became strangely unimportant and
could not matter. I think it unlikely that I ever sailed with a finer seaman nor yet one with whom I became a closer friend. From our first
meeting we were attracted to one another and our strong liking for
each other remained staunch for the short—too short—time we were
together. He was not an alcoholic but he was given to devastating
bouts of heavy drinking; during these he would become violent and
dangerously uncontrollable. None of these periodic spells of maniacal
drinking ever affected the resilient toughness of his seaman's body,
but of course they jeopardized his career; he was not always able to
control the attacks and confine them to times and places where they
would not matter, and as a consequence his career was always set
back and often came near to ruin. A lesser seaman would have been
beached and deprived of his certificates years before but somehow his
magnificent courage and superb seamanship made all captains loath
to 'break' him; in every case these indisputable qualities caused loop-
holes to be found for him through which he could escape and avoid
final relegation to the land. It was while we were in one of these ports
that he became overwhelmed by another of his bouts of furious
drinking. Our Captain once again gave him a chance, with the
ultimatum that he must take himself ashore and 'disappear'. A return
to the ship could only mean he would be irrevocably broken. This in
itself was all right for he was well able to look after himself in the
tightest spot—except one, at sea before the mast in a 'bad' sailing
ship, caught for a year or even more. It was into just this very plight
that—in besotted recklessness—he had plunged himself when, to
save his certificates, he had walked over our gangway.

Lying in the port was a large four-masted sailing ship loaded and
ready to sail but held up for lack of crew. She had a wicked reputation for being a bad ship, as indeed she was; in consequence she
always sailed short-handed. Her food was bad, her captain and mates
were known the world over for brutal driving bullies. She was not
English. Our Third in drunken bravado had signed on to her as an
able-seaman, but worse than this had gone aboard taking with him
all his money and gear including his sextant and other navigational

instruments, all his papers and his certificates. He had dumped all this in the fo'c'sle and with enough money in his pocket—but nothing else—had walked ashore to blind himself with alcohol for two days before sailing.

Word came to our ship: not from the Third himself—he was by this time incapable of any action—but from the Madam of the house where he had gone to do his drinking. He was well known and also well liked by this woman, as he was by many other Madams in many other ports. He preferred to go on his bouts of hard drinking in these houses, well knowing that in his incapacity he would be looked after instead of being stripped, if not knifed, if he was adrift in the water-front dives. In moments of lucidity he must have talked of having got himself caught for this ill-famed square-rigger. The Madam, greatly concerned, set about getting word to our ship: not—like the wise women she was—to the captain or officers, which could only in the difficult circumstances have complicated things but to us, the half-deck apprentices, with pleadings that we must somehow retrieve his gear from the sailing ship and bring it to her establishment; this done, she would be responsible for fixing up the Third when he came out of his alcoholic paralysis. If we did not succed in this, she would have to ship him aboard to sail before the mast in this 'bad' ship rather than let him lose his certificates.

It was a formidable task that faced us. We well knew that this disreputable, short-handed ship would never let go one of her hard-come-by sailors without a fight. The Third Officer was in the clutches of his alcoholic oblivion; in his sea-chest was everything that he would not only need, but must have, to get for himself another berth as Third or Fourth Officer in some decent ship. The mates of the sailing ship knew quite well—from long experience—that our Third dared not be separated from his papers. As long as they could keep these on board, sooner or later they would have him as well; even if he was incapable of getting himself aboard they could count on some of his friends doing this for him, conscious or unconscious, as indeed the Madam proposed to do if we failed to wrest his things out of the ship.

Stratagem in the first move seemed our only hope; an attempt at open, defiant assault could never succeed. The essential thing was to gain access to the inside of the fo'c'sle before alarming the ship. Our first step was to organize a raiding party. This was not difficult for the Third was liked and admired by the crew; we were able to pick our sailors and getting together we worked out a plan. We decided we would sneak up quietly and separately to the sailing ship and muster in a dark corner of warehousing just out of sight of her. Three o'clock in the morning would be the best time; our own ship would be quiet and so would the other. When we had collected together near the ship we would send forward two sailors letting them walk openly over the gangway with orders to engage the watchman with excited talk of someone climbing aboard over the poop. Specifically designating the poop was a last minute touch which, if our sailors played their part well, would take the three of them as far as possible away from the bows. It was on to the bows that the rest of us intended to drop silently; then stealing up to the fo'c'sle doors, we would fling them open and rush the ship's crew, grab the sea-chest and the other small gear of the Third's, and flee the ship with, we hoped, as little damage as possible to ourselves.

The sea-chest was the problem; the small gear did not matter. We knew that it would be impossible to outrace the crew of the sailing ship with such a cumbersome thing. Instead of attempting this, we planned that once we had seized the heavy box, encircling it in a body we would force our way out of the fo'c'sle, scramble across the decks, charge the gangway, and putting on a sprint run like mad for the cover of the dockside buildings. If we could arrive here still in possession, we planned without in any way checking our pace to drop it in the dark corner where we had congregated before the attack. The two men detailed for 'looking after' the watchman were to keep in hiding until we had drawn the chase away from where the chest would be lying—we hoped unnoticed—among the piled crates of cargo. When we were well away, the two men who were 'dealing' with the watchman were to pick it up and by devious ways, taking an opposite direction to us, make their way with it and hide it among the cargo and débris outside a warehouse near our ship where it could be collected later.

It worked splendidly. Everything was really on our side. We had the element of absolute surprise against them and, more valuable still, our eyes were accustomed to the darkness while theirs were not. The actual rush into the fo'c'sle was tremendously exciting and the mêlée which followed was quite tough going. For a moment or two it was ugly; knives were drawn—it was difficult to distinguish friend from foe; but somehow we consolidated and in a bunch surrounding the sea-chest raced across the deck and over the gangway. It was as we were crossing the deck that I felt a sailor lunge to throw me but I skipped over a hawser which luckily threw him down—as he crashed behind me I felt the point of a knife prick my leg. Once amongst the wharfside buildings (keeping up a racket) we dropped the sea-chest exactly where we had planned and keeping just in front of our pursuers, all the time yelling back ribald insults to provoke them, led them on; gradually we increased our distance, splitting up as we had previously arranged into three groups to confuse them further and then, when the chase cooled, peeling off singly to make our way to our rendezvous at the Madam's. Here we found a great welcome for ourselves, and a fine reception for our sailors. Madam, with graceful compliments upon the apparent success of our exploit, led two or three of us to her own apartments for wine and supper; but I was anxious to be away to collect the sea-chest in case anything had gone wrong over it. I begged her to produce some sort of transport and, seeing my eagerness, she went off and coming back told me that a fiacre and trusted driver had been arranged for and would be dispatched for the chest at the right moment. Gathering us up, she took us on again towards her rooms. As we went, she discussed with me, like the clever tactician she was, the inadvisability of rushing off immediately to collect the sea-chest, reasoning that if the chest was, as we hoped, safely hidden close to our own ship, it was safe; if it was not we could not now do anything about it—to go for it so soon might attract attention. The Clipper ship would not be likely to dismiss the affair or take it lying down—they would have their scouts out . . . no, no: it would be much better to do nothing until later . . . yes, yes: and when the time came it would be better to leave the collecting to her. She had her own excellent grapevine . . . would hear exactly how everything lay and act accordingly. . . . In the meantime we must have supper with her . . . after all the night was young . . . and there were cuts and bruises to be attended to—and looking down at my leg from which I was delighted to see the blood showing most effectively through my canvas trousers, she said, 'Ah, yes, and a leg to be dressed and bandaged.'

The next morning the Captain sent for me. I felt quite certain it was to do with the raiding party to the sailing ship. His first words confirmed this: looking at me very keenly but not, I was relieved to see, without a twinkle in his eyes, he said:

'I hear, Owen, there was some trouble in the four-master last night. Have you heard about this?'

'Yes, Sir, I have heard there was some misunderstanding aboard her.'

'Humph, humph, "misunderstanding" . . . you have a neat way of putting things I must say. Her Captain is raging mad, accusing every ship in the port of having stolen, stolen mark you, the gear belonging to one of her A.B.'s—not a very nice word, Owen, is it?'

'No, Sir.'

'He has been here to see me; he is convinced that this ship had something to do with it. He suggests that the A.B. concerned was our own late Third Officer. Fortunately I was able to deny any knowledge of the matter and you, Owen, must see to it that I never do hear any suggestion that my ship has been concerned.'

In a very stern voice he went on:

'Do I make myself clear?'

'Yes, Sir, perfectly clear.'

'Very good. Sailors talk, you know, and I hold you responsible that no rumours shall spread outside this ship. Is that understood?'

'Understood, Sir.'

'I have given orders to the Chief Officer to cancel all shore leave forthwith. By the way, have you seen anything of our Third since I had to send him ashore?'

'No, Sir, I have not.'

'I see. Well, he seems to have found a good friend on the beach. A bad, very bad business but not, it seems now, as bad as it might have been. But sit down, Owen, I really sent for you to tell you officially that we are now short of a Third Officer. I have decided to appoint you as Third. From now onwards you will stand your watch at sea. Do you feel confident to do this?'

'Yes, Sir.'

'So do I—my decision will be queried on account of your age but that is my worry. Good luck. That is all.'

Just as I had closed his cabin door, the Captain called:

'Mr. Owen.'

'Sir.'

'Humph ... Ah, yes ... a bit tricky ... but, well, there it is ... I am glad that windjammer will be sailing short of an Able Seaman. Now shut the door and report to the Chief Officer as our new Third.'

'Sir.'

We finished our loading and the next morning sailed. I cannot remember where we were making for, probably Montevideo, but we were not yet homeward bound; we had some weeks to go before we should be able to turn around for home. As we left Rio, my feelings

were very mixed. I was tremendously exhilarated at being pushed up
to Third Officer, but at the same time hated the idea of taking the
place of this friend of mine, the 'good sailing man', our real Third;
not having him on board seemed all wrong somehow. I was distressed
about leaving him in the middle of one of his fearful bouts. I thought
to myself he would just about be running into the violent stage which
always preceded his slow return to sobriety. The Madam and her
staff would look after him, but all the same he was now shipless and
stranded. Some of my anxiety was alleviated by the splendid relief I
felt that at least we had got him clear of the danger of being shipped
before the mast.

As we headed seawards through the incredible sparkle of the blue
waters of the South Atlantic, I could not know that this was to be
my last peacetime voyage in a merchantman, or that when eventually
we set our course for home waters, it would be to find England at
war with Germany.

24. *War*

4 August 1914. War. On this day we as a family were more separated
than we had ever yet been. I have an idea that my mother and Mary
were staying with my mother's sister and her family at their home
near Reading. My father was at home, Wilfred was in France. Colin
was in camp with the Boy Scouts in Aberdovey. I was in Uruguay—
Montevideo. We were lying off the port. I had leave from my ship
and spent the whole of the day ashore in my customary way, wandering about the city, enjoying the pleasant tree-shaded plazas and the
fine shops, altogether perhaps one of the pleasantest of my Merchant
Service days. I must have recently sold quite a number of water-
colours for I lunched, I remember, at the most expensive restaurant
and in the afternoon bought a costly piece of carved alabaster which I
had admired during the morning. The city was seething with rumours
about the imminence of war between England and Germany. The
general atmosphere was pro-German: I encountered no actual
hostility but in every conversation it was made abundantly clear that
the 'Gringoes' had no chance at all against the mighty German army
and that all the English ships in port—if they put to sea—would be
sunk by the wonderful German navy. But war was still not certain.
We were homeward bound and due to sail that evening; I did wonder
vaguely and a little uncomfortably if we should get home or not. But

I was very young, intent upon enjoying my day ashore, and beyond this slight wonderment as to what it would all mean if war did break out, I cannot really remember being greatly impressed; on the whole I think I found the tingle of excitement that was running through the streets and cafés rather exhilarating.

We sailed that evening not knowing if war would break or not. Unless we passed some non-enemy ship the next day, with later news, one that we could signal by semaphore (we had no Aldis lamps in those days and in any case we could not have used them for fear of flashing a German cruiser) we should have no means of finding out. No doubt the Captain had been given his secret orders but the rest of us knew nothing. Speculation of course ran high. We were supposed to run into Bahia and then Salvador or one of the more northerly ports before running across to the Cape Verdes and the Canaries, and then home. We did not think any of this was likely to happen now; as far as we knew the whole of the German fleet was at sea—the possibility that the enemy warships might be bottled up never occurred to us. It seemed certain that if war had been declared our chances of getting home were slim. At every first sign of a smudge of smoke the Captain sheered off, putting the greatest possible distance between us and it. This went on for some days until one hazy morning with the first light of dawn the look-out reported 'Cruiser on the port bow'. She was hull-down and we could only see her four funnels and top-hamper.

Every officer was on the bridge; argument waxed hot—English or German—nobody really knew. The Captain was inclined to think she was German and had altered course on sighting her, taking the thin and only chance of evading her by slipping into the thick mist; but she was closing rapidly; even with emergency speed we could not exceed ten knots.

A flash of livid crimson flowered from the cruiser and a warning shot, the signal to stop, ripped across our bows. I remember the Captain's quiet sharp order 'Stop'. As I pushed the handle of the engine-room telegraph from 'Full Speed Ahead' to 'Stop', I knew we were at war: seconds later I also knew we were not captured. Straining to distinguish her ensign I saw the cross on the grey-white was red and not black. A cheer rang out from the hands mustered on deck. A boat put off to board us, in charge of a fresh-faced sub-lieutenant two or three years older than I was myself, perhaps nineteen. I remember admiring his immaculate uniform and the smartness of the sailors who made up the seaboat's crew. The boarding officer had brought sealed orders for our Captain and instructions to collect any Naval Reserve sailors we might have on board and commandeer orders for stores. Speed was everything; in a matter of minutes, flour and food, tobacco and cigarettes were broken out and lowered into the tossing boat; our two naval reservist A.B.s said goodbye and boarded the cutter; the smooth-cheeked young sub-lieutenant climbed down the Jacob's Ladder, smartly getting his boat away from our heaving side and another cheer rang over the waters to speed her on her way. When she was clear the Captain gave the order, 'Full Speed Ahead'. I rang the engine-room telegraph again and as the ship instantaneously throbbed into life I felt very glad we had not been captured and our ship sunk. The Captain had mustered all hands and told us he had orders to get his ship to England taking all risks to do so. We were to put in to no port at all. If we ran short of coal—as was most likely—we were to burn everything combustible in the ship. Beyond being told that we were making for an Irish or English port with all speed, the Captain told us nothing else.

It was strange steaming home towards England knowing only that war had broken out, but knowing nothing of what might be happening. If we ever got home should we find the Germans in England? We just did not know. While I could not form any opinions, I did have the feeling that enormous changes were coming about, that from now onwards everything would be different; with it came an unsettling regret. I remember so well thinking during the long night watches what a pity it was if disruptions were going to come about for me now. For the first time in my life things seemed to be going well for me. I was selling my water-colours faster than I could paint them; my sea-faring career was I thought quite promising; my navigational studies were going well, logarithms were no longer a mystery, and surprisingly trigonometry was unfolding itself; with this I had lost all my fear that my neglected education would prevent me obtaining my sea-going qualifications. I had a fine feeling that I had caught up with many things.

Obscurely and unhappily I sensed a threat to all this, in this business of war between us and Germany, and wished very much that it had not come just now. As usual with me when confronted with change or uncertainty about what might lie in front, my thoughts would fly backwards conjuring up a synopsis of what had gone before. As we sailed through the weeks between us and England, expecting any day to be captured by an enemy ship or sunk by a submarine, flashes from the last few years crowded into my mind, mostly in conglomerations of smells and sounds ... the tortilla vendors of the Valparaiso nights with their cries made musical by distance and choral by their dispersed numbers ... 'Tortillas ... Tortillas ...' the cries shrilling out sweetly from the strident criss-cross of the police whistles which, in glorious abandon, were blown in their hundreds all night long; the sailing ships of Iquique beautiful with tracery of masts and spars as they lay, sometimes fifty or sixty, clustered together in immobility. Mixed up in my ruminations came the hot heady coffee smells of the Brazilian ports: Montevideo with its cool and pleasant plazas; music from mouth organs and accordions drifting across still water, coming from the fo'c'sle of some distant anchored ship; waterside dives with doors swinging open to throw out hot blasts of thick rancid air and debouch reeling sailors and women tottering on high heels; the dark heat of dockside warehouses, the hot strike of the sun from molten water shooting sparks as if from a myriad tiny anvils. . . . Callao, with its Peruvian Navy of one gunboat, or was it two? Mejillones, with its yellow cliffs; Lima where I made pen and ink drawings of the cathedral ... the gruesome bones of Pisarro and the more gruesome paths mosaiced with human knuckle bones—the harvest of some Peruvian-Chilean massacre ... the ports of Eten and Payta ... somewhere in a remote village a Peruvian Indian woman suckling little piglets one at each of her own breasts ... the howling of the Cape Horn winds ... the completely naked men and women, natives of Tierra del Fuego, long-haired and emaciated who would come within throwing distance of a ship—but never nearer—in primitive dug-out canoes, to glean scraps of food ... the loneliness of the first watch at sea in charge of a bridge ... pinpoints of light from the charcoal cooking fires of the little houseboats lining the Ganges. The cold blue beauty of the curving glaciers of the Magellan Straits ... a masthead light pricking the horizon ... and always the white frozen stare of the malignant albatross. . . .

I was thinking like this on the voyage home, going backwards perhaps instead of forwards because, with this outbreak of war, to look forward seemed difficult; for me the details of what might happen in wartime were hard to visualize. I seem to remember I was surprised about it all so that until we sailed, still in doubt, from Montevideo, I must have given hardly any thought to the possibility of it happening: being out of England I had missed the infectious excitement of the weeks preceding the declaration. In a vague way, I realized that excitements of a different sort might be waiting for me, very different from these kaleidoscopic recollections that were occupying me so much at this moment; altogether I think I was quite resentful of the threatened disturbance; I had an uncomfortable feeling that my own little personal adventures and my secret pleasures would not only leave me but lose their romance for me. In a very young and boyish way I sensed rather strongly that this was the end of a chapter.

This then was the beginning of the 1914 War for me; I was already caught up in the routine of war. The beginning for Wilfred was altogether different; there he was tutoring in France, worried perhaps about his future and worried too that his entrée into literary circles still seemed remote. His immediate reaction was, I am certain, his usual one when any disrupting influence threatened his absorption with his poetry—one of exasperated nervous intolerance. He saw in it not only infinite threat to his poetry but as well possible death to all his literary ambitions.

It is manifest from the letters he wrote to my mother during these first few months of the war that the declaration of war between England and Germany could not, and did not, stir in him any patriotic ardour; he felt no personal call to do anything about it at all. Not for him the fine first flush of rushing enthusiasm upon which he could be swept—before more serious thoughts could assail him—into the irrevocable decision to 'join up' as it was called in those days. Far from anything like this, his only strong feeling and determination at this time was to safeguard his writing and to preserve for himself the opportunity to continue with his poetry at all costs. The fact that his contemporaries were joining up in their tens of thousands did not seem of any importance to him; it did not deflect his design. He only had one purpose in living—to write poetry. If a war was likely to destroy or even retard his poetry, he would have nothing to do with a war.

Wilfred in those first months was never troubled in himself about NOT enlisting. What harried and distressed him was the thought that he might succumb—take the easier way and join up before he was convinced inside himself that this was a right action. Written down it all sounds rather smug and over-selfconscious but to understand Wilfred it is necessary to understand the importance to him of this thinking at that time.

It was not until the spring of 1915 that grave doubts about what his own personal reaction ought to be towards the war began with nagging unsettlement to assail him. His letters to me were becoming more frequent now. In one of them he wrote freely about not having yet made his decision to be combative or non-combative: bodily he found himself curiously impersonal, mentally he was torn with most personal perplexity. At times the temptation to smother his conscience, succumb, and doing so become a *hero* overnight was almost overwhelming. The alternative, being branded with lack of courage, and the ostracism which would follow—this prospect and all its consequences he found appalling, and much more frightening than the horrid thought of Army discipline and barrack square drillings. . . .

In all of this there was no suggestion of detraction of those who so unhesitatingly and immediately joined up; on the contrary his admiration was both natural—unusually so for him—and unstinted, touched only with envy. He wrote to me how he envied his contemporaries, how clearly they could see things, for them their course seemed open and straightforward—they had only their personal doubts and aversions to contend with—while he seemed to be fogged and blinded with all these obscurities and inward questionings which he could not answer . . . how he wished he could be like them, and like them feel he had only the disagreeableness of it all to contend with.

Wilfred, of course, was not by any means alone in this reserved attitude; while the surge of patriotic eagerness appeared to sweep all the young men of England into the Army, there still remained the few hundreds of other thinking young men who found it difficult to accept the War unquestioningly. Wilfred and the small core of those like him, refusing to be mass-persuaded, insisted upon their right to decide the issues for themselves.

Wilfred told me much later in the War during one of our rare short meetings, how inestimably glad he was that he had not allowed himself to be swept into the fighting on some wave of emotional excitement. He was, I could see, savagely depressed over the fearful waste and futility of the violence of which he was a part. It was then that he told me, not fluently but in disjointed sentences often barely audible, of the relief he felt that he had not been coerced, that what he was doing had at least come from reasoned thinking and not from patriotic hysteria. 'Sometimes when I think too much this does make it worse, I cannot claim the excuse of being caught . . . I alone must be responsible for myself. . . . But I would rather have it so . . . I can

think more clearly ... and later ... if there is time ... time to do it ...
speak more clearly ... I must always remember it is my war ... I am
acting from my own volition ... but others are not ... perhaps I can
speak for them ... can my poetry do this? ... I do not know ... I
must do this ... but shall I have time or will my poetry—not yet born
—be killed with me?'

This is not intended to be an account of the personal war
experiences of either Wilfred or myself; not of Wilfred's because his
are fairly widely known through Edmund Blunden's *Memoir*—and
from his letters—and differed little in actual encounter from those
of the thousands of other young officers fighting in France; not of
my own because I do not like talking about my war experiences, and
they too differed little from those of thousands of others in wartime.

Except for the short time while I was being taught to fly, I was at
sea for the whole of the War and for a year afterwards. I did not see
much of my family and less of course of Wilfred. I was still to do
another two years or so sailing short voyages running the submarine blockade carrying food and war materials before I could get
free of the Merchant Service and transfer to the Navy. I had a short
stay in the newly formed arm of the Royal Navy—The Royal Navy
Air Service. Instruction was given on Graham-White and Maurice
Farman aeroplanes and after only ninety-one minutes' dual instruction I was sent up for my first solo flight. ... The aeroplane was badly
smashed up. This was the first of a number of similar misadventures
and, as only a very few accident incidents were allowed (usually
only two), until we were posted to a fighting unit, it was suggested
by the Commanding Officer that it might be less costly all-round if I
returned to sea. Thereafter I served as a midshipman in various
battleships and finished the war as the sub-lieutenant of a light
cruiser.

Meetings between Wilfred and myself were, as I have said, few,
but they remain vividly in my mind. For in those hours of all too
short leaves, sometimes at the camp where Wilfred was stationed,
sometimes in London, sometimes at home, we came to understand
each other and to be aware of each other as individuals. We dropped
our trivial hostilities of speech—the elder and younger brother,
student and Philistine relationship gradually disappeared—and we
became less diffident and reserved about voicing our innermost
thoughts and capable at the same time of a rather silent communica-

tion. We did not speak of this; it had come about too naturally, it was the order of things; it was functional, it was expected. Early in 1918 when we had a night at home together with the family, the mutuality of our understanding was complete. This was the last time that we saw each other.

25. *Armistice Day*

The last weeks of the War were for me extremely unhappy ones. I find it difficult to explain satisfactorily why this should have been so. Certainly there were no special happenings that might cause me to feel like this; it bothered me that I could not—to myself—account for my restless unease. Letters from home were intermittent and usually came in collected numbers covering several months but I had just had one of these collections which had brought me fairly recent news. They were all well at home—anxious about Wilfred, actually fighting in France, but not immediately worried, for they were getting letters regularly from him. In them he sounded well and confident and strangely complete in his mastery of himself and his ability to lead and fight. My mother in her latest letter had told me of this, and reading between her lines I sensed almost a hopefulness in Wilfred as if he had begun to recognize the possibility that he might yet survive the fighting. Curiously though even this news failed to revive my lowered spirits.

November 1918: I was on the African Station, serving in the light cruiser, *Astræa*. The eleventh found us anchored in Table Bay. When the news of the Armistice came through, the Captain cleared mess-decks and addressed the assembled ship's company. When this was over he invited all officers to his day cabin for drinks to mark the cessation of hostilities. It was champagne of course and after an informal and happily worded little speech from the Captain we settled down amongst ourselves to the usual ship's party: but it was no good. I could not enter into any spirit of gaiety, I felt horribly flat, everything else seemed flat, the ship and the champagne—the champagne certainly wasn't but it tasted so to me and I would not drink much. I could sense all round me an atmosphere of intense relief—most especially did I feel this relief myself; perhaps it was reaction from this relief which made me so disinclined for gaiety. I had I think had enough of war, I did not want its celebrations. In spite of my recent letters I was unhappy and worried about Wilfred.

I could not rid myself of a constant nag of acute anxiety about him and Colin too: where was he . . . perhaps entangled in a crashed aeroplane . . . I was glad when the Captain intimated that the party was over.

After lunch another lieutenant with whom I was very friendly asked me to go ashore with him to see what was happening. I wanted to get out of the ship but I did not really want to spend the whole afternoon jostling about amongst the throngs of excited people. In the end I compromised and told him I would dine with him in the hotel; I would meet him there in time for a drink before dinner, after which, if we could get there, we might go along to the club in Simonstown. We went ashore together and with this arrangement parted company. There was some excitement, but not as much as I had expected. The real hysteria was to come later. Adderley Street was very full of course, and mostly orderly, but I did not want to stay in Cape Town. I wanted to get away from the city and find somewhere where I could be alone, so I made my way to the outskirts and from there to the coast. I don't quite know where I got to on that Armistice afternoon. I remember walking through a pleasant residential district— peculiarly deserted which gave it a Sunday-like atmosphere; from here I was able to walk along the coastline cliffs which was what I wanted. It may have been False Bay but I never really knew; I remember walking along cliffs for some miles with no one else in sight. I lay down on the springy herbage of the cliff-edge with my back to the sky and my face turned seaward. I stared out over the incredibly blue expanse of glittering sea, and perhaps something in the limitless stretch of water and sky affected me. I felt lonely and curiously isolated, but this was not unpleasant although it steeped me in a strange sadness.

It was I remember a very still day and the sun was hot on my back. As I lay motionless, just staring out to sea, the solitude began to work on me, until slowly a peace of mind worked into me so that tranquil thoughts drifted pleasantly into my pattern of contemplation . . . I realized with a surge of happiness that the War had not broken my own family. Wilfred and Colin must be all right now . . . they were a long way away from me . . . it would I thought be two years before my ship returned to home waters but with the War finished how could that matter . . . they were safe and so was I . . . Wilfred would go on writing his poetry and I would go on with my painting. . . .

I thought how nice this sounded, Wilfred writing and me painting

—both of us doing what we wanted to do. With the memory of our last few snatched meetings still so fresh in my mind I knew that although the vituperation might remain there could never any more be real discord between us; although we could not travel together— each of us was too individualistic to share another's path—yet the love between us would be there and if we could not share we could help and encourage each other onwards.

The sun I saw was lowering, I must hurry back to Cape Town to keep my dinner appointment. I wished I had not made it. I would have liked to stop somewhere here where I was and finding some small coast hotel dine alone. I sprang to my feet.

With my sudden movements my apprehensions about Wilfred began to gnaw me again. Why couldn't I be certain . . . I must know . . . I made up my mind—I would cable my father for news of him. I hurried towards Cape Town. Once there, I had to fight my way through the dense crowds to gain the Post Office but I hardly noticed them so intent was I on my purpose. I had actually written out the cable when I hesitated. I remembered too well the dread fear that telegrams inspired in England—the sight of a red bicycle within a hundred yards of your own house could make your heart jump and miss a beat . . . at home, perhaps secure in the knowledge of Wilfred's safety, might not a cable from Africa mean only one thing . . . slowly I tore up my telegram and threw it in the waste-paper basket . . . it *must* be all right. After all I had had no cable from home and the War *was* over. . . .

With my frustration through not having sent the cable came a return of my flat empty feeling. I felt completely out of sympathy with the milling crowds of shrieking people thronging Cape Town and choking Adderley Street. It was early yet so that I was still able somehow or other to force my way through the streets and reach the hotel but I did not achieve this without a struggle and some altogether unpleasant jostling as people crowded in on me or surged me into a tide of unwanted direction. For the most part the mobs were good-humoured enough although I could already sense in some sections an undercurrent of distinct hostility towards English people. But as yet I had encountered no serious incidents; these were to come later. Dinner was a scrambled affair, the dining-room overflowing and the service disorganized, but this interlude was the only bearable part of the indescribably unpleasant evening. I had secured a veranda table on the first floor and because of this we were able to look down on the waves of people surging below us. Maudlin songs and shouts of drunken laughter broke through the undertone of throbbing sound that pulsated with steady rhythm from the packed streets.

The vulgarity of the scene turned my flat feeling into desperate depression: the weighted force of this threatened to overwhelm me. I became possessed by only one thought—to get away from it all, right out of Cape Town, if possible back to my quiet ship and the clean freshness of the wind across Table Bay. I realized I was rather spoiling things for my companion but this I just could not help; to make amends I ordered a bottle of whisky and siphons for I could see he was infected with the jubilations and intent upon making a long gay night of it. I wished I could share this excitement with him, I even tried, but it was no good—I could not rid myself of disillusion; the throngs of excited sweating people nauseated me to a degree which surprised me. I thought the whisky might help but when it came I found I could not drink any; I had a curiously strong and strange feeling that I did not want to lift my depression falsely by drinking. It was the same aversion I had experienced only that morning during the Captain's celebration party.

By now the hotel was uncomfortably overcrowded so we decided to go out into the streets again to see what was happening. We arranged that if we became separated, as we most likely would in these eddying and, as we could see, quarrelsome crowds, we would act independently. He would seek his amusement where he could find it; if this did happen, I for my part would do my best to get back to *Astræa*.

As we tried to struggle through the crowds we were jammed to a standstill by the people in front of us; peering over and between them we could see a gang of street roughs and very drunk individuals stripping Union Flags from parked cars and windows and throwing them on the road to be trampled on. Resentment flared immediately from other sectors who at once retaliated with equal violence. The situation was combustible. Ugly rushes followed during which my companion and I became divided; there was nothing either of us could do except be carried along with our separate tides of people. I was fortunate in being swept into a side street where there seemed to be only normal excitement. I felt sure this was an isolated incident but even discounting this, I was aware that—at this moment anyway —feelings were running dangerously high in Cape Town.

When things had quietened down I made my way back to Adderley Street to see if I could find my companion again but, as I knew it would be, it was quite hopeless; I felt I ought to look around for him for quite a long time although I was hoping fervently that I should not find him. I could not get Wilfred out of my mind and wondering about him perhaps sharpened my sensitivity so that revulsion was all I could experience—revulsion for the mawkish patriotic songs, the drunkenness which was becoming more evident everywhere, men lying senseless in the gutters, young women and some girls drinking out of bottles in the streets, empty bottles being thrown down to splinter on the roadways. I must get out of it all; with a force that in itself must have been provocative I charged and elbowed my way through the crowds.

Later on, when at last I got to the naval jetty, I looked upwards to the clean brightness of the night sky, while I was waiting for a launch to take me off; and once again my thoughts flew back to home. What were they feeling and thinking now the fighting was ended. Was Wilfred all right, was Colin? I wished now I *had* sent that cable. I could not be happy about any of them at home. Something I knew was wrong. Monstrous depression clamped hold of me. I was glad to be back in my ship again.

A few days later we sailed for Walfish Bay and the Cameroons.

In Victoria, limp and enervated with the moist heat and recurrent malaria, insects plagued us day and night. Victoria itself, since the occupation by us of the Cameroon territory, had no white people at all except for two or three up-country planters—only negro population. I found it difficult to throw off a lowness of spirits. Now that the War was over it seemed somehow less necessary to do so, which made it harder. Malaria of course was doing its undermining work. It may have been something to do with this unusually low state of mind that I was going through which brought about for me an extraordinary and inexplicable experience.

We were lying off Victoria. I had gone down to my cabin thinking to write some letters. I drew aside the door curtain and stepped inside and to my amazement I saw Wilfred sitting in my chair. I felt shock run through me with appalling force and with it I could feel the blood draining away from my face. I did not rush towards him but walked jerkily into the cabin—all my limbs stiff and slow to respond. I did not sit down but looking at him I spoke quietly: 'Wilfred, how did you get here?' He did not rise and I saw that he was involuntarily immobile, but his eyes which had never left mine were alive with the familiar look of trying to make me understand; when I spoke his whole face broke into his sweetest and most endearing dark smile. I felt no fear—I had not when I first drew my door curtain and saw him there; only exquisite mental pleasure at thus beholding him. All I was conscious of was a sensation of enormous shock and profound astonishment that he should be here in my cabin. I spoke again. 'Wilfred dear, how can you be here, it's just not possible. . . .' But still he did not speak but only smiled his most gentle smile. This not speaking did not now as it had done at first seem strange or even unnatural; it was not only in some inexplicable way perfectly natural but radiated a quality which made his presence with me undeniably right and in no way out of the ordinary. I loved having him there: I could not, and did not want to try to understand how he had got there. I was content to accept him, that he was here with me was sufficient. I could not question anything, the meeting in itself was complete and strangely perfect. He was in uniform and I remember thinking how out of place the khaki looked amongst the cabin furnishings. With this thought I must have turned my eyes away from him; when I looked back my cabin chair was empty. . . .

I felt the blood run slowly back to my face and looseness into my limbs and with these an overpowering sense of emptiness and absolute loss. . . . I wondered if I had been dreaming but looking down I saw that I was still standing. Suddenly I felt terribly tired and moving to my bunk I lay down; instantly I went into a deep oblivious sleep. When I woke up I knew with absolute certainty that Wilfred was dead.

The certainty of my conviction of Wilfred's death amounted I realized to absolute knowledge; I could not any longer question it. That I had not heard that he had been killed—that weeks had now passed since the fighting had stopped—made no difference to me at all; all that could be explained. What I found impossible to explain was this self-existent awareness of mine, unrelated to any facts; I did not try, I accepted his death completely without hope and without pretence. My awareness was so profound that knowledge could not be denied.

I was so absorbed with the truth of his death and my own adjustment of myself in order that I might receive it, that I did not think to probe deeply into the strange manner of the conveyance of my certainty, indeed to me there had never been any strangeness: after my first quite ordinary surprise at seeing Wilfred in my cabin the whole happening had been completely natural both at the time and in memory ever afterwards. Even the sadness of its portent could not make it unnatural nor yet unhappy. I did vaguely wonder of course whether I had not in the first place gone into my cabin, lain down on my bunk and fallen asleep and afterwards dreamt that I had stepped into my cabin to find Wilfred there. Yet I had no recollection of anything like this happening. I could not reconcile my thinking to such reasoning: my inward perceptiveness refuted this utterly. I knew it just wasn't true. My belief that it was otherwise was intense and unqualified. I was glad about this—I did not wish to think differently, to have to do so would I realized bring to me a sense of deprivation which could only be profoundly disturbing. Strangely I did not seek nor did I want full understanding, much less explanation; my preparedness for acceptance was so powerful that I did not need them. I was immune to curiosity—I had only this extraordinary awareness of a privileged access to rare experience. With equal strangeness, I could sense the isolating singularity of the experience; I felt possessed of inner knowledge which made me absolutely certain that it could never happen again.

I went about my duties and carried on my normal routine. The loss of Wilfred would not leave me, but the unease of terrible wondering had gone: in its place I had indisputable certainty, but strangely, now, this was accompanied by understanding—a comprehension only dimly revealed and only barely apprehended. In a bewildered way I was conscious that although I should never again see Wilfred or speak with him, that physically he had irrevocably disappeared, yet I had not lost him . . . his body was dead but Wilfred, the real Wilfred, would remain. What he had left was mine: this I could never lose. While I myself lived neither war, accident, nor illness could separate me from it.

It was Christmas week before I got any letters from home. Something had gone wrong and we did not get our mails from England, but except for news of the others at home these were not important to me now: I had no doubts and did not need confirmation about Wilfred. What I did need very badly was news of them all at home; I could not forget what Wilfred's death must be meaning to them.

When in this Christmas week of 1918 my letters did at last catch up with me, I collected my large package which I could see were nearly all from my mother and took them to my cabin to read. My mother never failed to post at least twice a week to Wilfred and once a week to me—and later Colin—throughout the War. Before I opened any of them I searched quickly through for Wilfred's hand-writing . . . there might be a last letter from him . . . but it wasn't there. . . .

Seeking the latest postmarks I opened my mother's letters until I found the one I knew would be there. It was.

They had received the dreaded telegram at 12 noon on 11 November, Armistice Day. The church bells were still ringing, the bands playing and the jubilant crowds surging together. Bitterly I recalled the Captain's party and remembered the brawling mobs in Cape Town. Later that day I went ashore and cabled my love to them at home.

26. *Cameroon Country*

This post-war period on the African Coast was a strange one for us in *Astræa*. We were peculiarly isolated from contact with the world and apart from rare visits to up-country planters—always masculine establishments—we had no social life; the planters were more cut off than we were. In this way we missed some of the most immediate post-war reactions. For entertainment and recreation we were forced over long periods to rely upon our own wardroom associations. We all suffered in different ways from the monotony of one another. Malaria was general and as such came to be accepted as part of living; the frightful overdoses of quinine acted as malignant depressants and the source of violent head-singings. The incidence of other tropical illnesses apart from malaria was serious so that we became a rather gaunt yellow-skinned ship's company.

On the whole, the remainder of our commission in *Astræa* was not really very pleasant. We were a happy enough ship in ourselves, but the War after all was over, reaction was setting in, and every one of us wanted to get home. The West Coast then was not the healthy or the pleasant place it is now. Victoria consisted only of disused German colonial buildings and unoccupied barracks, overgrown pineapple gardens and of course the cocoa and banana plantations —all relics of one-time German colonization.

Still between spells of lying off Victoria we moved up and down the coast from Sierra Leone to Walfish Bay. Whenever we were in port I seized every opportunity for going ashore. My insatiable curiosity and love of fresh places drove me—to explore every town and village within my reach. In this way, my little adventures and incidental happenings came to me to relieve monotony as they so often had done before; we had some good cutter and whaler sailing on fishing expeditions; big game fish abounded and gave us good sport especially as we had to construct all our own flies and lures. Lagos lagoon was full of tarpon, beautiful great fish. Almost every evening, attracted by our gangway light, they would come in their scores to swim and dart at surface level within inches of our feet as we stood on the gangway platform. We tried every device of lure and fly to try and get into one, but they would not look at any of them. The lovely creatures, seemingly fashioned out of ten-foot bars of pure sea-washed silver, would only glide with incredible smoothness of movement, fascinated by the mesmeric allure of the circle of light-charged water. Anxious to obtain a specimen we got the engineers to make us iron harpoons with which we tried to spear them. Whether it was refraction or the scales which glanced the point off I do not know, but although only a foot or two of water separated us from the fish we could not strike them: only once my harpoon held perhaps for twenty or thirty seconds and as the line burned out through my fingers, an alien stain of blood marred the crystal water. After this I never tried again; there was something horrible about this wilful, senseless damage to a living creature of such superb silver beauty.

The West African Coast, in spite of the fever and the constant physical disagreeablenesses which its climate of steaming swampy heat bred in us, held for me an enormously powerful attraction. I liked the eternal mystery of its tropical bush; as I penetrated inland and traversed the areas as yet hardly touched by western civilization I became more and more aware of how these lands of swamp and impenetrable jungle—bush we called it—breathed: sometimes the breath was repellent but always with it was this sensation of the land itself being alive and breathing. On the surface appeared only lassitude and eternal decay. The very trees rotted as they grew, the vines and innumerable creeping, climbing, and spreading bush vegetation sprawled their tentacles of lurid green to overgrow themselves in a heat spasm of gross cannibalistic living, until overreaching they fell back and became food for the younger growths; these with avid greed would fasten on their dying brothers and with orgiastic abandonment suck life from decay. The rottenness spread in dangerous patches to the soil itself and what might look like firm ground would, if trodden on, fall away like decomposing flesh and spew up from its slime hosts of living parasites obnoxious with the white creepings of buried life. But deep underneath this exhibitionism of growth and dissolution, the land of Africa breathed and pulsated with the ascendancy of primeval mysticism. It affected me strangely so that I could never free myself from the fascination of this feeling of being confronted with the evolution of millions of years. Far from experiencing any sensation of superiority for being a white man I had a disquieting unease that not only was I not superior but that the black peoples were in many of their customs, philosophy, and manners quite often superior to me.

I well remember one African night when the impact of this profundity had impressed me most strongly. I had been sent up to the foothills of Mount Cameroon—Beaua I think it was—for leave and recuperation. Here was a bungalow—a Government rest house —which was at the disposal of service officers. We usually went up in pairs but for some reason or another I had had to go alone. I did not mind this; I had the company of a Negro cook and a Krooman servant from the ship who would also act as interpreter. I looked forward to a week or ten days alone with the Negro people. The journey up was great fun too; we went by a little narrow-gauged mountain railway, the 'train' consisting of a primitive little steam engine attached to an open box-like arrangement with wooden seats and an awning supported by four uprights from each corner. The engine was wood-burning which meant frequent stops on the way for the Negro driver to dismount, cut wood from the bush, and re-fuel his tender. I thought it was great fun, for there were always excitements: some of the gradients were very steep, and on these the picturesque little engine, her tall smokestack red-hot and palsied with the steam that gushed from its decrepit boiler, would puff and pant until her speed lessened to walking pace. As soon as this happened the driver, grinning happily, would jump off and armed with small tree trunks for chocks would walk behind ready to block the wheels when finally, with jets of steam and water spurting from every part of her, she defiantly stopped. But she was a gallant old lady and after being given time to cool off her burning joints, she would start off again with joyous bangs and rattles. On the down-grades she really showed off and with squeaks of excitement and joy hurtled around bends until the track itself bounded and undulated to whip back in efforts to derail her; but with whistle shrieking she spurned all caution. The damp wood fuel made fearful smoke charged with sparks which blowing back choked and stung and burnt holes in drill suits, but it was all great fun and I enjoyed every minute except when charging across the ravines on flimsy, swaying native-built bridges—this was distinctly alarming.

It was while I was in Beaua that this particular night came to me and the influence and drag of Africa impressed itself on me with such imposing force. It had been a burning day of still, suffocating heat and night had come down with brooding heaviness. I had eaten a solitary dinner and was looking forward to two or three hours reading before turning in to sleep. My only light was a small paraffin lamp. Every evening it was difficult enough to read by this because of the hosts of insects which circled around in gyrating myriads; on this evening it was worse than usual for in addition there was an invasion of flying beetles of all shapes, colours, and sizes, some of them as big as mice. They charged the lamp, they struck me in the face, and smothered my book. I had to give up and retired to bed, but even with the light out the maddening vibrating hum went on as the cloud of flying creatures blundered into and crawled about the mosquito netting. Sleep was impossible and after some hours of restless discomfort I decided to dress and go for a walk. It was nice walking alone in the hot African night: it was dark but not too dark, so that I was just able to see my way; the stars were brilliantly alive and I remember thinking that this really was starlight, the sky was lit up enough to silhouette the hills and emphasize the undulations of vast expanses of the plain-like tracts of scrub and rock. The great masses of bush-forest were the only really dark things and I thought they looked couchant and vaguely sinister in their heavy clothing of unbroken indigo as they lay brooding in the nightlight.

I climbed up into the foothills and finding a rock sat down and with my chin cupped in my hands stared out over the great living breathing land. I felt again the drag and draw of this negroid country: as I watched I thought it swelled and sank with simmering motion as if deep beneath its surface bubbled the primeval stirrings of primitive wisdom and mystery. As I sat through the dark hours of the night I became obsessed with this feeling of primitive power that surged up from the hot earth and the darkness of the enigmatical forests. I felt the rightness of the men this dark land bred, it was right that they should be black and altogether fitting that being nude they could not comprehend nakedness.

Suddenly for no reason at all a vision of London, Piccadilly Circus, Shaftesbury Avenue, and Oxford Street flashed across my mind. So greatly was I absorbed with the immensity all about me that this sudden picture, out here in the lonely beauty of the African night, of white people milling about in narrow spaces between houses that were nothing more than brick boxes, all fussed and bothered about trivialities that had nothing to do with really living, all of it, our cities and towns—so carefully insulated from the earth—the useless ships of war, the armies facing one another intent only on impersonal destruction, the whole senseless pattern of it, suddenly—as if focused from the wrong end of a telescope—looked pygmean, childish and toy-like, and surprisingly funny. I laughed out aloud . . . some beast in the forest, disturbed by my laughter, answered back and I thought laughed with me. . . .

I knew at that moment that I did not care if I never saw London again. Was I off my guard? I had heard strange things about what this power of the Coast could do to white men . . . of course it was the malaria, but all the same I must watch myself. The forest was coming to life. Far in the distance I heard a barking roar—I was certain it was a gorilla although I thought it was a bit high up for one here: but perhaps he too was sickened by his tribal vendettas and like me had sought higher ground and the solitude that the night could bring. Unlike me he could not laugh—perhaps because of this he roared instead. I felt a strange link with him and very friendly towards him. The light was flushing where sky met earth; I waited and listened hoping to hear him again; perhaps his unguarded sounding, as had my own, had reminded him that he too must watch himself, for no echo came. I stood up but before I turned I waved with an understanding gesture to my huge companion of the night somewhere down there deep in his forest fastness and wished him well. In the swiftly flooding light I looked up towards Fako Peak and saw that it was lovely with morning rosiness. I walked back to my bungalow hoping that when I got there I should sleep. I took a double dose of quinine.

27. Butterflies

Although the climate, especially in the rain seasons, was so dispiriting and the recurrent malaria so energy-sapping I always managed to find something to interest me. Unlike many of the others in the ship I was not easily bored; even when we were anchored for longish spells in deserted Victoria, which was the dullest part of our commission, I was able to keep tedium at bay. I had re-started my water colour painting; whenever I could I wandered off through the bush and into the villages making sketches. This had a double advantage for not only did I collect some drawings but better still it gave me a reason for being in the villages. At first my entries into the small communities caused unobtrusively swift withdrawal of all the inhabitants either into their palm-thatched huts or into the protective bush. After a few visits their curiosity would prove stronger than any remaining temerity and they would cluster up behind me. Their instinctive good manners kept them at a most respectful distance; when I beckoned them to come nearer they only did so with the utmost diffidence. If they could bring themselves to come close enough to examine my sketch they would chatter excitedly amongst themselves, and like children they would cast knowing looks at one another. Sometimes as they peered at what I had done, my painting would strike them as extremely funny and they would shake with laughter, again with the inoffensiveness of children.

While I was in the Cameroon country I formed a valuable friendship with an old man—a white man—an extraordinary eccentric, universally known up and down the Coast as 'The Butterfly Man'. All sorts of rumours regarding this old man's story circulated freely but they were mostly unsubstantiated. What was known with certainty was that he had not left the Coast since he had first come out as a very young man some forty or fifty years ago. It was vaguely thought that before he became the recluse he was when I met him, he had been some sort of government official, but in the blur of time even this was uncertain.

My first meeting with him had been curious. I had gone a little up country to make a water colour drawing of some swamps that I liked, and I was sitting on a fallen tree washing in my colours when from the bush behind me I heard the sound of running and a distinctly English voice shouting, 'I'll get you this time, my beauty, you see if I don't.' A moment later an old man—gasping for breath—came hurtling out of the scrub thickets holding in front of him an enormous butterfly net.

'Which way did it go?'

'Which way did what go, Sir?'

'The butterfly, the butterfly, where is it?'

Nonplussed, I looked keenly at him and realized that my presence had made no impression upon him at all—he had not really seen me; my surprise was cut short by his excited shout:

'There it is!'

Following his outstretched shaking arm and trembling forefinger

I did indeed see a butterfly hovering low to ground about twenty yards away: rushing at me he thrust the net into my hand and in an agonized voice implored me:

'Get it, get it.'

I hesitated for I was no hand at butterfly catching and did not fancy rushing about in the afternoon sun but something of urgency in the exhausted old man made me set off in pursuit. It was a nerve-racking performance for every time I got within striking distance and raised the net for a capture the old man yelled to me, 'Wait, wait, not yet, you'll miss it.' After four or five of these abortive efforts, I really thought I had a chance and ignoring the frenzied shouts brought the net slamming down. For a glorious moment I thought success was mine but the next I knew it wasn't for there spiralling up to freedom was the blue and gold creature. I watched it zoom into the forest and then I walked back slowly.

I saw that the old man was sitting down—I expected recriminations and was astonished when he rose up and demanded:

'Who are you?'

Not knowing quite what to say, I answered:

'I'm from the cruiser in the Bay, Sir.'

'Good God, you a butterfly hunter, too?'

'No, I am NOT.'

'But you've got a net.'

'This is yours not mine.'

'This is preposterous, what are you doing with my net? This is mine!'

I handed him his net.

'Ah, yes, of course, but you missed it, didn't you, you should have waited.'

Seizing the net he strode off without a word. As he went, I was able to take note of his somewhat wild appearance. He was I saw wearing very dirty shorts but instead of the usual bush-shirt he wore only an old and frayed tweed jacket; in place of a sun helmet he wore an extremely ancient deerstalker cap from underneath which his over-long grey hair straggled about his face and neck. I remember thinking how exactly he conformed to the caricature of a stage or fictional professor. In spite of the exaggeration there remained something professorial about him.

I went on with my painting; it was just as I was packing up to go that I espied the Butterfly Man re-emerging from the bush. I waited until he came up and then asked him if he had got the one he wanted:

he shook his head and walked on. When he had gone about ten yards
he turned and called out:

'Will you come and dine with me one night?'

I called back that I should be delighted to do so.

'Thursday be any good?'

'Thank you, yes.'

'Eight o'clock then.'

When Thursday evening came along I walked up to his bungalow
wondering not a little what sort of an evening I was in for—I had
heard strange tales of my host. The veranda was in darkness and I
could see that only one of the rooms was lit. The absence of servants
was queer too; I could neither see nor hear any 'boys' about anywhere. I stumbled up the steps and called out; the old man called
back telling me to walk in. I fumbled along the dividing passage
until I saw a door with a strip of light underneath it. Opening this I
saw the old man sitting at a table mounting butterflies. He got up
and welcomed me warmly enough; at least I was expected, which was
something I had seriously begun to doubt during these last few
minutes. He rose and motioning me to a chair sat down again and
continued with his setting. I noticed that he was still wearing grubby
looking shorts but had discarded the old tweed jacket for a freshly
but badly washed shirt. I wondered if this was a concession to the
dinner invitation, which reminded me that there were no signs of any
preparations for a meal. The building was soundless and except for
our two selves obviously deserted. I glanced across at the old man.
He was immersed in his delicate work, quietly muttering to himself
and quite oblivious of me. Immediately upon arrival I had made
some polite remarks as a sort of opening gambit but in return he had
merely stared at me uncomprehendingly so that I had desisted. I felt
diffident about breaking into his absorption. I lay back in my cane
chair quietly smoking—it was not unpleasant, indeed there was
something peaceful about watching the old man manipulating his
paraphernalia. We must have sat like this for an hour before he
pushed back his chair and rising came around to my side of the room
and in a most rational manner exclaimed:

'My dear boy, I do apologize and you must forgive me. I just do
not know what has happened about dinner. It should have been
served long ago, I hope you are not too hungry. In the meantime
help yourself to a drink; perhaps you will be good enough to mix one
for me.'

I assured him I was not in the least hungry. Looking around I saw that there were no drinks so I let this pass and resumed my chair. After another long silence, he said quietly, 'Everybody on the Coast thinks I'm mad: the whites because I never took my leaves in England and now in my retirement choose to live here—they despise me for this; the blacks because they think I am singled out by important Gods to be different—they exalt me for it. To be different is not to be mad . . . I suppose forty-five years away from white civilization does make you different, and of course Africa has done something to me . . . but she has given me my butterflies. Ah, yes, my lovely butterflies, I must show them to you.'

Springing to his feet he picked up the lamp and leading the way preceded me into another large room. This I saw was lined with beautifully-constructed tiered frameworks filled with specimen boxes: the centre of the room was similarly built up to surround a central table. The narrow alleyways thus formed gave the effect of a museum; surmounting the tiers of closed boxes and running all around the room were hermetically sealed glass-fronted frames in which, superbly set, were richly hued and gorgeously marked butterflies. The enhancement this gave lent to the room the brilliance of an exhibition. After we had made a tour the old man placed the lamp on the table and gently pushing me into a chair proceeded to lay before me box after box of the glorious insects, some of them no more than minute jewels. I was entranced as I studied them and heard from him what must have been an extremely erudite dissertation upon the classification, breeding cycles, and habitat of the innumerable species. I was amazed with the great beauty of the preserving and mounting and as I realized the superb craftsmanship and meticulous labour this involved I found it curiously baffling to connect these delicate processes with this unkempt, uncared-for and vague old man, often so disconcerting with his lapses of reality and memory.

It must have been well after midnight when with a rather vacant expression he suggested we might go into the other room and drink some beer. In the other room we sat down again and he talked to me of the Coast, which was now his only interest in life, but neither then nor at any time in the months to follow did he ever speak of himself; if by chance in some of his recountings he was caught on the verge of even trivial allusion to himself, a wary look would come into his eyes and he would break off in the middle of a sentence. This happened on this first evening—stopping abruptly in mid-talk he looked at me in a distant way and muttered, 'Ah, yes, some beer, wasn't it. I must go and find some.'

Taking up the lamp he shambled uncertainly out of the room, leaving me in darkness. He seemed to be gone a long time. I could hear him wandering about the deserted place, opening and closing doors and muttering to himself. I was thinking the beer must be very difficult to find and wondering if I should go and offer help when I heard his footsteps returning. As he came into the room I saw that instead of beer he was carrying two butterfly nets, one large and one small; not without diffidence he pushed them towards me saying, 'Take these and start a collection of your own, you will enjoy it. We will go out together. I will show you how to set them up.'

Thanking him and telling him how much I should like to go out with him, I was able to take my leave. He walked down the path with me and as we went he said, 'I do hope you enjoyed your dinner, I can't remember. Tell me, was it very bad? My cook I fear is a little primitive.' Before I was out of earshot he called out, 'I'm sorry about the beer, being so warm I mean, but I could not find any ice. Good-night, come again soon.'

As I walked on down to the beach I smiled thoughtfully to myself over the old man's concern for the niceties of a dinner and drinks neither of which had materialized: too much of the Coast could certainly play the strangest tricks. I had enjoyed my evening and was determined to see much more of the old man.

28. *Elephants*

There is a curious discrepancy between chasing butterflies with a butter-muslin net and hunting elephant, but things like this happened on the Coast which perhaps accounted for its impelling fascination for me. It was customary—almost obligatory—for all young lieutenants from the gunboats and cruisers which were stationed in turn in the Gulf of Guinea to try for an elephant. This was made particularly easy for Naval officers by the generosity of the Department concerned; instead of having to pay one hundred guineas for the privilege of attempting to find and kill, we were allowed our organized attempt without fee; only if and after we had killed our elephant did we have to pay, and then only ten guineas.

I had some leave due to me and an invitation from a planter who proposed I should spend it with him on his banana estate in the interior; if I would do this he promised to obtain the services of a good black hunter—whose only duty would be to take me within shooting distance of an elephant. He would also organize the hunting party of trackers and porters, these latter to be armed with powerful hacking knives—pangas—for cutting a path through the bush. I would have to make my try alone, without another white man—my planter friend could not leave his plantation and in any case had lost his shooting eye in the War.

I was to wait a day or two before setting out on the hunt so that I might be shown around the banana groves while final preparations for my hunt were put in hand. During these few days of waiting I became rather badly perturbed. When it had first been presented to me that it would be possible for me to have a try for an elephant, my excitement had known no bounds; with the youthful thinking of my twenty-one years I had thought only of the perfect triumph of returning to England with my trophies—the great feet and the ivory: here within my grasp was the highest achievement of big-game hunting—my only fear had been that I should be deprived of the opportunity. Now on the eve of this possible great attainment and actually in the heart of first-class elephant country, horrid doubts began to assail me the most persistent of which was the awareness deep inside me that I did not in the least want to bring a magnificent beast crashing to its knees in blood and splintered bone . . . and behind that indecision I was horrified to recognize in myself a personal tension . . . would it not be me—not the elephant—who would soon be a mass of slashed and trampled pulp? I had had no experience at all of elephant shooting but from talking to hunters I knew well enough that there were only two vulnerable spots in an elephant which would bring instantaneous death, and only one for a .303 service rifle, which was all I had.

I might even now have withdrawn over my scruples about bringing death to a fine animal had I not felt the onslaught of my own strain. It was difficult to decide satisfactorily which emotion was really actuating my desire to abandon the project. One good thing came out of this indecision: my moral aversion to the attempt to slaughter a beast took second place, my physical nervousness became the only important issue—I knew now that I was committed. If I was ever to enjoy peace of mind about the whole affair, I must go through with it.

My arrival at the banana plantation did nothing to lessen this conviction. My host was aghast when he learnt that I had no elephant gun but proposed to try for an elephant with a service .303. It had been done before but it was a suicidally dangerous undertaking. He did his best to talk me out of it and to persuade me to wait until a hunter came to the region from whom I would be able to borrow a heavy gun. All this well-meant persuasion for some curious reason made it all the more difficult for me to back out. He explained to me —he had himself got his quota of elephant before he lost his eye— with somewhat unnerving detail the hazards of using a light calibre rifle; while a .303 was capable of killing, it had no stopping power— it could only kill if the bullet was placed in the circle of thin bone in the forehead and this was no bigger than a saucer. It was he told me not easy, even with a standing but head-weaving animal, to place a shot accurately in so small a circumference. Apart from this the great danger lay in the truth that although a bullet so placed would in fact have killed, there was so little impact that the elephant though technically dead could and would still charge as if alive. On the other hand the shock power of an elephant gun was so great that even if not mortally wounded the animal would be stopped with the first shot; the second if well-placed would bring it to its knees. A second shot from a .303 would be almost useless.

I had already known all this but the way my planter friend told it to me made it sound most alarming; it certainly did nothing to ease my mounting tension. However in a day or two word came through that a herd might not be too far distant. I arranged to start before sun-up the next morning. In the evening my host and I sat on the veranda in the blue-black of the African night and talked. He gave me a somewhat vague brushing-up upon the procedure for killing an elephant, mostly pessimistic warnings—I wanted something more positive; however I did manage to find out from him just exactly where in the elephant's head was this vital small circle of thinner bone, through which I must put my bullet. I had not been at all certain about this: I thought it rather important.

He was more communicative in a cynical way about the personnel who would make up my hunting party, stressing the conditions under which I was engaging them. It appeared they were not professional hunters, but just chosen and recruited from the villages. Their only obligation was to guide me within range of elephant: having done that they reserved their right to take to the trees. The native responsible for the party was the Headman of a neighbouring village with, as he put it, a fair enough reputation for integrity and steadiness. The trackers were good at their job. The Headman would act as hunter and guide and take charge of the bush-cutting porters—the unreliable element. I had brought up with me a spare service rifle, and suggested that if the Headman was really trustworthy and could use a rifle it might be a good idea—in case of emergency—to let him carry this; but my planter friend was adamant in not sanctioning such a course. Mine must be the only rifle and when my gun-bearer was carrying it the clip must be removed. My heavy service revolver must never under any conditions be unstrapped from my person. All of this I thought sounded frightfully serious; it had as well, I was beginning to think, a rather lonely ring about it. My host told me that the trackers would call me in the morning with one of his ponies, on which I could ride to the village where I was to pick up the Headman and the porters. This would save me many hours of weary walking. From the village we might pick up spoor in a matter of hours or it might be days—the going in the heat of the day would be very hard especially if we had to cut through bush. Telling me when I got my elephant to send a runner back, he said that if I wasn't too far away he would try and get out for a photograph. With this pleasing thought I wished him good night—no, he would not be seeing me off. That might bring bad luck.

I walked across the grounds to the little guest-house and skipping up the wooden steps went along the veranda straight to my room.

Climbing inside the mosquito netting I lay down on my cot hoping that I would be able to get to sleep. At first my thoughts were racing rather a lot and I cursed myself for my inability to prevent these attacks of pre-action nerves which projected me so mercilessly into the future. . . . When I had the great head in my sights would I be able to find that undefined, seemingly mythical saucer-sized circle of soft bone . . . if the beast was close I *must* remember to take evasive action to avoid a charge and be instantly prepared for a second shot . . . would I act swiftly enough to avoid the post-death momentum . . . there seemed an awful lot to remember. . . . Suddenly I felt drowsy and rather bored with the whole thing. I must have fallen quickly into a dreamless sleep, for the next thing I remember was a black face lit from the light of a hand lantern peering at me and a soft deep voice speaking to me to awaken me. It was one of my trackers come for me. A pleasant tingle of fine excitement ran through me which brought me wide awake. I shaved rapidly and took a quick sponge-down in the hip bath calling out to my lazy 'boy' to bring in tea and biscuits. In no time at all I was in shirt and shorts; a final pull-through of my rifle barrel, a testing slide of the bolt-action, a collection of revolver and ammunition and I was ready. I went out to greet my trackers. The light was just coming up and the niceness of morning overlay everything. Africa was superbly at her best.

I vaulted on to the waiting pony and was delighted when she responded to my high spirits with a playful rear and a naughty buck. I smiled at the two trackers and they grinned back at me. I motioned them on to lead the way. As I gathered the hard rangy pony under me to keep her at walking pace, I felt surge over me splendid exhilaration—we were started and come what may I was going to enjoy every minute of it. Gone was all my tension, I felt confident and young and strangely gay. Excitement and real living was just in front of me, and who knows perhaps great triumph too, but this did not matter; all that mattered now was the intensity of being alive—the past was gone . . . the future did not concern me, I had the moment . . . just then it was all that I wanted. I called out to the trackers to make them turn; this time it was I who grinned at them and they who smiled back at me.

Our arrival in the tiny native village created a gala air. Every man, woman and child was out to greet us; not only the people but the dogs and domestic animals took on a festive air, the pigs trotted about grunting a welcome, the dogs rushed about and yelped, the baby pigs stood and stared—looking I thought rather like miniature elephants—the scrawny chickens fired with the general excitement flapped about in their silly way and the cocks to show their disdain exhibited their superiority with blatant immorality as they chased the screeching hens and trod them in the dust. In the centre of the ring of grass huts standing aloof from the turmoil I saw the upright figure of a fine negro: this I knew must be the Headman and my hunter. I slid from my pony and as he advanced towards me I offered my hand. His returning grasp was dry and firm—I liked him immediately. He told me his tribal name was Ngobi, this was the nearest for pronunciation I could get. He was a man of medium build. I was glad of this, for I had a mistrust of very tall powerfully-built men.

He had I found quite good pidgin English so that in a restricted way we were able to converse. When the excitement had died down he gathered his party together and in an authoritative manner—which I was quick to admire—addressed them in dialect; from the way they kept glancing in my direction he was I thought talking about me. I had an idea he was excusing my youthfulness. While he was doing this I took the opportunity of weighing up my native party. The Headman I was sure was a man of courage. He gave me the impression that in a tricky situation he would remain cool and stand firm; with this conviction came to me a fine feeling of being less alone. I judged him to be about forty-five, charcoal-black, well-built but tough and wiry. His natural courtesy and innate dignity I found impressive; I felt my heart going out to him with friendliness and respect. I had a grand feeling that if we were forced into any tree-climbing we would be doing it together. The two trackers looked competent but their duties ended once they had brought me within range, this done they would retire to safe positions; if the hunter and I got in a tight fix they might rise to negative usefulness but sizing them up I had my doubts about anything better. Of the rest—the bush-cutters—I had no doubts whatsoever: they looked a poor lot. At the first hint of even distant danger they would be leaping for the trees like demented monkeys.

When he had finished talking to the others Ngobi came over to confer with me about our plans. He told me that reports coming in indicated that elephant were in the district but not immediately close. If I agreed he thought now would be a good time to give the rifle a test for sight-setting and accuracy. I had of course already done this but as he really seemed eager about it I consented; it occurred to me he might be staging an exhibition to impress the party. He sent off a boy to string up five or six coconuts at different distances. I was not bothered about this, for the only thing I was at all certain about over this elephant shoot was that I knew myself to be really good with a .303.

When the targets were ready Ngobi and I headed our party and with the entire population—pigs, chickens, and babies—following at a respectful distance behind us we entered the grove.

As I took up my stance to commence firing I remembered with startling clarity the day nine or ten years ago when Wilfred and I had done our 'dual act' in a village fair in Wales, shooting off our rows of clay pipes and dancing coloured balls to win prizes for the beautiful London actress who came down to open it. How skilfully we had covered up each other's misses then . . . what wouldn't I give to have his slight figure beside me now, perhaps later in the day to cover up some fatal miss. . . . The roar and kick of my rifle shattered my day-dream.

When I had finished, Ngobi I could see was hugely pleased; the rest of the party were excitedly grinning and chattering amongst themselves like mad. Ngobi came up and patted the rifle. All were eager to be on the way; a few sharp words from Ngobi restored quietness but did not damp the cheerful spirits and forming up, the bush-cutters and trackers in front, we entered the forest. The serious business of hunting had started.

As we struggled along I thought over Ngobi's tactics of arranging the pre-shoot and the surprising enthusiasm that had been the outcome. Had he really been only concerned with impressing the others or had he, unarmed himself, wished to satisfy himself—before accompanying me—that I could shoot? If it was really the latter, far from feeling resentful I felt pleased with his good sense and if it was this, I was touched by the delicate way in which he had brought it about. In their own surroundings what sensitive people these were, what beautiful instinctive manners they possessed until, I could not help thinking, they became corrupted by us.

Whatever had been his motive he had got his party moving off on the right foot. I knew how easy it was to do just the reverse with Africans—and turning to him I tried to tell him, in our constricted pidgin English, of my pleasure at the evident good start. He called out something to the others in his own tongue and back along the line came musical chortles. I was feeling fine. After this Ngobi enjoined silence. The trackers did not think we were near elephant yet but any time we might come on fresh signs; in any case the sun was getting high, the going was very hard and it was too hot to talk. Flies and stingers of a hundred sorts stung and bit, horrible leeches made themselves fast on us and had to be removed. Ngobi had warned me to be vigilant for snakes but in the intense heat I found that the effort of forcing myself through the narrow tunnel only roughly hewn out by the cutters, and the climbing over rough undergrowth took all my energy; by the time I had dealt with the insects that encrusted my mouth and eyes I had no concentration left to give to the possibility of snakes; like the bare-footed natives I became fatalistic. This disregard of theirs was to cost me dearly before the hunt was ended.

All that day and all the next we cut our way through forest or in grilling heat traversed open country. Signs of elephant were everywhere but not fresh enough to tell us how far away they might be. I was beginning to think we should never come up with them, and my time was getting short. Whenever my disappointment showed too plainly Ngobi would reassure me always with the same words, 'Bimeby plenty big elephant, trackers plenty good, he know plenty good, bimeby plenty big bull come soon plenty much ivory.' He would with enormous confidence place his hands one on each side of his face and sweep them down to the ground and up a bit to illustrate for me the great size of the tusks of the bull he was so determined to track for me. In spite of his 'bimebys' I could see by the earnest expression in his eyes that he was quite sure of himself and certain that he would bring me up to a herd.

It was about noon on the morning of my last day when both trackers, fingers to lips, came creeping noiselessly back: they had hit fresh spoor, elephant were very near, they were moving slowly and stopping to feed and churn soft ground for mud-baths, and within an hour we should be close enough to manœuvre for a shot. I felt myself tense with excitement and my heart begin its usual uncomfortable thudding. Ngobi and the trackers—with much wind-testing of wetted fingers—conferred; satisfied, we moved into position, Ngobi and I walking abreast with one tracker just in front of us. Ngobi with much whispering and pointing had indicated where the herd was; between us and it there was a piece of elephant grass eight to ten feet high through which we must pass. This was the nastiest cover to be caught in when near a herd, for visibility was confined to the immediate grasses surrounding us. Ngobi with dumb show and breathed whispers had made me understand that if we came upon them in the grass we would not try for a shot while in it but wait until they moved out. Ngobi I could see was nervous about being in this fog of grass; he was shaking his head and with lip-movements was saying 'Plenty bad, plenty no good.' From time to time we would stop and listen: at each small open space he would lie down and put his ear to the ground. We moved with the utmost stealth. Away over to our right we could hear the swishing grass as the great beasts pushed their way through. Ngobi pointed that way and then to the front; I nodded to let him know I realized the herd was in two groups. Presently we started to hear the group in front of us tearing down branches and pulling up young trees. They sounded very near, so I knew the screening grasses must be coming to an end. The trackers had fallen back and retreated to the rear; of the rest of the party there was neither sight nor sound. Ngobi and I were alone. We could hear the animals' footsteps and the brushing of branches as they moved about. Ngobi edged up close to me, patted my rifle, and signalling for me to go on fell-in a little to one side and a yard or two behind me. As soundlessly as I could I commenced to steal forward expecting any moment to see through the green of the leaves the rough greyness of hide or the yellow gleam of ivory. Then from behind me came with terrible urgency the warning cry from Ngobi as he leapt to my side: advancing upon us with head raised and tongue darting ready to strike was a large deadly looking snake.

'Shoot, Master, SHOOT.'

As the revolver shots shattered out with reverberative clangour the whole forest to our front and on our right hand filled with the noise of confusion. Shrill frightened squeals and angry trumpetings were all mixed up with the frightful cracking of smashing timber as the herd milled about in panic, until the steadier sound of a concerted rush told us that the great beasts were crashing their way through the bush in an organized stampede for open country. As soon as the herd was safely distant the trackers came running to us, jabbering excitedly, and saying something to Ngobi they set off after the elephants. Ngobi beckoned to me with indications that we should follow them; this we did by keeping to the cleared swathe made by the herd in its impetuous flight. The destruction of the bush was frightening; the implication of weight and power was awesome. Coming out of the forest we came up with the trackers who were standing looking over the open country. We followed their pointing fingers and tracing the dust clouds caught a glimpse of the herd as they broke from high grass to enter another forest. They were travelling fast.

Ngobi called the trackers over to us and we went into conference; there was much head-shaking and pointings to the sun . . . we could not possibly come up with them in daylight. We must commence the return journey. Our hunt was over. Ngobi I could see was very downcast and in his nicely-mannered way blamed himself for disturbing the snake and spoiling the chance of a shot: he kept on telling me we could still come across more elephant on the way back and harangued the by now rather sullen trackers to this effect. I too—after the keyed-up state of the last few hours—felt the dreariness of reaction and bitter disappointment that I had not got my elephant. The porters, deeming it safe now, soon joined us; they too showed discontent and disappointment but for a different reason. From the very start their mouths and minds had been drooling with thoughts of juicy steaks and unlimited meat.

I had told Ngobi that we would rest for a few hours before turning back, but in less than an hour he came over to me and said he thought the men were getting quarrelsome. He suggested it would be a good thing to get them moving again. Rather dispiritedly we set off. The men were sulking like children but I knew that by next day, still like children, they would have forgotten all about it and be as bright as crickets again.

We were on the last trek to Ngobi's village when both trackers came in and reported fresh spoor of a single elephant close at hand.

An argument ensued between Ngobi and the two scouts. Ngobi looked very angry and kept shaking his head in denunciation, the other two gesticulated in fierce argument; but Ngobi sent them off with the already disappearing porters and as they turned he spat insultingly twice on the ground, saying, 'Two, plenty good bad.' Then pointing at me and then at himself, he said, 'You me go, plenty good brothers.'

As we moved quietly along Ngobi kept trying to explain something to me—I thought it was about his quarrel with the trackers but I did not pay much attention. This development was unexpected and came to me as something of an anti-climax; I was occupied with reorientating myself for the fresh ordeal in front of me. Ngobi was intent too with wind-testing and studying the ground. We walked for a mile or more over scrub ground until we entered forest again; it was well screened but good silent walking. Ngobi signalled to me for extra caution and side by side we crept and sidled, stopping every few yards to peer and listen. I shall never know how long we were in this forest—time for me had stopped. Presently Ngobi froze. We heard the sound of a branch being pulled down and the swish as it sprang back stripped of its leaves—a feeding elephant, we had got our direction. Ngobi nodded to a screen of bushes. I understood. Behind that we should sight our elephant. With racking caution we edged almost without movement nearer and nearer until we were behind the screen of cane and bushes. Seeking a view we manœuvred and twisted, shoulder to shoulder, until Ngobi nodded his head forward. . . . There in front of me, thirty yards in clear sights, was my elephant. It was a three-quarter view, stern nearmost, a perfect target for a behind the shoulder shot . . . I remember reminding myself that with only my .303 I must wait for the head shot. Slowly I raised my rifle to get sighted; when it turned I would fire. . . . As my rifle arm crept up I felt Ngobi's hand gently laid on it and then slight pressure. I thought he was warning me to wait for the head shot . . . I nodded my understanding, but the pressure grew firmer and signalled urgency. Barely turning my head I saw him shake his and then nod vigorously beyond and to the side of the elephant and there camouflaged in the bushes I saw the calf . . . the elephant was a cow and of course unshootable. I turned my eyes to Ngobi. Still shaking his head and speaking with his eyes, he increased his pressure on my arm— but this time with an upward movement; in those seconds we were in absolute attune. I understood him perfectly . . . I was to keep the elephant covered for safety. . . The cow idly stripped a leaf and lumbering around looked straight at us. I felt Ngobi's signalled pressure. . . . It was a perfect head shot. At that moment the calf moved out and the cow turned to it; she had not seen us but she was weaving uneasily, scenting with wavering upswinging trunk. I could feel through his hand the tension of Ngobi. Still dangerously uneasy the cow gathered the calf to her with her trunk and moved silently away from us deeper into the forest. The little calf made a funny bubbling noise. The cow stopped and nudged it with her knee, I think to silence it, and went slowly on. I heard Ngobi breathe deeply again—I was glad to do the same. We waited a long time and then stole out of the bush as quietly as we had come in.

Out in the open we both stopped and looked at each other with pleasure: this fine black man was my friend, I felt humble and proud that this was so. He was I could see quietly triumphant that he had been able to show me this rare sight; we both felt it had put everything right.

While we were walking over the open country to re-join the others, I asked Ngobi what it was that had made him so angry with the trackers. He told me that they had tried to persuade him to arrange things so that I would be forced to shoot the cow in self-defence. In their simple way they argued that by doing this I would get my elephant, and much more important they would get their meat and extra 'present' for a kill, and everybody would be exceedingly happy.

We arrived at Ngobi's village in the early afternoon. I settled up with the trackers and when they were out of the way Ngobi invited me into his hut; leaving me for a moment he came back with a small elephant tusk which with much diffidence he presented to me. I was deeply touched by his friendly gesture and his thoughtfulness in seeking to allay as far as he could any lurking disappointment in me.

It was not until long after I had accepted his parting gift that I realized the dual compliment of his action: it was illegal ivory—in disclosing it to a white man he took serious risk. I suppose I ought to have felt compunction, but I never could, for the simple sincerity of his action outweighed with me anything else. It was a small tusk not more than twenty inches long. It was probably from a cow caught in a pit-trap. Today it forms the handle for my studio door.

As I rode back to the plantation I suddenly realized that for once I had the best of both things; I had had the experience, I had been within shooting distance with all the excitement of proximity, but I had not killed a fine creature. I thought of the comically sweet little calf making its bubbling noise and felt infinitely glad that I had not—earlier in the day—murdered what might have been its father.

I rode along in slack relaxation; I was happy and contented.

29. *Return to England*

Soon after I reported back to *Astræa*, we moved out of Victoria and made short visits to different parts of the Coast, with longer stays in Lagos and Freetown. It was when we returned to the Cameroons that the wretched fever really began to undermine me. Our surgeon became gravely concerned and finally insisted that I should be invalided off the Coast and sent home. Admiralty was informed and steps were taken to bring this about, but transport was extremely difficult and before anything came of it *Astræa* was herself ordered to sail for England. I was very pleased about this for although the War was over I hated the thought of not finishing the commission.

The news that we were ordered home for paying-off swept through the ship with invigorating effect. I, like everyone else, was relieved and happy to be leaving the breathless moisture of the Coast. I knew what I was leaving, to what I wondered was I going: freedom from malaria—this was doubtful; our surgeon had told me I would never be passed fit for sea again and had warned me that recurrent malaria might make life in Northern climates so miserable that I would find it unbearable.

It was late in 1919 when we anchored in the Thames Estuary. As I heard the cables run out and the roar of iron striking iron, as well as the sensation of finality this sound always produced in me I felt suddenly and inexplicably depressed; this return to England, unlike any of my other returns, was charged with uncertainty. Virtually I was finished with the Navy and the sea; there would be some medical boards and other formalities but in a matter of months I should be on the beach and except for my naval gratuity, penniless. Life for me would have to begin all over again. My father was having a hard enough struggle to keep the house going, financially he would be unable to help me at all—I thought a little bitterly that three or four months at home, whilst I looked around for something, might be an embarrassment. I must see to it that I did not place this upon him. My depression, I tried to convince myself, was a result of malaria combined with the somewhat hopeless uncertainty of my own future, or more simply the cold uninviting English afternoon; but I knew it was not really so. I was too used to driving off these more ordinary doubts. My sadness went deeper than any of this; I wanted Wilfred to be in England, or peace-time France if the awkward old wretch must—I didn't really care where he would have been, I could always have got to him somehow . . . I wanted terribly to see him again . . . why did he have to die . . . looking over the bleak and dreary Thames Estuary I felt the physical loss of him hit me like a blow . . . out there on the Coast the inevitable impossibility of meeting him, even had he been alive, had I knew acted as a buffer. Out there, for this reason, his spiritual loss had been the greater but now in England again I was re-faced more acutely with the physical realization that I could never see or speak to him again. I saw now that out there this truth had not had the absoluteness that it had for me now; the buffer was in the knowledge that had Wilfred survived the War, I would still not have been able to see or speak to him until this moment. In the hot nights and days of Africa, I had contemplated the *world* without Wilfred: in England again I knew I should have to contemplate, almost with fresh shock, *England* without him. The compression of thought this brought about stabbed me with sorrow for what I had lost. I could not send a telegram to Wilfred, but I could and must send one home. As I wrote it out I knew I was writing the last words of a chapter. No, not a chapter, the last words of a whole series of chapters. When I joined them again in a few days' time, I would be starting a preface for a fresh beginning, all over again, on page one.

I remember being really surprised over my despondency, it did not seem quite like me somehow. What had happened to my determination to paint? It had thrived in the early sea-going years and survived the war years . . . was it to die in the years of peace? I felt unambitious as if living in a void and, because of this, intolerably futile.

My telegram home arrived when they were all away. My father and mother and Mary had gone to stay for a few weeks with my father's sister in Torquay, but knowing I might arrive in England at any time they had left a forwarding address and wired back asking me to join them there as soon as I could.

When my train ran into Exeter in the early hours I got out on to the platform in the hopes of finding some coffee; I had forgotten momentarily that the ministering women volunteers who had run

buffets for travelling troops during the War years would no longer
be there. I was walking up and down the platform when I noticed
unusual activity; all the odd porters, ticket-collectors and guards
were hastily going from carriage to carriage searching the train. I was
idly wondering who it might be they seemed so intent on finding—
when I saw charging up the train the well-dressed stocky figure of a
civilian. It couldn't be. . . . My goodness it was. . . .

'Father.'

He responded to my voice immediately and turned towards me.
For one awful moment I thought he did not recognize me but his
shock passed swiftly as we rushed towards each other to grasp
hands; it was a good moment for both of us. I was delighted when my
father in order to cover up any emotion he might be showing reverted
to his more usual fussing and fuming self. On his arrival at Exeter
he had made himself known and ordered the search for me to be
carried out, so that he could be sure of joining me for the last part
of the journey—now he marched off to thank and dismiss the
searchers. Returning to me he furiously demanded, 'Now, Harold,
what on *earth* have you been doing to yourself to come back looking
like this? I don't understand it at all. What *have* you been doing?'

I was nettled by his hasty assumption that my appearance was
somehow my fault but much more moved by the deep concern I saw
so plainly in his eyes.

'I'm awfully sorry, Father, but it isn't quite my own fault, you
know.'

Gripping my elbow he pulled me warmly towards him.

'Fault, dear boy, who's talking about it being anybody's fault. It's
just that I'm worried about Mother, not much more than a year
ago . . . Wilfred . . . and now you looking like this. . . .'

'Yes, Wilfred. . . .'

'But come on, we can't stand here gossiping like women, we're
keeping the train waiting.'

He hustled me into my compartment, some station official came
along—saluted my father:

'Everything all right now, Sir?'

'Very much so, thank you.'

And then my father with his natural courtesy introduced me:

'My son just home from West Africa.'

I shook hands.

'Best of luck if I may say so, Sir.'

The door slammed, the whistle blew and we were off. I was feeling fine, I'd got my grand tough little father all to myself, and the station official, a complete stranger, had genuinely wished me luck. Perhaps after all things weren't going to be so bad. . . . On the floor I saw a jug of coffee, a plate of enormous sandwiches, and two canteen cups.

Just as the train moved off a piercing screech tore out from the far corner seat of the carriage and my poor father sprang up as if he had been shot at.

'What . . . what on earth's happening?'

'It's all right, it's only a parrot that I've brought home for Mother. I reared it from the nest.'

'Did you. Well the confounded creature nearly frightened the life out of me, why didn't you warn me?'

I thought he looked pleased but also a little dubious.

'Does the beastly thing always make noises like that?'

'Oh, no, it's a very highly-trained and well-behaved bird.'

We burst out laughing.

After an initial medical board and some other formalities I was sent on indefinite leave prior to coming out of the Navy for good. I had some foreign service leave due to me as well so I went home. Although I had been looking forward to this I also found myself rather dreading it. In all the familiar family surroundings the loss of Wilfred was going to hit out at me with renewed force. I was anxious as well over what I had heard from my father and mother about Colin and troubled that they should contemplate his futureless prospects with so much complacent resignation. It did not help my unease to realize that I myself, unless I could get to sea again, was in exactly the same position, unqualified even untrained to do anything else at all— not even bricklaying or carpentry—and faced with the absolute necessity to earn an immediate living. All the same how fine it was going to be to see old Colin again after all this time. Perhaps between us we would be able to find some way out of this hopeless-looking blind alley, although I could not begin to see just how we were likely to achieve this.

Colin was out of the Royal Flying Corps and getting on for twenty. When he was demobilized it had been difficult for him to know what to do for a career and he finally decided to go as an 'assistant' on a farm. This usually meant for unpremiumed boys, living with a farmer ostensibly to learn farming. What it really amounted to was exceptionally hard work for a quarter of the pay of a farm labourer. No doubt it was a good way of learning the business of farming and provided capital would be available in a few years' time to buy or rent and also to stock a farm it could lead to a pleasant life in the country. When Colin came home we talked things over for a few days exchanging news and ideas. I told him if I could get passed fit for sea again I should, as I had always intended to do, combine a seafaring life with my painting until I was established enough in painting to wean myself from the sea. If I could not go back to sea I would take stop-gap jobs until I could somehow get myself to London and paint seriously. He told me that he thought he would have to go on with the farming as there did not seem any chance of Father or himself finding anything better—perhaps later on things might alter and he would be able to get a small place of his own. I was of course still on leave but I knew I could not be happy just sitting about at home doing nothing much. While we were talking like this it suddenly occurred to me what a good idea it would be if—while waiting to hear how things were going to work out for me—I could get some work with Colin on his next farm. Though, with no chance of enough capital to start even a small holding of our own, for Colin and me the occupation was a sheer waste of time, but the alternative in those dreadful 1920's was just simply to be out of work.

I had kept up periodic visits to the Appointments Bureau, but nothing came of them, nor did it seem likely that anything ever would. I had also been persistently writing to the Departments concerned with applications for a grant to study painting. Finally I was informed that no Government provision was made for officers for the study of painting, but my name had been forwarded to the Agricultural Department for favourable consideration.

Shortly after this I received two letters by the same post. One was from the Admiralty offering me a lump sum in settlement of my disability, and the other from some Government Department offering me a working pupilship in practical farming. . . . It went on to explain that this carried a grant of one hundred and fifty pounds per annum for approximately two years. . . . The major part of this amount I should be required to pay to a selected farmer in return for board and tuition . . . the letter went on to state that applications for further grants to assist in buying or stocking farms would not under any circumstances be considered.

That, I thought, was that: another dead-end.

I was sick to death of this England who smugly looked on while her young men just out of the War peddled boot-laces and collar studs or lined up in their scores for the chance to sell goods—not for a salary, but on commission only. All around there seemed to be riches in plenty, new motor-cars, new houses . . . and as I eyed the flagrant prosperity of the new rich I felt rising in me the wormwood of disillusion—I did not want security, but I did bitterly want opportunity. I read the two letters through once more and then I sat down and accepted both offers.

With the coming through of my wretched agricultural grant, Colin and I decided that as there seemed nothing else for it but to go on with this pseudo farming occupation we would do it together on the same farm. In this way not only would it be more bearable for both of us but we should undoubtedly find pleasure and happiness in being with each other and between us would somehow contrive, now and then, to get a little fun out of it, which was something we felt at this time we could very well do with.

After one or two abortive efforts—the independence my grant afforded allowed us to be selective—we hit upon a first-class farm requiring an assistant. Colin applied for this post, a meeting was agreed upon, and during this it was not difficult to arrange for me to be taken on as a pupil under the Government scheme. It was a large farm, the owner was in need of further assistance, and so it was very pleasantly fixed.

From what we had gathered during our interview, the immediate prospect—in its negative way—looked pleasing enough. The owner and his family were completely delightful; they possessed a charming house and an excellent farm. All of them were interested in other things besides the farmyard, which made for good conversation. Colin and I had been most warmly welcomed and quite soon were made to feel we were an integral part of the household.

We all of us worked fantastic hours on the land, in busy seasons from first light until after dark, but so harmonious was the spirit amongst us that this never really seemed to matter. Indeed there developed a healthy rivalry between us as to who could accomplish the most work; there was a pleasantness about this which we all found entirely satisfying.

This was all very well, and while for a little time the strenuous work and the ease of the social surroundings had a soporific effect; just the same as the months sped by I found I was more frequently asking myself where it could possibly lead to—I was certainly learning how to farm but to what end? None at all that I could see. . . . Worrying at me was the old nagging knowledge that failure in attempted achievement was easier to live with than the safety of success without true attainment. Was my painting pricking at me again . . . or was it something else, which the vicissitudes of the last six years had so tangled and clouded that I could no longer think clearly, nor yet see plainly? My thoughts turned back to Wilfred and thinking of him I remembered his passionate cries for three years at Oxford . . . at last I understood. . . . What would I myself not now give for three years in a University—two years, yes one year might be enough in which to lose myself and absorb from older, more vital minds—not scholarship, I was too old for that, I had already lived too intensely, I did not now want scholarship for itself: I wanted illumination and a clarifying of this inner urging that I had something which I must use. A career even did not seem really necessary . . . what I needed was direction; without this I would be lost, or worse still take the wrong turning thinking I was on the right road. A University was out of serious thought, but direction I must find. I would not find it on this pleasant farm among these pleasant people. . . . I must look for it elsewhere. . . .

I became restless and ill-at-ease with myself; with returning health I wanted the real fight and the real struggle to be on again. I would go to London and study painting, I would take an unfurnished room. A camp bed, a chair and a gas-ring would be all I would need. I counted up my money: I had saved a little, enough to see me over a few months, if School of Art fees weren't too high or painting materials too costly.

I said a regretful good-bye to the nice family—in the year or fourteen months I had been with them we had got very fond of each other—resigned the rest of the agricultural grant and went home for a week to break the news to my father and mother, sort out my things and substantiate my plans.

I went up to London for a few days to find a room for myself. I had at first hoped I could manage a furnished room with breakfast, but a tour of the more likely apartment districts and the enquiries I made soon told me that anything like this was far beyond the sum I intended to lay out on accommodation. I began looking for a different class of room. In the end I came across one in Campden Street, Kensington. It was small and dark and a bit unsavoury but I thought it would do for a few weeks just to get me to London, after which I could look around more carefully. I took the room.

The night before I left home for London I went up for a few hours to Wilfred's room at the top of the house. I wanted to look at his books and feel his presence. Perhaps I was seeking a blessing, or was I just saying good-bye? I felt that a disintegration was taking place in our family life: Wilfred was gone for ever, I was turning into an unknown road. Stranger still, although I was only going to London, for the first time I knew I was really leaving everything behind. . . . How often had I sailed for Peru or India or Patagonia but always knowing that everything would be the same when I came back. Now I was only going to London, but I sensed that when I came back nothing would ever be quite the same again. . . . I could smell the taint of family dissolution: tonight our family was still complete, Wilfred, not actually with us, shared our life; I was about to diverge from Colin, from now on our paths must be tangential. Tomorrow I should be gone, more separated from all of them than I had been when thousands of miles of sea had lain between me and home. . . . What might tomorrow bring. . . . My mind probed forward into the darkness but no light showed, I could not see. . . . I gave up trying; tonight I would think only of Wilfred, and taking out his books, one by one, I dipped into them.

OXFORD

MORE OXFORD PAPERBACKS

Details of a selection of other books follow. A complete list of Oxford Paperbacks, including The World's Classics, Twentieth-Century Classics, OPUS, Past Masters, Oxford Authors, Oxford Shakespeare, and Oxford Paperback Reference, is available in the UK from the General Publicity Department, Oxford University Press (JN), Walton Street, Oxford OX2 6DP.

In the USA, complete lists are available from the Paperbacks Marketing Manager, Oxford University Press, 200 Madison Avenue, New York, NY 10016.

Oxford Paperbacks are available from all good bookshops. In case of difficulty, customers in the UK can order direct from Oxford University Press Bookshop, 116 High Street, Oxford, Freepost, OX1 4BR, enclosing full payment. Please add 10 per cent of published price for postage and packing.

ALONG WITH YOUTH

Hemingway, The Early Years

Peter Griffin

Foreword by Jack Hemingway

Peter Griffin has drawn upon much previously unpublished material—including numerous letters and five early short stories—to trace the formative years of one of America's most celebrated writers. His compelling biography is the first part of a three-volume life which promises to become the definitive Hemingway biography for this generation.

'This book has shown me insights into my own father's character and behaviour I would not have thought possible.'
Jack Hemingway

'brings to sparkling life the Hemingway legend' *Financial Times*

'the first critical biography to appear for sixteen years . . . abounds in fresh material . . . highly readable and well-researched' *Irish Times*

'surpasses all previous work on the subject . . . adds a great wealth of detail' *Scotsman*

JOURNALS OF DOROTHY WORDSWORTH

Edited by Mary Moorman

The cherished companion of two great poets, William Wordsworth and Samuel Taylor Coleridge, Dorothy Wordsworth is herself a poet in prose. Her *Journals* combine an intense and minute observation of nature with a genuine poetic imagination.

Oxford Letters & Memoirs

THE DIARY OF A COUNTRY PARSON,
1758–1802

James Woodforde

Edited by John Beresford

James Woodforde was parson at Weston Longeville, Norfolk, from 1774 till his death in 1803. His life was obscure and tranquil, his character uncomplicated; he loved his country, sport, good food, and established institutions, and was warm-hearted and generous. His diary covers nearly every single day in his life from 1758 to 1802. What makes it a classic as well as a remarkable document of social history is Parson Woodforde's rare ability to bring vividly to life the rural England of two centuries ago.

'compulsive reading' *The Times*

Oxford Letters & Memoirs

PETER FLEMING

A Biography

Duff Hart-Davis

Peter Fleming is remembered as the author of some of the best—and funniest—travel books ever written. His godson, Duff Hart-Davis, describes Fleming's privileged background and his relationship with his brother Ian, creator of James Bond. He creates a picture of an unusually fascinating man who, though very much the English squire, was drawn to bizarre and dangerous adventures all over the world.

'tantalising and fascinating' Jan Morris in *The Times*

'enormously readable' *Daily Telegraph*

Oxford Lives

FURTHER PARTICULARS

Consequences of an Edwardian Boyhood

C. H. Rolph

'So the twentieth century and myself set off boldly into the unknown, myself keeping prudently a few months behind.'

With these words C. H. Rolph ended his earlier volume of memoirs, *London Particulars*. Now, in *Further Particulars*, he picks up the threads at the end of the First World War through to the present day, and reveals what that 'unknown' was to hold for him. Entertaining and provoking as ever, he describes the remarkable variety of this period of his life, and stands out, as he always has, as both a reformer, a realist, and a man of exceptional honesty and compassion.

GLADSTONE

1809–1874

H. C. G. Matthew

'the account of the private drama which co-existed with the public epic . . . brilliantly recaptures the Victorian soul in torment' David Cannadine, *Observer*

Gladstone was *the* Colossus of Victorian politics. He became an MP at 23; his political career spanned over 60 years; he became Prime Minister four times; and formed his last administration in 1892 at the age of 83.

These recently discovered diaries of Gladstone indicate his private life was every bit as dramatic as his controversial public career. For the first time this book sets his early achievements as Chancellor of the Exchequer, and then Prime Minister, against the private crisis in his life—the guilt ridden struggles with sexual temptation as he sought consolation from the trials of office in reading pornography, rescuing prostitutes, and self-flagellation. The figure of Gladstone that emerges is the most plausible and complex yet presented.

Oxford Lives

AN ENGLISHWOMAN IN INDIA

Harriet Tytler

Edited by Anthony Sattin
With an Introduction by Philip Mason

On 11 May 1857, mutiny broke out in Delhi and Harriet Tytler, eight months pregnant, with two children to look after, was forced to flee from the city. Yet when her husband, Captain Robert Tytler, returned to Delhi, she went with him, and for the next three months was the 'only lady' present at the so-called Siege of Delhi, sharing the dangers faced by the soldiers.

This is her story, not just the Siege of Delhi, but also of her childhood and travels in India and England: the record of a courageous, endearing, remarkable woman.

'extraordinarily vivid . . . should appeal to every type of reader' *British Book News*

SELECTED LETTERS OF OSCAR WILDE

Edited by Rupert Hart-Davis

When Sir Rupert Hart-Davis's magnificent edition was first published in 1962 Cyril Connolly called it 'a must for everyone who is seriously interested in the history of English literature—or European morals.' That edition of more than 1,000 letters is now out of print; from it Sir Rupert has culled a representative sample from each period of Wilde's life, 'giving preference', as he says in his Introduction to this selection, 'to those of literary interest, to the most amusing, and to those that throw light on his life and work.' The long letter to Lord Alfred Douglas, usually known as *De Profundis*, is again printed in its entirety.

'In Mr. Hart-Davis's *The Letters of Oscar Wilde*, the true Wilde emerges again for us, elegant, witty, paradoxical and touchingly kind . . . I urge all those who are interested in the contrasts between pride and humiliation, between agony and laughter, to acquire this truly remarkable book.' Harold Nicolson, *Observer*

CLOSING TIMES

Dan Davin

In *Closing Times* the novelist and former publisher Dan Davin has set down his recollections of seven writers, all of whom were close friends: Dylan Thomas, Julian Maclaren-Ross, Louis MacNeice, Joyce Cary, W. R. Rodgers, Enid Starkie, and the Yiddish poet Itzik Manger.

'It would be heartening to think that "Closing Times" is only one of many such consolidating works but also unduly optimistic. All the more reason to cherish Mr. Davin's stylish book.' Melanie Lowy in the *Jewish Chronicle*

LEAVES OF THE TULIP TREE:

Autobiography

Juliette Huxley

It was as a governess at Garsington, Lady Ottoline Morrell's mansion outside Oxford, that Juliette Huxley met the glittering Bloomsbury set, and among them her future husband Julian Huxley. She recalls the excitement and occasional chaotic moments of their courtship, and their later life together in London. She also describes with affectionate humour friendships with D. H. Lawrence and Frieda von Richthofen, Aldous and Maria Huxley, and H. G. Wells.

'This is the story of a real-life Jane Eyre, her romantic courtship and stormy marriage to a brilliant masterful and ruthless Mr Rochester.' *Observer*

'Against a background of two World wars and enormous social change, Juliette Huxley's autobiography has a fascinating and at times sad immediacy.' *Times Educational Supplement*

Oxford Letters & Memoirs

JONATHAN SWIFT

A Hypocrite Reversed

David Nokes

Winner of the James Tait Black Memorial Prize for Biography.
Dr Nokes presents a gripping and authoritative portrait of
Swift in his multifarious roles as satirist, politician, churchman,
and friend. He puts into perspective the legends of madness,
and the mysteries surrounding Swift's romantic attachments
to Stella and Vanessa, that have so often distorted our picture
of the writer.

'should remain the standard one-volume life for years to come'
New York Times

Oxford Lives

R. V. W.

A Biography of Ralph Vaughn Williams

Ursula Vaughn Williams

'Mrs Vaughn Williams presents a crowded picture of the composer's ceaseless activity right into extreme old age, his persistent concern with new music and young musicians, his unabated
instinct to compose and, at the end of his life, the new-found
pleasure in travel and relaxation that was reflected in his last
two symphonies.' *Daily Telegraph*

In addition to his great powers as a composer, Vaughn Williams
was a man of strong character and unflagging energy, who
lived a long, full life. He was at the centre of musical events
in England for sixty years, a period which for sustained musical
achievement is probably unequalled in the history of this country.

This intimate and detailed biography by his widow uses
much material not available until recently.

Oxford Lives

DOROTHY WORDSWORTH

Robert Gittings & Jo Manton

This brilliant biography is the first to treat Dorothy Wordsworth as a person in her own right rather than merely as an adjunct to her brother, or to Coleridge. Her devotion to her family and friends is well known, but she was also a woman of problems and contradictions, often connected with the changing social and political climate of her day. Her uncertain health and the nature of her final breakdown are fully examined for the first time, throwing light on several controversial actions in her life. She emerges as a more strange, wayward, and human figure than convention has portrayed.

'the authors have done what only the best biographers do; they re-create living people . . . it is a relief to have a real Dorothy presented' Patric Dickinson *The Times*

CHARLOTTE BRONTË

The Evolution of Genius

Winifred Gérin

Winner of the James Tait Black Memorial Prize, the William Heinemann Award, and the British Academy's Rose Mary Crawshay Prize.

'surely one of the great biographies of recent times'
Sunday Times

'a book to end all books about the Brontës' *Sunday Telegraph*

Oxford Lives

THE LIFE OF KATHERINE MANSFIELD

Antony Alpers

Until recently it has not been possible to deal freely and frankly with all the events of Katherine Mansfield's life. Conventional mores, respect for the privacy of her lovers, family, and friends, and the lack of some crucial material, have all prevented it. Little was known, for example, of her disastrous one-day marriage, her elopement with her childhood friend, Garnett Trowell, and her subsequent affair with Ida Baker. Now, drawing on newly opened manuscript collections, private papers, and personal contacts to which he has had exclusive access, Antony Alpers has been able to expand his 1953 biography in a new, award-winning interpretation of this volatile and vulnerable genius.

'This is in the way of being a definitive biography, and as such utterly engrossing, simply because Katherine Mansfield herself is always engrossing.' Kay Dick in *The Times*.

STRINDBERG: A BIOGRAPHY

Michael Meyer

This outstanding biography of Strindberg reveals previously unknown details about his three tempestuous marriages, his dabblings in the occult, his recurrent bouts of madness, and his friendships with Gauguin, Munch, and Delius, that were the touchstones of his tormented life.

'This will remain the standard life in English for many years.' Anthony Storr in the *Spectator*

Oxford Lives

LETTERS OF JOHN KEATS

Edited by Robert Gittings

Written in a fraction over four years, 1816 to 1820, the large body of Keats's letters forms the most complete portrait we have of any English poet. With extraordinary candour and self-knowledge Keats gives us his experience of almost everything that can happen to a young man between the ages of twenty-one and twenty-five; an all but day-to-day account of the working processes of a poet; and finally, as Robert Gittings says, 'some of the most profound comments on art, philosophy, and the human condition that any single person has produced.'

Robert Gittings has selected 170 letters, each elucidated by explanatory notes. He has also provided a Preface, and Introduction, and an Appendix.

Oxford Letters & Memoirs

EDWARD THOMAS

A Portrait

R. George Thomas

Some years before her death, Edward Thomas's widow gave George Thomas open access to her husband's correspondence—some eighteen hundred letters rich in significance and quality. It is these letters that lie at the heart of this superb biography, which reveals so much about Thomas both as a writer and as a loving husband and father.

'an absorbing book [which] provides an indispensable aid for any future study of the poet and his work' *Guardian*

'takes its place as the standard work' *Times Literary Supplement*

Oxford Lives